SHOW ME THE WAY
TO GO HOME

Form AR-8   Registration Number   **6158360**

ALIEN REGISTRATION RECEIPT CARD

Kenji TAKEUCHI
c/o Officer in Charge
Immigration & Natz. Service
Tule Lake WRA
Newell, California

KEEP THIS CARD. Keep a record of the number.

UNITED STATES DEPARTMENT OF JUSTICE
IMMIGRATION AND NATURALIZATION SERVICE
ALIEN REGISTRATION DIVISION
WASHINGTON, D.C.

To the Registrant:

Your registration under the Alien Registration Act, 1940, has been received and given the number shown above, your name. This card is your receipt, and is evidence only of such registration. In writing to the Department of Justice about yourself, always give the number on this card.

16—15416   Director of Registration.

This Alien Registration Receipt Card should be sent to the Alien Registration Division, Department of Justice, Washington, D. C., (1) if it is found; or (2) if the person named hereon departs from the United States, or becomes naturalized, or dies.

I am signing under protest for I consider myself as an American citizen.

Kenji Takeuchi

(SIGNATURE OF REGISTRANT, OR PERSON REGISTERING THE ALIEN)

ADDRESS REPORTS—Read Carefully

The Alien Registration Act, 1940, requires all resident aliens to report each change of address within 5 days of such change. Other aliens, for example: Visitors, students, and others not admitted for permanent residence in the United States, must report their address every 3 months whether they change their address or not. Prepared forms for such address changes and reports may be obtained at any post office. A penalty of fine and imprisonment is provided by law for failure to make the required reports. Address letters and reports to the Alien Registration Division, Department of Justice, Washington, D. C.

When reporting, give both your number and name.

16—15416

Show Me the Way to Go Home

The Moral Dilemma of *Kibei* No No Boys in World War Two Incarceration Camps

Takako Day
Edited by Michael Day

WREN SONG PRESS
MIDDLEBURY, VERMONT

Show Me the Way to Go Home
First Edition, April 2014

Text copyright © 2014 by Takako Day

Author photo: Michael Day

Design by Winslow Colwell/Wren Song Design

Published in the United States by Wren Song Press
PO Box 6, East Middlebury, VT 05740

The text of this publication was set in Minion.

Cover photograph: Elaine Yoneoka. *Graffiti in Tule Lake Segregation Center jail. Translation: "Defeat the U.S.!"*

Title page photographs courtesty of Kenji Takeuchi. *Tule Lake Segregation Center and Dai Toa Juku.*

Wren Song
Press

ISBN: 978-1499148695

TABLE OF CONTENTS

EDITOR'S
FOREWORD

In 2000, after spending several years collecting the oral histories of ten men who endured the double hardship of wartime incarceration and subsequent ostracism from the Japanese American community for having answered "no, no" to the U.S. government's loyalty questionnaire, Takako Day published *Nihon no heitai o utsu koto wa dekinai* [I Cannot Shoot a Japanese Soldier] in Japan. A few years later, she realized that since these men were American citizens, but their stories had never been told in English, U.S. audiences needed to hear them. She engaged the services of two professionals to translate the book into English.

Those who have been immersed in two or more languages or who have used translations provided by online services will understand that direct translations from one language to another *may* capture literal meanings but often fall short of conveying idiom, nuance, and feeling. Furthermore, what passes for "logical" structure and transition in one language may puzzle readers of another language if the translation is direct and literal. To tell the stories properly, maintaining the dignity, character, and wit of both the author and the interviewees while also providing appropriate historical context, the translation had to be reworked for readers of English.

Thus, as the author's biggest fan in the U.S., the task of recreating a new manuscript in English fell to me. Although I am not a scholar of U.S. history, I have studied Japanese rhetoric and have a personal interest in the wartime history of Japanese Americans. At the 2008 Tule Lake Pilgrimage, I participated in events and met key figures such as Tsutomu "Jimmy" Mirikitani and Kenji Takeuchi, deepening my commitment to helping to bring the stories of the "No No Boys" to English readers. Here is what I jotted down on an index card as part of my reflection on that pilgrimage:

On the far desert in a forgotten corner of California, under the pristine white gaze of Mount Shasta, is a monument to the indignity and insult to law-abiding, hard-working American citizens who came to this country of hope and promise and had their hopes destroyed, their dreams dashed to bits, their families torn apart, their possessions confiscated or stolen, their pride and dignity stretched to the utmost limit. This was the ultimate test of spirit, of strength in the face of injustice. With the tenacity of sagebrush holding on with bare claws to the rough volcanic soil, they embraced the birth of possibility as agricultural geniuses sprouting plenitude from the barren desert. In the face of uncertainty, they held fast to both culture and conviction, many of them later not only surviving but even prospering.

*   *   *

As I have a full-time job and my own professional commitments, I was only able to work on this project sporadically — an hour here and an hour there — in fits and starts over an eight-year period. Along the way, I encountered many puzzles. First among them was the issue of showing respect to all stakeholders mentioned in the book while still allowing the author to express her opinions about them. Second, I needed to strike a balance between the author's necessarily complicated syntax (these are complicated issues!) and my sense of what would be most direct and understandable to English readers. Finally, I needed to check her sources to the best of my ability, but those sources range from oral interviews and publications in Japanese, to typescripts of U.S. wartime reports, to newspaper articles spanning eighty years, to scholarly books and articles. With my current commitments, it would take another eight years just to verify all the sources. But this book, with its moving stories of loyalty, language, and culture, is long overdue. Despite its shortcomings, it needs to be made available to readers of English.

This is my way of saying that I have done my best to balance the author's view with the interviewees' stories and the interests of stakeholders, but, as with most complicated endeavors, the result will never be perfect.

Michael Day
DeKalb, Illinois
December 15, 2013

A NOTE ON TERMINOLOGY

In writing this book, I have been grappling with the relationship between political power and language. As a *shin issei* [post-World War II immigrant from Japan; the prefix "shin" means "new"] coming to grips with my own understanding of U.S. history, I have had to make decisions about terminology that affect the reader's interpretation of, and attitude toward, that history. This has been a difficult process, fraught with concern about taking sides or with using terms such as "concentration camp" that have taken on meanings associated with other historical events.

After consulting several resources, such as *Power of Words Handbook*, a document from the Japanese American Citizens League (JACL) and Greg Robinson's "A Note on Terminology" (pp. vii-viii), I have chosen the terms "forced removal" for "evacuate/evacuation, relocate/relocation," and "temporary detention center" for "assembly center." The most difficult terms to reconsider were "internment" and "relocation center/internment camp," as they have been used in the public media for many years, to the point that they have become customary. The currently recommended terms range from "American concentration camp" to "incarceration camp," "prison camp," and "illegal detention center." Keeping in mind "the fact that there is no commonly understood term to describe such an action [of the government] with precision" (Robinson, p. vii), and that "incarcerate is generally defined as to confine or imprison, typically as punishment for a crime" (*Power of Words Handbook*, p. 10), I have chosen to use the term "incarceration" or simply "camp," depending on the context.

continued

However, looking at the above definition of "incarceration" as a punishment for a crime, I had to ask myself: "Why did Japanese Americans have to be "punished"? And the only answer I could come up with is that, to white Americans, they were considered "Japanese" and therefore enemies. With this in mind, I do not hesitate to use "incarceration" when I focus on the history of the humiliation of an entire ethnicity, although I certainly understand that "these institutions were not penitentiaries" (Robinson p. vii). I use "camp" in more conversational contexts, especially since those I interviewed always used that word. Technically speaking, Japanese Americans were "inmates" in confinement camps operated by WRA, and became "internees" in Justice Department internment camps for enemy aliens. However, I decided to use "prison camp" and "prisoner" for War Relocation Authority (WRA) punitive camps, such as the camps in Moab, Utah, and Leupp, Arizona, instead of the euphemism "Citizen Isolation Camp."

I use quotation marks around the words "disloyal" and "pro-Japan," which are political labels used by one group to describe another. These expressions relate deeply to the theme of this book: how the names one group chose to describe another determined the destiny of those targeted groups. The issue of what could be considered "disloyal" and "pro-Japan" is indeed arguable.

I also often use the word *jun nisei* in the book. *Jun* is literally translated as "pure." "*Jun nisei*" has been defined as "educated only in America" (*Thomas*, p.105) in contradistinction to the "impure" *kibei nisei*, implying "contaminated" by Japanese culture. The *kibei* I interviewed often used the word *jun nisei*; thus, I would like to place *jun nisei* alongside *kibei nisei* as an important historical term in Japanese American history.

– T.D.

PREFACE

Language is transmitted from parents to children. It is "in the blood" — belonging to the realm of destiny, without the slightest room for choice — and this makes it one of the most unreasonable things a human being will ever encounter.

— Katsuhiko Tanaka

In the summer of 1986, I migrated from Japan to California. For six years I lived in California, the energetic land where Asian people and culture are steadily making inroads into the mainstream white community. After California, I spent seven years in South Dakota, an isolated state on the northern plains where it is often said that there are more horses than men and where the history of Native Americans still survives. And after South Dakota, fourteen years quickly passed in Illinois.

My eastbound migration — from California to the harsh badlands of the inland West and on to Chicago and beyond — parallels the history and path of Japanese American "assimilation" in this country. Some Japanese Americans, believing that the severe discrimination that they experienced before World War II had resulted from their hesitation to assimilate into American society, did not go back west to California but instead decided to scatter and move to the east after being released from incarceration camps during and after the war. In fear, and wanting to be accepted as Americans, some of them wished that the Japanese language and culture would become extinct.

Unconsciously, I have traced the same eastbound route the Japanese Americans took in their wartime and postwar history. Has my "assimilation" into the United States somehow advanced in the past twenty-seven years, against my own will?

No, it has not. Wherever I move within the United States, there is one thing I cannot erase that forever keeps me from becoming totally assimilated — the Japanese language.

Born, raised, and educated in Japan, I am a person who provides evidence of my own existence through self-expression in the Japanese language; I am a Japanese-language being. This will never change, even if I continue to live in, became naturalized in, and die here in the United States. Even though I have lived here for nearly three decades, I still feel that prohibiting immigrants the use of their mother tongue as a condition for assimilation is a violation of basic human rights.

For many people, the term "bilingual" carries with it a kind of glamor or allure, the power of living in two languages, two cultures. However, people rarely talk about the power of language, the sense of fate that accompanies language, or the influence language exerts over one's personality and life, especially if one's mother tongue ever becomes the enemy's language.

Today, largely due to Japan's global economic power, the modern Japanese language has status as an international language in the U.S. to the point that in 1992 it became the first Asian language to be included as an option on the SAT test. To enhance business and communication between the U.S. and Japan, and to further expand and deepen the international roles of the two countries, more and more people have elected to study Japanese over the last twenty years. Japanese has risen in importance among world languages.

In contrast with its current popularity, the Japanese language had very little influence in the United States before World War II. It was largely confined to the Japanese American community, which was segregated from mainstream white society. At that time, the Japanese language was like a small piece of fish bone stuck in the throat of mainstream U.S. society; the harder they tried to swallow it, the more firmly lodged it became. The Japanese language was what some Japanese Americans clung to as proof of their existence; the more U.S. society tried to exclude them because they could not be assimilated, the more fiercely they stuck to their mother tongue.

The outbreak of war between Japan and the United States on December 7, 1941, suddenly changed the status of Japanese from an ethnic language used only among families and friends to a hostile tongue regulated by the State. Speaking Japanese became synonymous with connection to the enemy, Japan, and speakers of Japanese were suspected of being traitors who would incite the Japanese war spirit and trumpet Japanese nationalism.

The U.S.-Japan war deeply divided a Japanese American community in which the Japanese and English languages had previously coexisted in a delicate balance. Against the backdrop of war, language had a decisive power to determine how people lived as well as their ultimate destiny. Between the centripetal force of the English language and the centrifugal force of the Japanese language in the U.S., a confrontation emerged along a spectrum of attitudes: from those who could pursue total assimilation to American society by speaking English to those who could not speak English well and wanted to preserve their ethnicity by speaking Japanese, including those who could utilize their ability with the "enemy language" as interpreters and translators working for the U.S. war effort. Their decisions reflected, in different ways, their personalities, family backgrounds, and attitudes about the future. Because it determines outlook and worldview, the power of language overshadowed all of the decisions of these conflicted people, to the extent that no one could reason clearly about what to do. This division within the community produced a climate of distrust in which each side accused the other of betraying either their original or their adopted country and language.

Even today, so many decades after the war, the Japanese American community is still divided about issues of language, loyalty, and "betrayal." In the last decade or so there have been a few visible signs of Japanese Americans initiating harmony within the community by positively facing the painful history of their brothers' "betrayal." However, some of the survivors and their descendents still appear to be unconsciously avoiding the pain they would have to go through in order to acknowledge what has happened. It almost seems as if they are waiting in silence for the parties involved to simply pass away. But with the passing of these survivors, the inside story of the Japanese American incarceration, some of the history of a Japanese American community divided against itself — by shame, blame, and betrayal — is about to be erased from history without a trace.

This book is an attempt to throw into relief the anguish of Japanese speakers living in the English-language world of the United States. What I have attempted to introduce here are the lives and struggles of Japanese-speaking Japanese Americans (known as *kibei nisei,* a minority within a minority) who survived the tempestuous period of World War II when Japanese was an enemy language.

Because of prejudice, the *kibei nisei,* especially the *kibei* "No No's," have been forced to fall silent in spite of having lived in the United States for so many years. The dawn of the new millennium has seen the term *kibei nisei* itself become nearly extinct.

The stories of these men must not remain buried like a dirty secret in Japanese American history. Their voices should be heard.

★   ★   ★

My interest in this historical moment began when I was living in South Dakota. One day in spring 1995, I received a letter from California. I did not recognize the name of the sender, but he had a Japanese name. I found out, however, that he had been a fan of my articles when I was a reporter for the San Francisco *Nichibei Times* for nearly two years before I moved to South Dakota. In Japanese, he wrote that he was Japanese American *nisei* and wanted somebody to write his story. In the envelope, along with the letter was a legal document titled "AFFIDAVIT," as well as letters from an attorney, Wayne M. Collins.

With those documents in my hands, I thought back to a night that I had spent at a powwow in Bismarck, South Dakota, a few years earlier. I felt as if I were holding someone's life in my hands, sensing an almost palpable energy of purpose, of fate, circulating around me. I thought, "I have to do this because I now live in South Dakota, the almost barren land the U.S. government had chosen for Indian reservations." With the same reasoning, the same government had chosen locations for incarceration camps for Japanese Americans during the war. "I have a reason to be in South Dakota," I said.

My research started from that moment. I met the man who had mailed me the documents and visited his *nisei* friends in California. Over time, the group of people I was destined to meet extended from California to Washington and eventually to Japan. I visited their homes and spent hours talking with them in Japanese while the tape recorder was running. In so doing, I was able to meet fifteen Japanese American *nisei* men and collect their stories. Yes, they were all men. Because of traditional values of hierarchical Japanese family dynamics, they were the ones assumed to have political power and therefore the ones who were singled out and punished for expressing their beliefs. They were considered "troublemakers," "disloyal" to the U.S. during the war, and long stigmatized in the Japanese American community. I interviewed the following men, some of whom wished not to have their full or real names used:

Tsutomu Umezu
Kenji Takeuchi
Harry Ueno
Susumu Kako (pseudonym)
Tadahiko Okamoto (pseudonym)
Yoshio Nishikawa (pseudonym)
Ichiro T. (pseudonym)
Jiro T. (pseudonym)
Saburo T. (pseudonym)
Masashi Nagai (pseudonym)

★　★　★

In summer 1992, I visited United Tribes Technical College in Bismarck, North Dakota, for a Native American powwow. During the four days of the powwow, dance contests kept the arena alive with music and color from early morning deep into the night. The powerful drumbeat was accompanied by eerie singing, and the cadences in an exotic language shook the tar-black sky. The heat of the dancers' steps seemed to rise from the abyss to warm the chilly night air of the region's short summer.

Absorbed in the almost tangible excitement that seethed in the dark under a foreign sky, I was engrossed in a blissful moment, liberated from the cares of daily life, strolling casually among the brick buildings of the campus. Suddenly, a door in front of me creaked open. In the narrow beam of light cast through the door, I glimpsed the face of an older Native American man with black-framed eyeglasses. Probably thinking there was something strange about an Asian woman hanging around an Indian gathering, he introduced himself as David Gipp, president of the college. Upon learning that the suspicious woman was Japanese, he said in a lively, nostalgic voice, "You remind me that about eight years ago someone visited here from Japan. He told me that he had been here before."

A Japanese had been here? Hearing those words, I was plunged back into reality as the dark excitement of the exotic night suddenly waned. Unlike the East or West Coasts, with their large Asian populations, how could there have been any Japanese people so deep inside the United States, in this distant and harsh terrain that sometimes reached -30° F in the winter and felt as if it had been abandoned by the rest of the world?

Becoming more and more curious about this history, I visited the North Dakota Museum in the center of Bismarck adjacent to the cultural center. It was there that I first saw a photo exhibit of Japanese and German prisoners detained together. One of the photos in the exhibit was of a group of Germans, titled "Enemy Aliens Enjoying Poker." Next to it was a photo of a group of Asians in hats getting off a train at gunpoint. The photo's caption read, "Japanese brought to Fort Lincoln – February 1942." Then I remembered seeing that one of the old three-story brick buildings at the college still had bars on the windows.[1]

It did not take long before I learned that more than fifty years ago the buildings of United Tribes Technical College had been used as a wartime enemy alien incarceration camp, overseen by the United States Department of Justice during World War II.

---

1. In fall 2003, Dennis Neumann, Public Information Director at United Tribes Technical College, found a Japanese inscription on the brick wall of the Sitting Bull Residence Hall on campus. The inscription is the name of a historically stigmatized pro-Japan/anti-U.S. radical group (Ishimaru Family History, p. 15; Yanagisawa, 2007, pp. 144-145).

*　*　*

Six years later, during my South Dakota years, I boarded a bus leaving from San Francisco's Japantown on a pilgrimage to Tule Lake Segregation Center in northern California. Two hundred fifty people in four tour buses took part in this pilgrimage. Almost all of them hailed from the Pacific Coast states of California, Oregon, and Washington, the states from which the Tule Lake inmates had forcibly been removed. I found myself comfortable on the bus, listening gratefully to the sounds of English spoken the way I speak it, sounds that were not harsh or pronounced with emphasis on certain consonants and syllables, but more gentle and flowing. I could tell that this was San Francisco, not South Dakota. I basked in the relief of not being alone.

On the second day of the pilgrimage, our tour bus made its first stop at the former site of the stockades. Under the control of the Army, these buildings had held as many as 350 people during insurrections such as inmate protests and strikes for better living conditions. Even now, they are surrounded by barbed wire and bear a placard that reads, "No trespassing."

Of the original six buildings, only one remains. For a prison, it had an excessive number of conspicuously large windows. Inside, a pale gold concrete wall caught my eye. This wall no longer had the heavy, oppressive feeling of a prison; there were cracks and chips in the paint here and there, and for some reason the doors had all been removed, revealing only the white wood frames. Just inside the entrance was a large rusty gas stove, perhaps where a guard had been posted. There were eight rooms in all. None of the rooms appeared to be for individuals. With as many as three hundred crammed into a facility with capacity for only one hundred, it was no wonder that dissatisfaction and antipathy toward the government escalated further.

Wondering how many people had been confined in this room, I was looking around when an older man spoke to me in Japanese: "There is some controversial material over there."

"Controversial material"? Did he mean traces left behind by the people considered extreme-right radicals?

I walked over to the place he had pointed out and found a lot of graffiti penciled on one of the walls. The words were inscribed in Japanese so darkly, firmly, and forcefully that you would have thought the pencil would break. Suddenly, across more than fifty years, the twisting, breast-rending anguish of the people imprisoned in this place came vividly to life.

There was evidence that bunk beds had been lined up against the walls, and the most extreme Japanese-language graffiti was concentrated on the upper third of the wall. The writer must have scrawled the graffiti while lying on the top bunk, seized by violent emotions. I could not read them without straightening my spine and tilting my head ninety degrees. "Great Japanese Empire." "Down with America." "Fist." "Revenge." "Humiliation." "Fools." The words read more like intense anger toward the United States than allegiance to Japan. "Why have I been treated this way? I am an American citizen, born in America. Imagine putting citizens in a place like this! Don't trifle with me! America can eat shit."

I felt the ghastly force of his anger, which seemed to leap into my eyes like the sudden strike of a coiled cobra. I had to avert my gaze, brushing the wall with my forehead to let go of the pent-up resentment now revived after the passage of fifty-odd years. I also found Japanese characters: *ryokoku kitto*. Had the writer perhaps meant *shikkoku kitto* [chained without freedom]? Was he expressing determination to someday break free of the shackles that bound him? On the bed below, it seemed that someone had been counting off the days on his fingers. Where the lower bunk would have been, I saw the word for "July" and the Chinese character *sho* written three times. Like the four vertical lines crossed though and "bound" by a fifth horizontal line to keep a tally, here in the States this five-stroke character is drawn line by line to keep a count of 5. Had the prisoner been keeping count of the days in July and stopped at July 15?

Where the opposite bed would have been, I found the English words, "Show me the way to go home." No doubt a *jun nisei* ("pure" second-generation Japanese American) youth, whose native tongue was English, had been here too. The beautiful script belied his aching desire to return home. Under such circumstances, to what home could he go?

Some of the prisoners had been here following Japan's defeat in World War II. Written on the wall in Japanese was, "Entered on Sept. 29, 1945. Born Aug. 20, 1919, Iwakuni City East, Yamaguchi Prefecture." This prisoner also had been young. The "green season" of youth comes but once in anyone's life. To think that he had to spend it here…

After reading these words, I remembered the voice of one of the men I had interviewed: "At a time when life should have just been beginning, the forced removal and incarceration caused us to lose everything. It was a bitter pill to swallow."

The more calmly and philosophically the experience is spoken of, the more evident the depth of the wounds sustained becomes. Such voices have I heard in San Francisco's Japantown. Even the fire and passion of youth are supplanted by a meek expression with the passage of years. Did the single-minded fervor of this man, who had been counted as one of the "disloyal," turn into a number, merely a statistic, and vanish just like that from this world?

More Japanese writings have been discovered in what is known as Farmer Brody's Garage. The camp's residential barracks were sold off after the war for one dollar each to veterans who settled in this area. Mr. Brody had been one of them. He used the former barrack purchased from the government as a garage. The exterior had been refurbished with new wooden panels and painted a bright green, but the interior remained unchanged.

The stained cream-colored walls were covered with graffiti written in ideographic *kanji* (Chinese characters) and the simplified syllabic characters of *katakana*. Here, too, I found strings of political messages whose meaning was not entirely clear to me, as I was born after the war.

"The America of Asians. The Japan of Asians. Land inhabited by the sacred people." "His Imperial Majesty of Japan is of Urajio, Russian, and Primorski stock; he is from not of the land of the gods, the land of the Buddha, nor the land of the stars." "… is the right wing, is a white fig." "… is left wing, is red, is Russian, has come from Russia." "Natives of Wakayama, without exception, will be rounded up by the American government for repatriation to Japan." And so on.

Words like "spy," "*Kokuryukai*" [Black Dragon Society] (a nationalistic group), "Hirohito," "East Prussia," "the Crimea," "Tojo Hideki," and "Empire" were clearly visible among the countless strings of graffiti scribbled in pencil and incoherent at first glance. There was also one that read, "Japan was the one that started it. This war is Tojo."

This Japanese graffiti reminded me of the plight of Native Americans in the U.S. At the end of the nineteenth century, the American Indians, fearing that their ethnic culture would be forever lost, began to hold Ghost Dance ceremonies imbued with the emotional power of prayer. These dances were their own parting gifts to themselves as they confronted the fearful possibility that they would soon vanish from the face of the earth. The American government, mistakenly believing that these dances were rites designed to summon evil spirits in opposition to the white man, suppressed the ceremonies with a heavy hand, fearful of something they did not understand.

Exactly half a century later, the government took the same course in its handling of American citizens who sought salvation in Japanese culture and language, having been roundly rejected in their bid to be accepted as American. Despised as "disloyal" even by other Japanese Americans, Japanese speakers were hounded to the point of being driven from the country.

Through this book, I would like to emphasize the fact that one hundred years ago, long before the war, the *issei* (first-generation immigrants who by law could not be American citizens) believed that understanding the Japanese heart through the Japanese language would contribute to a multiethnic, multicultural ideal, an ideal even today still thought to be at the center of the American spirit. To honor their pursuit of this ideal, I still must struggle in my own small, steady way — even if I do it alone — as proof that I have lived.

ACKNOWLEDGEMENTS

In 2000, I published *Nihon no heitai o utsu koto wa dekinai* [I Cannot Shoot a Japanese Soldier]. In 1999, when the book manuscript was selected as a finalist in the Rennyo Award competition sponsored by Kawade Shobo Shinsha publishers, I then thought that it would be important to translate the book into English. The translation finally became a goal in 2004, but I had no idea how difficult and time consuming it would be. Since then, for nearly ten years I struggled to make this book happen, with hope of seeing the faces of aged men satisfied to know that their voices had finally reached an American audience. Sadly, the translation process has taken so long that I will not see many of them ever again.

First, this book would have been impossible without the sincerity and trust of N. D., Kenji Takeuchi, K. H., Tsutomu Umezu, the T. brothers, Harry Ueno, I. F., J. E., Mitsuo Aoyama, Masatoshi Aoyama, Tom Akashi, Tetsuo Asano, and Teruo H., who generously shared their stories with me.

And although the sheer volume of research materials covering the injustice committed by the U.S. government is far beyond my reach, I received generous scholarly and research help from Teruko Kumei, Akemi Yamashita, Elaine Yoneoka, Haruo Kawate, Takasumi Kojima, Eileen Tamura, Kaoru Matsushita, Hisayuki Ishimatsu, Mikio Okada, Dennis Neumann, J. K. Yamamoto, Bill Yoshino, Ikumi Yanagisawa, Mariko Mizuno, Sachiko Takita-Ishii, Art Hansen, Barbara Takei, Satsuki Ina, Eric Muller, Takeya Mizuno, and Greg Robinson. For primary research, I made two pilgrimages to Tule Lake in 1998 and 2008. These visits were warmly welcomed by Kokuho Kasai, Keiko Asano, and the members of the Tule Lake Committee.

When I mentioned the translation project to Takeo Shimizu, he did not hesitate to offer me a generous gift to make sure I could bring the translation to completion; his understanding and encouragement inspired me not to give up on the project. Since he passed away in 2007, all I can do now is to imagine his big smile and laughter, congratulating me for a "job well done!"

The book's theme — the political power of language — is reflected in all the work that went into making a new English book from the Japanese original. This work would have been impossible without the efforts of two professional translators and two editors. Hisako Ifshin was courageous enough to be the first translator to tackle my Japanese writing, and Cheryl Fujimoto also contributed to the translation task. To fine-tune the English version, I was very lucky to have a capable editor in my husband, Michael. On top of his heavy professional load directing a writing program, he served as my editor for many years, wordsmithing the translation to make it suitable for English readers. The book could not have been finished without the expert copyediting assistance of Carolyn Law, who grappled with and brought together the two distinct citation systems I used to document the English and Japanese source materials, Winslow Colwell, who crafted the book design, and Jan Vander Meer, who put the finishing touches on the book with expert proofreading assistance.

Finally, I wish to express my sincere gratitude to my family: Michael again, who has encouraged me to be a writer since before we were married, and my daughter, Emi, who has lived in and embraced two cultures, Japan and the United States, since her early childhood. They put up with me and supported me even when I neglected the everyday tasks of daily life through all the years I was writing the original Japanese book and working on the translation. And although my late mother and father, like most pre-war-educated, old-fashioned Japanese parents, never put their encouragement in words, I still feel their final silent support.

The meaning of a word changes with time and context. One word, *gaman,* brought by Japanese immigrants into pre-war America, has survived in the Japanese American community until today. Originally it signified Japanese obedience to authority, but in this country it has come to mean a more American-style resilience and patience to struggle for one's integrity and dignity. With this book, I convey my whole-hearted respect to all Japanese Americans, whose struggle for the last 150 years will keep giving me the energy and spirit to survive in America.

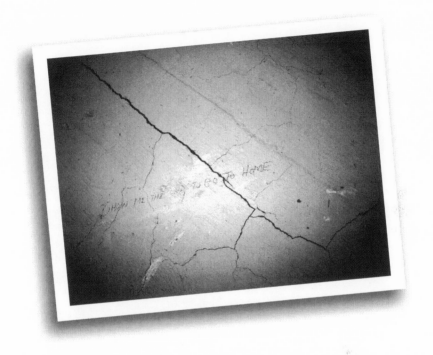

SHOW ME THE WAY
TO GO HOME

CHAPTER ONE

FORT LINCOLN ENEMY ALIEN INTERNMENT CAMP, DEPARTMENT OF JUSTICE, BISMARCK, NORTH DAKOTA

The Japanese and the Germans

The book, *Enemies: World War II Alien Internment*, by John Christgau (1985), features a picture of a German casino at Fort Lincoln Internment Camp in Bismarck, North Dakota, during the last world war.

In the picture, all the ceiling beams are decorated with German signboards, and the scene looks so festive that it could be from a real beer hall in Germany, far across the Atlantic. According to Frank Vyzralek, historian and retired North Dakota State Archivist, "The Internees themselves decorated the place following a Bavarian Beer Hall motif" (2003, p. 6). And, as recounted in an article in the *Bismarck Tribune*, at "one end, an artist [had] painted a mural depicting an Austrian dance; other painted scenes of scenic spots in the fatherland attested to the internees' homesickness" (Moen, 1946). In the picture, two long counters frame a door at the far end of the room. In front of the counters are square tables arranged in three lines, and each table is surrounded by four chairs. According to Vyzralek, the capacity of the hall was two hundred.

It was January 16, 1944, when the beer and wine casino, long awaited by internees,[2] finally opened (Christgau, 1985, p. 119). Many of the prisoners gathered every night to drown their sorrows in the casino, which

---

2. "In May 1943 the German group obtained permission to establish a Casino, converting one of the frame barracks so that it contained a complete kitchen, wash room, coffee counter, cake and cookie counter, beer and wine bar and tables and chairs to seat 200" (Vyzralek, 2003, p. 6).

sometimes even opened at ten in the morning. The sale of beer and wine was discontinued in May 1945 to prevent trouble that might stem from the expected German surrender leading to increased drunkenness among the German detainees (Christgau, p. 165).

The men smoked to their hearts' content and drank seven-cent glasses of beer and wine (the wine was mixed half and half with sparkling water) until their curfew at 10 p.m. The smoke of the men's cigarettes filled the large space so thickly that they could not even recognize each other. Although the beer was only three percent alcohol, not strong enough to make them *very* drunk (or so their captors thought), they gradually did get drunk and sang in German. Among the Germans were men with Japanese faces, humming along to the melody of the German songs they did not know, drawn along by the Germans' excitement.

It was an abnormal world, composed only of men, nearly a thousand of them, secluded from the outer world by high walls, barbed wire, and guard towers. And beyond the barbed wire was a stretch of lonely farmland expanding far beyond the horizon without the slightest trace of human civilization. Even if someone could get over the wall, there was no place to hide. In this place that seemed like the end of the earth, where the horizon was so distant that it appeared slightly curved, the men desperately but patiently waited for the time to come when they would be released. Some Germans did try to escape, only to be shot dead.

Susumu Kako, a kitchen worker, was one of those who went to the bar every night to drink beer to pass the time away.

> On the train on the way there, they checked on what kind of work I could do at Bismarck. I wrote down "cook" and "shoe repair." Then, when I got to Bismarck, they said they didn't have enough cooks and asked me to cook. For a while we, the six cooks, prepared all the food. We got up at five in the morning and prepared meals. We couldn't serve everyone at once, so the men from each building would come at different times ... you know. I would make breakfast, lunch, and dinner one day, then another cook would come and prepare it the next day. I didn't work every day; I worked every other day. Internees took turns

by room doing the dishes. We made meals for five hundred people. The food was relatively good. They paid me eighteen dollars a month, plus three dollars pocket money. We had a lot of meat, and we cooked three hundred pounds of rice per meal. I would make six hundred pounds for lunch and dinner. Breakfast was usually something like bacon and eggs and toast. As I said, the food wasn't that bad! The kitchen was large, so we divided it in half: one side was for Japanese; the other for Germans. The Germans had a ration of rice as well, but they didn't eat that much rice, so they said, "I'll give you rice if you give me potatoes."[3] A barter, you know. Also, they asked me to fix the Germans' shoes because they had nobody to fix them, and I said okay. They tipped me.

"Bismarck life was good," Susumu Kako said with a smile. "There were only men. It was fun. We could even play tennis, baseball, and other games."[4]

Yoshio Nishikawa, who worked as a negotiator with the authorities for the kitchen crew, said that he yearned for some interaction with the Germans in those days. "I had studied a little German in high school. I couldn't really converse in German but I could speak a little broken

---

3. "Consideration of the different nationalities was given in the way of food, luxuries and other goods. The Germans were given an abundance of potatoes. The Japs were given rice…. The mess hall was divided by a partition. An ordinary line was later substituted. Upon arrival, the Japs had no cooks. The Germans did all cooking and later trained Jap cooks" (Moen, 1946).

4. "Recognizing that athletics and other recreational activities were vital for a smooth running camp, the INS administration cooperated fully in providing both equipment and facilities, including three tennis courts, one concrete and two clay, a regular size soccer field, three softball diamonds, three outdoor basketball courts and skating facilities. Almost unique was the ski slide built one winter, to fit within the fenced enclosure. The activities were wide and various: billiards, soccer, fistball, handball, gymnastics, tennis, badminton, table tennis, swimming, ice skating, hockey, softball, basketball, volleyball, judo, wrestling and boxing. In addition there were theatre and cabaret performances, movies twice a week and a sizeable library of both scientific and fiction books. Also there was a band, orchestra and chorus in addition to three pianos and a small organ" (Vyzralek, 2003, p.10).

German. I could say the numbers in German, and they seemed to think of me as a bit special. It was broken German, but because I spoke in their language, they seemed to feel close to me somehow. I worked at the canteen for just a short time, and we could buy candy and cigarettes there. The Germans came to the shop and we traded jokes then."

About seven hundred Germans were confined in the Fort Lincoln camp (Vyzralek, 2003). They lived in barracks, separate from the old three-story brick buildings where the Japanese-faced[5] men were housed. As their mess halls were also separate, the two groups hardly ever saw each other. But in the evening, because they had time on their hands, the men from both groups gathered at the casino in twos and threes and talked in English about the war and their lives, usually complaining about their internment (Christgau, 1985, p. 163).[6]

On arriving in Bismarck, Nishikawa and others were supplied with boots, jackets, and gloves by the U.S. government. He remembered, "They warned us that winter in Bismarck was so cold. We were told to never grab a doorknob with bare hands, otherwise our skin would stick to the knob."

At the end of April, when spring finally came and melted the snow and ice that had shut the men inside for more than half a year, the German and Japanese-faced men played baseball and soccer together. The Germans were not good at baseball, but they were strong at soccer. In summer, they held the Japan-German Swimming Competition. The young Japanese-faced men were bewildered by the Germans, who swam in the nude "without embarassment" and "began to chide the Japanese for their reserve" (Christgau, 1985, p. 163).

---

5. Because the men had been American citizens but were educated in Japan, had Japanese features, and had renounced their American citizenship (some of them were actually stateless), I use the term "Japanese-faced" to refer to them.

6. "'Rumors that Germans and Japs had to be segregated because of their inability to get along are not true,' [Ike] McCoy said…. 'Germans and Japs drank beer together, patronized each others' stores, and cooperated excellently. There were no major incidents between the two'…., McCoy said that the main difference between the two nationalities was that the Japanese were more community minded. The Germans were more selfish and greedy" (Moen, 1946).

Fort Lincoln, 1942

Fort Lincoln was built on the east side of the Missouri River in 1900, and, until 1939, had hosted only a few infantry regiments there in the middle of the Plains. In early 1941, the U.S. government decided to turn it into a camp for enemy aliens, who allegedly were a threat to the security of the United States. In June that year, 220 Germans and 162 Italians were brought by train from the East Coast to Bismarck Station. Only the Germans got off and were sent to Fort Lincoln in military trucks. Among them were sailors who had been arrested for illegal overstays (e.g., stranded on board ships in U.S. harbors) or who were alleged members of German loyalist groups supporting the Nazis. The Italians did not get off and instead were taken to Fort Missoula, Montana (Christgau, 1985, p. 8).

On February 9, 1942, at the break of dawn, 415 Japanese men arrived in Bismarck from the West Coast on a special thirteen-coach Northern Pacific train. The unloading of the Japanese was not completed until about 9:30 a.m. (*Bismarck Tribune*, February 9, 1942). In wind so cold that it numbed the skin in an instant, the Japanese, wearing hats and long coats and aware of the submachine guns trained on them, stepped carefully out onto the snow-covered ground. They were taken to Fort Lincoln packed twenty-five to each truck. The Germans, who had already settled into the camp, watched the Japanese get off the trucks from the other side of the barbed-wire fence. Between the areas designated for the German and Japanese internees was a buffer zone ten feet wide (Christgau, 1985, p. 34).

Two weeks passed. On February 26, a second group of 715 Japanese dressed only for a typical California winter, many of them thinly clad and bare headed (*Bismarck Tribune*, February 26, 1942), was sent from Terminal Island in Los Angeles in a nineteen-car immigration train. Because they had been engaged in fishing from radio-equipped boats, they were regarded as the most dangerous and most likely to guide Japanese troops in the event of an invasion. As these newcomers arrived at Fort Lincoln and found old acquaintances among the Japanese already there, they called out greetings and slapped each other on the back, delighted at their reunion in this bitterly cold weather. The Germans looked upon this with a kind of awe (*Bismarck Tribune*, February 26, 1942; Christgau, 1985, pp. 34, 76).

In its sixty months of operation, the Fort Lincoln camp saw the deaths of nine Germans and three Japanese. Of these deaths, two were suicides: one Japanese and one German (Vyzralek, 2003). One of the Japanese was Jinnosuke Higashi, fifty-five years old, from the first group that had arrived on February 9. On March 19, prior to his hearing before the Alien Enemy Hearing Board, Higashi hung himself from a ceiling beam in the washroom after conducting a farewell ceremony with his colleagues.[7] The funeral services were held at Fort Lincoln, as his wife had already died and his only son's whereabouts were unknown[8] (*Bismarck Tribune*, March 20, 1942; Christgau, 1985, p. 76). As if to console Higashi's desolate soul, a severe blizzard blanketed Bismarck for a week after the incident. The remaining men refused to occupy the building until the beam used in the suicide was replaced (Vyzralek, 2003) and spent their days in monotony, confined indoors (Christgau, p. 76).

After Higashi's death, a Japanese man from Wakayama Prefecture died of a heart attack in the barber shop on March 12, 1942 (*Bismarck Tribune*, March 20, 1942; Itoh, 1982, p. 104; Yanagisawa, 2007, p. 158). There was one even earlier death recorded — an elderly Japanese man from California. It was said that he was shot to death by a guard when he left an assembly to go to the bathroom (Itoh, p. 104).

The arrest and internment of enemy aliens (Japanese nationals) from the Japanese American community began immediately after the Japanese attack on Pearl Harbor on December 7, 1941. By February 16, 1942, more than two thousand Japanese on the mainland and 879 from Hawaii had been arrested and sent away (Niiya, 2001, p. 209). In North Dakota before the war, there were about eighty Japanese residents (Yanagisawa, 2007, p. 148). One of them, Harry Hayashi, a successful Japanese businessman who had settled in Carrington, North Dakota in 1920, was arrested by the FBI on the night of February 25, 1942, for failing to comply with enemy alien regulations, and was sent to Fort Lincoln soon thereafter (*Bismarck Tribune*, February 26, 1942; Yanagisawa, 2007, p. 155).

---

7. According to FBI report file 100-10177, Higashi was born in 1888 in Wakayama, Japan, and came to San Francisco in 1905.

8. When Higashi died, his son Tsutomu became an orphan at 18. Later, Tsutomu became a leader of a "radical pro-Japan" group (H. Ueno, private papers).

During the war, there were over fifty detention and internment facilities for aliens spread across the United States, including eight Immigration and Naturalization Service (INS) internment camps. Fort Missoula, Montana, was for Italians and Japanese; a huge camp in Crystal City, Texas, was for Germans, Japanese, and their families; Fort Stanton in New Mexico was a maximum-security facility for German prisoners; Santa Fe, New Mexico, and Kooskia, Idaho, were for Japanese internees; and camps in Kenedy and Seagoville, Texas, were for Germans, Japanese, and their families *Snow Country Prison Exhibit Guide*, 2003, p. 4; Yanagisawa, 2007, p. 152).

Most of the Japanese were held at U.S. Department of Justice enemy alien internment camps in Fort Missoula, Montana; Fort Lincoln, North Dakota; Santa Fe, New Mexico; and Crystal City, Texas (Niiya, 2001, p. 11).

As time wore on, these original Japanese internees gradually disappeared from Fort Lincoln. Some were repatriated to Japan by boat through wartime exchanges; others were relocated to ten War Relocation Authority (WRA) incarceration camps, which the U.S. government called "relocation centers," across the United States, or to other enemy alien internment camps in such places as Santa Fe, New Mexico. According to Vyzralek (2003), "By September 1942 all of the internees but the original group of German seamen had been 'paroled, released or transferred to the custody of the Army'" (p.4).

Fort Lincoln, 1945

On a quiet Saturday, February 3, 1945, three years after the arrival of the first Japanese internees, Acting Chief Parole Inspector Ike McCoy received an inquiry out of the blue asking whether he could accept 650 new Japanese-faced prisoners. He was also asked in the same message about the possibility of taking on thirty-five Italians. Worried about possible problems, McCoy conferred with Dr. Gerhard Sprenger, the German detainees' representative. Sprenger replied that he was agreeable to having Germans living with Japanese but added that their cohabitation with Italians would be impossible. With this advice, McCoy said no to the Italians but had no reason to reject the Japanese (Christgau, 1985, pp. 144-145).

On February 10, it was announced at the Tule Lake Segregation Center near the California-Oregon border that 650 Japanese Americans who had renounced their U.S. citizenship would be sent to North Dakota the following day. Upon hearing the news, a crowd gathered outside the Tule Lake office to shout for joy, cheering, "Banzai! Banzai! Banzai!" in the traditional manner (Christgau, 1985, p. 146).

The next afternoon, a large group of young men waited for departure. Their heads were shaved and they wore grey sweatshirts bearing the characters *hokoku* [patriot], signifying *Hokoku Seinen-dan* [Patriotic Young Men's Group to Serve the Homeland]. After lunch, these vigorous young men, suspected of having made an oath of loyalty to Japan, were loaded onto trucks, taken to the station, and put on the 2:30 p.m. train (*Tule Lake News*, February 15, 1945). Of the 650 renunciants, 632 were Japanese Americans and 18 were Japanese (Otani, 1983, p. 304).

In contrast to previous *hokoku* departures, which were similar to send-offs for soldiers going to war[9] (Otani,1983, p. 304; Shirai, 1981, p. 198), there were no Japanese flags for these men, and they heard neither *Kimigayo* (the Japanese national anthem) played on a trumpet by their fellow *Hokoku Seinen-dan* who remained behind the barbed wire nor the three cheers of "Banzai." "It was a quiet departure," said Yoshio Nishikawa, remembering that day.

The train that Nishikawa and others boarded was a specially prepared transport train composed of ten coaches, two dining cars, three sleeping cars, and two baggage cars. The train windows were blacked out, shutting out the scenery. Fifty-two armed patrol inspectors escorted the internees, and early in the trip, Senior Patrol Inspector Red Selland of Fort Lincoln went through each compartment informing everyone that they would arrive in Bismarck on Wednesday. It was a three-day train journey from the West Coast to the center of the continent. The train first went north to Portland, Oregon, and then straight east. From time to time it would stop in a station to let other trains pass (Christgau, 1985, pp. 145-146).

According to Nishikawa:

---

9. For example, the departure to Santa Fe had a spectacular farewell with bugling and drills (Collins, 1985, p. 99).

When we went through Montana, the train stopped from time to time for construction. When people saw us, they most likely thought that we were POWs from Japan. We all had shaved heads, you know. On the train trip, although we were not wearing Rising Sun headbands, we did have on sweatshirts with the *hokoku* characters on them. So people who saw us seemed to think that we were captured Japanese soldiers. They had probably never seen a Japanese person before.

Nishikawa added that no one threw stones at them or used abusive language toward them.

According to most accounts, the "troublemaker" renunciants were very courteous toward the authorities on board the train. Some had difficulty communicating in English, but in general they were quiet, well mannered, and cooperative (Christgau, 1985, p. 146).

The train carrying the 650 men arrived in Bismarck at 8:00 a.m. on Wednesday, February 14, and the young men were taken off the train at gunpoint. Nishikawa still clearly recalls their collective fear at that moment: "When we got off the train at Bismarck, I got so frightened when they said, 'Japs, get in there!' while pointing guns at us. And then we got on the bus."

They were soon transferred to army trucks and sent to Fort Lincoln. At the entrance to the fort stood two tall stone gateposts between which a big signboard reading FORT LINCOLN was hung. From the northwest corner of the entrance they could see a guard tower in the distance.

The young men were told to gather in the gymnasium, where they squatted on the floor. They saw a big sign: "Welcome Japanese People." Officer-in-Charge McCoy made a short greeting to the 650 shaved-headed internees, then Dr. Jung greeted them in Japanese. Jung, who had taught high school in Sapporo, Japan, and represented the German internees, offered to share the bars, shops, and entertainment with the new residents. The doctor continued, "It is certainly a pleasure to bid you a hearty welcome.... It was our intention to greet you with a band, but it was too cold.... We know why you were segregated and sent here. We are proud of you for being loyal to Japan" (Christgau, 1985, p. 161).

Two additional groups of *Hokoku Seinen-dan* members were sent to Bismark, one group of 125 on March 4, 1945 (Takei, 2005, p. 89), and another group of one hundred on June 5, 1945 (Yanagisawa, 2007, p. 156).

Soon after starting their new lives at Fort Lincoln, the leaders of the *Hokoku Seinen-dan* demanded access to Japanese doctors, dentists, and Buddhist monks (Christgau, 1985, p. 161). By mid-March, they had received Japanese textbooks, at which point they started studying Japanese language and traditional culture five hours a day. Despite the U.S. government's concern that Japanese language study could be dangerous because of the possibility of propaganda in the texts, McCoy permitted them to study, commenting that the youth needed activities that let them work off their energy and that it was reasonable for them to study Japanese since they intended to return to Japan (Christgau, p. 162).

A weekly Japanese-language newsletter, *Hokoku*, published articles about the camp, along with folktales from Japan that would entertain the internees. No news about the war was available in Bismarck (Otani, 1983, pp. 309-310). One former internee told me that he learned Japanese, calculation on the abacus, and math from a member of the *Hokoku Seinen-dan* who had graduated from the University of California.

Nishikawa recounted those days in a quiet, halting voice:

> We didn't get up terribly early; it was probably around six o'clock. We slept in bunk beds, one on top and another on the bottom, like soldiers. Every morning, the government officers came to check on us, so we had to stand next to our beds. When they entered our barracks, which held about fifty men, the soldiers came in groups of three. They were not allowed to carry guns into our bunk room. At one point, after checking us, one of the soldiers said, "Fifty Japs." Since we were all in such high spirits those days, we said, "What did you say?" and surrounded him, the soldier. His use of the term "Japs" touched a nerve; he should have said "fifty men." Saying "Japs" made it sound as if he was insulting us or looking down on us. On the other hand, it's true that we were waiting for an opportunity to find fault with our captors. So that soldier really touched a nerve, but since he

said, "I'm sorry," we didn't threaten him or try anything.

Nishikawa, who was in charge of the kitchen, was asked to take responsibility for reading General Heihachiro Togo's teachings in his bunk room every morning. "The victory or defeat of the Empire depends on this battle," he would read. The young men sat up straight, listening with their eyes closed. They were driven by an enthusiasm that made them feel as if they had to prove their Japanese dignity to the U.S. government. At meal times, they bowed politely before entering the dining room. The authorities could not hide their surprise at the well-mannered Japanese.

In his report to the Justice Department on March 2, 1945, McCoy said that there was nothing of note to comment on about the behavior of the Japanese. He reported that each morning they "pay some sort of individual homage to the emperor or someone" and that "it is apparently a matter of their religion and I believe it would be going rather far to try to prevent it." He also noted that in the dining room, after carrying their trays to the table, they seemed to say a short prayer. Keeping in mind that most of the Japanese were still young boys and that they were very cooperative, McCoy said, "If they desire to pray silently there is little we or anyone else can do about it and I think it foolhardy to try to interfere" (Christgau, 1985, p. 162).

The Fort Lincoln camp was very much like a self-contained city and included a well-equipped seventy-five-bed hospital, with two doctors and four nurses available to take care of the sick, and a seven-thousand-volume library (Moen, 1946; Rogers, 2003). Each barrack room had a shower, and the camp even had an indoor swimming pool and an ice-skating rink. Life was much better than at the Tule Lake camp, where a family of four or five was crammed into a space of about twenty by twenty-five feet. In the Bismarck community, rumors even circulated that the internees were living and eating better than the civilian population (Moen, 1946; Vyzralek, 2003).

In addition to their assigned tasks, together with the Germans, the Japanese-faced men worked at making suitcases by hand, played mahjong, and wrote letters to the families they had left behind in Tule Lake. One man, Itaru Ina, wrote more than seven hundred haiku poems in Japanese and exchanged a total of 180 letters with his wife in Tule Lake during less than a year of internment at Fort Lincoln (Yanagisawa, 2006, p. 34;

Yanagisawa, 2007, p. 158). His haiku poems spoke of his "fence sickness" in bitterness and sorrow (Nakagawa, 2004). Sometimes Ina " shreded [sic] his bed sheets to use as writing paper, and then had sewn the cloth note inside the waistband of his pants for his wife to find.This was how he got around military censors, ... telling her that his pants needed mending" (Nakagawa, 2005a).

Movies such as *Major and the Minor, A Haunting We Will Go, Lloyd's of London, Castle in the Desert, No Time for Love, The Iron Major,* and *Rainbow on the River* were shown every day (Nozaki, 2007, p. 133). To keep the mood lighthearted, administrators showed dance movies featuring Fred Astaire and Ginger Rogers (Nozaki, p. 142). And the young people also read *manga* (graphic novels) to while away the time (Yanagisawa, 2007, p. 158).

Even so, some people were desperate to find a way out. German internee Max Ebel recounted the story of a Japanese internee who tried to commit suicide. "One night he and another German heard the toilet flushing repeatedly. When they went to investigate, the two found the Japanese internee with his throat slit, flushing his blood down the toilet bowl. Ebel and his friend got help and saved the Japanese man's life." Another Japanese internee gave Ebel a rosary, declaring that he no longer believed in the Christian God because a small opening in the crucifix had led to his arrest by the FBI; Ebel has treasured that rosary all these years (Nakagawa, 2004).

Sometimes the men even made unexpected discoveries. Nishikawa recounts:

> There was a barbed-wire fence about twenty feet back from
> our building. Beyond the fence was a field, and on the other side
> of the field was a house for the interpeters. We all had families
> in Tule Lake, so of course we sent letters to them. The interpret-
> ers checked all the letters; read them all.[10] The interpreters all

---

10. Outgoing and incoming internees' mail was censored. Internees could subscribe to magazines and newspapers, providing the publication was received direct from the publisher. An internee was not allowed to have his family send him a publication because of the possibility that words might be underlined for a code (*Bismarck Tribune,* February 22, 1946).

lived in that house. We noticed, from a distance, that they were women ... Japanese women. We, all men of course, were curious. When we looked through the fence and saw four or five women walking in front of the building, we called to them, hoping they would hear us.

Lowering his voice nostalgically, he commented that there had truly been all sorts of people in the camps.

A considerable number of letters must have been sent and received by the 750 *Hokoku Seinen-dan* members to and from their families in Tule Lake. The task of the interpreters at Fort Lincoln was to inspect these letters, which were written by American-born men in the Japanese language, and to censor portions that were considered dangerous. Some letters had so many parts cut out that they looked like beehives, checkered with holes.

At the end of the short summer in North Dakota, news of the Japanese defeat arrived. According to Nishikawa:

When we heard that Japan had been defeated, of the fifty of us in the room, each may have had a different feeling, but we *kibei* burst into a fit of rage. Some kicked the walls and furniture around them; others threw things across the table. Speaking from the point of view of the *kibei nisei*, who had been educated in Japan, ... well, it was natural that they would get angry. But I just felt sad and could summon no harsher feelings.

About thirty out of the fifty *kibei* went back to Japan on the first repatriation boat. Quite a few of them were hardliners who believed only in Japanese victory. We could not converse with them because they never agreed with people who accepted Japan's defeat, nor did they treat them as human beings. And some of them forced their ideas on others. Some were argued down. I felt sorry for those *jun nisei* who had never been to Japan, but I didn't know what would happen if I stuck my nose into these matters, so I kept my mouth shut. But at that time I thought they were normal; their feelings about Japan came from the bottom of their hearts. We felt the same way about Japan, but we honestly accepted the defeat. Some could not.

★   ★   ★

Removed forcibly and incarcerated at the Tule Lake Segregation Center in California were those considered "disloyal": the Japanese Americans who did not answer "yes" to the following questions:

"Are you willing to serve in the armed forces of the United States on combat duty, wherever ordered?"

"Will you swear unqualified allegiance to the United States of America and faithfully defend the United States from any or all attack by foreign or domestic forces, and foreswear any form of allegiance or obedience to the Japanese Emperor, or any other foreign government, power or organization?"

The tag of "disloyalty" — having been labeled traitors for failing to take an oath of allegiance to the United States — still haunts the Japanese American community like a ghost, undermining the spirits of both those who did the labeling and those who were the victims of this label. In particular, the *Hokoku Seinen-dan* and its parent group, *Sokuji Kikoku Hoshi-dan* [Volunteers for the Immediate Return to the Homeland to Serve] have been reviled and looked upon with prejudice up until this day. Having insisted on returning to Japan as "genuine Japanese," members of these groups were blamed for renouncing their American citizenship, agitating rebellion, and threatening to use violence to force others to give up their U.S. citizenship as well. They have been described as radical right-wing political terrorist groups in Japanese American history and are now dying off with this dishonor. This sad state of affairs has come about mainly because most of the members of this group lived their entire lives in the United States as Japanese-language speakers, and few people ever tried to get beyond the Japanese-English language barrier to understand them.[11]

---

11. Recognition and acceptance of the long-ignored and stigmatized resisters, especially the renunciants who were labeled as pro-Japan radicals in the history books, has finally begun to occur in the twenty-first century. In 2003, the North Dakota Museum of Art organized an exhibit titled *Snow Country Prison*, featuring several photos of Fort Lincoln and its internees, along with haunting haiku poems by Itaru Ina. Ina's haiku poems were also featured in the Emmy Award–winning documentary film, *From a Silk Cocoon* (2005), produced and directed by his daughter,

Looking back at his past, an aging *kibei nisei*, a former member of *Sokuji Kikoku Hoshi-dan*, said regretfully, "After the war, too, probably because I was on the government's blacklist, I could not get any kind of job related to the federal government. Here, the Japanese language and my Japanese education were just a hindrance, of no use at all. Recalling those days before and during the war, I feel so angry. I can't get along with the Japanese Americans who speak English."

Even now, in the final chapter of his life, the "burden of language" he has borne for so many years wells up in hard feelings from the bottom of his heart.

Sympathizing with his parents, who wished to return to Japan, one internee I met on the Tule Lake pilgrimage joined the *Hokoku Seinen-dan* and was sent to Bismarck. After the war, he went to Japan for the first time in his life with his parents. "I thought it was meaningless to remain in the United States, the country that betrayed us. So, I said, 'Let's go to Japan. America betrayed us, so what's wrong with favoring Japan?' This arguing among us Japanese Americans is needless, don't you think?"

When an interviewer, Phil Shigekuni, summing up the feelings of the divided Japanese American community, suggested, "Rosa Parks, King, and the rest of them had the support of their people. Many white people, and other minorities were with them. But you ... you got support from nobody," Kentaro Takatsui (*Oral and Documentary History*, 2000) replied with emphasis, "Not even from our own people."

Satsuki Ina. The opening ceremony of the *Snow Country Prison* exhibit was held at the United Tribes Technical College, Bismarck, on October 4, 2003, finally revealing to the public the scarcely recorded history of Fort Lincoln during the war. Another documentary film, *The Cats of Mirikitani,* about Tsutomu "Jimmy" Mirikitani (a *kibei* artist who renounced his U.S. citizenship, became a homeless street artist in New York City, and ultimately reclaimed his citizenship) was also well received by audiences in the U.S. and Japan. Mirikitani passed away in 2012.

CHAPTER TWO

ENGLISH OR JAPANESE?
A MANIPULABLE IDENTITY

The "Whitening" of Japanese Americans

In 1988, the translation of Mike Masaoka's autobiography, *They Call Me Moses Masaoka: An American Saga*, was published in Japan. The book's Japanese subtitle is "The life of a great populist leader emerging from the turbulent experience of Japanese Americans in the United States." Masaoka was decorated twice by the Japanese government after the war for his efforts to change U.S. law to help Japanese nationals in their quest to be naturalized as well as to improve the social status of Japanese Americans. Masaoka received the Order of the Rising Sun, Gold Rays, in 1968, and the Order of the Sacred Treasure, Gold and Silver Star, in 1984.

Harry Ueno, a *kibei nisei* born in Hawaii in 1907, wrote bitterly about Mike Masaoka's decorations:

> I am quite aware that I am not qualified to say a word about who the Japanese government decorates ... but I feel sorry for a lot of people who were harmed by his organization. It is an interesting country that honors the enemy with the highest decoration of a man who made thousands of Japanese American women and children miserable by informing on his fellow *issei* who made an effort to help Japan, selling them out to the United States government. I am distressed because the Japanese government looks down on and is contemptuous of Japanese in the United States. (Unpublished)

Ueno was one of many Japanese Americans recorded in history as a "troublemaker" because he denounced the U.S. government's injustice at the Manzanar camp in California.

Ueno had no words to vent his pent-up anger about Mike Masaoka, who, on April 6, 1942, when people of Japanese ancestry were being evicted from their homes and herded into temporary detention centers, sent an eighteen-page letter to Milton Eisenhower, director of the War Relocation Authority in the President's Office. In the letter, Masaoka recommended sixteen methods of using the incarceration camps, sites to which his fellow Japanese Americans were moved from the detention centers for training, to reform their behavior and force them to become "better Americans."

Here is a section of Masaoka's letter:

> We do not relish the thought of "Little Tokyos" springing up in these resettlement projects, for by doing so we are only perpetuating the very things which we hope to eliminate: those mannerisms and thoughts which mark us apart, aside from our physical characteristics. We hope for a one hundred percent American community.... One thing is certain: there should be no Japanese language schools. Special stress should be laid on the enunciation and pronunciation of [English] words so that awkward and "oriental" sounds will be eliminated. (qtd. in Chin, 1991, pp. 58-59)

To Masaoka, an "American" meant only someone who acts white and speaks English without an accent. In other words, the only distinction between the Japanese and Japanese Americans bearing the same physical features was language: whether one could speak English with or without a Japanese accent. Interestingly enough, an event from Masaoka's youth enables us to imagine how sensitive he must have been about his English ability. He had done very well in a speech contest in his student days, but a newspaper editorial "erroneously referred to [him] as an alien and piously expressed confidence that if Masaoka could learn to express himself in English, any real American boy should be able to do as well" (Masaoka, 1987, p. 42). Years later, the episode still must have haunted him. For

Masaoka, for Japanese Americans to be accepted by white Americans as fellow Americans, despite their obviously different appearance, they had to at the very least demonstrate a superb command of English.

Mike Masaoka was the product of U.S. society and education. His mother tongue was English; he himself said that he "understood virtually no Japanese" (Masaoka, 1987, p. 87). Born in Fresno in 1915, in the midst of California's strident anti-Japanese environment, Masaoka's family escaped from California soon after his birth, moving to Utah, where such an environment did not exist. Growing up Mormon in Utah, he said that he had "never been to Japan to fall under the evil spell of militarism and emperor worship" (p. 87). The Mormons respected the Japanese because of a certain sense of connectedness with them. Both had experienced persecution and they shared commonsense values. "Historically, the Mormon settlers of Utah generally admired the Japanese" because of "similarities between Mormon and Japanese value systems.... Mormons, like the Japanese, were people of vision" who had "a great admiration for [Japanese] industry, patience, frugality, strong family ties, and their willingness to sacrifice for the future of their people" (Arrington, 1991, p. 92).

Raised in a much kinder environment than California, Masaoka recounted his upbringing thus:

> The *nisei* of our generation were the products of an educational system that promoted Americanism by rejecting one's ancestral heritage. Youngsters were told in grade school to speak English, to forget the alien tongue. The popular reasoning of the times was that if the old-country culture was so good, why had immigrants left it to come to the United States? In America, it was important to reject the past and embrace the present. (Masaoka, 1987, p. 66)

In August 1941, Masaoka, the "great populist leader," was asked to become the first executive secretary of the Japanese American Citizens League (JACL), a Japanese American *nisei* organization. The JACL had begun in San Francisco in 1918 as a small community group consisting of six college-educated *nisei*, and by 1930 had developed into a national organization. It had solid *issei* backing (Kurashige, 2000, p. 1636). *Issei* "counted on the Nisei's American citizenship as a bulwark against new developments of the antagonism that already prohibited Japanese immigrants from becoming American citizens and owning land in California" (p. 1633). In the early 1930s, it had only a few branches outside Washington state, in California and Oregon. But by the time Japanese troops attacked Pearl Harbor, it had expanded to as many as fifty branches spread across those three states. And, as many of the founders of the organization held professional degrees, and because it drew members from higher social positions, "the politics of the JACL was very conservative and staunchly Republican" (Niiya, 2001, p. 219).

As previously stated, just before the war broke out in 1941, the JACL needed to hire a full-time executive secretary to overcome their shortcomings, and they agreed that the person must be "fluent in Japanese as well as English, have good rapport with the *issei*, have a knowledge of Japanese community affairs and JACL history, be able to speak in public, and have the poise and experience to meet with government officials on their own terms" (Masaoka, 1987, p. 57). Mike Masaoka first declined the offer on the grounds that he was "totally unable to meet most of the requirements." Indeed, he was a *jun nisei* who had never been to Japan, didn't speak the language, and had very little knowledge about its culture. And since he had grown up in Utah, he knew very little about the Japanese American communities on the West Coast. The JACL persuaded him, however, promising "to tutor him on the fine points of Japanese American psychology and Japanese community politics," so he assumed the office on September 1, 1941 (Masaoka, 1987, p. 57).

Masaoka, having rejected his ancestral past and embracing "loyalty" to the U.S. as his strongest weapon, was fiercely ambitious to gain status in the white world. Japanese Americans called him a "genius lobbyist with genius eloquence, and surprising persistence in getting what he wanted" (Takeshita & Saruya, 1983, p. 108). In an FBI survey of the incarceration camps, Inspector Myron Gurnea pointed out that in Masaoka and the JACL's outspoken proclamation of loyalty "there are some indications that their views [were] as political as patriotic" (Lim Report, 1990, p. 71). Masaoka impressed the government as being "exceptionally intelligent,

shrewd, wily, quick-witted, persuasive, and not altogether scrupulous"
(Ladd memorandum, 1943). To the government, Masaoka must have
seemed the most appropriate person to lead the Japanese American community, as he was such an eloquent speaker, aspired to become a lawyer,
and was blessed with extraordinary talent as a lobbyist as well.

Even to this day, the Japanese American community is still split in its
evaluation of the activities of the JACL before, during, and after the war,
with a substantial degree of underlying resentment, particularly about
the JACL's enthusiastic cooperation with the U.S. government when it
incarcerated people of Japanese ancestry. It could be said that this lump
of resentment has solidified enough to seal people's lips, and young *sansei*
and *yonsei* (third- and fourth-generation Japanese Americans) rarely ever
mention the name "Mike Masaoka."

Of course, no one can forget the heroes of the Japanese American 100th
Infantry Battalion, the 442nd Regiment Combat Team in Europe, and the
Japanese American intelligence officers in the Pacific Theater in World
War II. But in reality, as soon as the war broke out, Japanese Americans
were disqualified for the draft. Interpreting this as an act to deprive
Japanese Americans of the right to swear their loyalty to the United States,
Masaoka began lobbying the U.S. government for "the right to fight." And,
as a consequence, the brilliant accomplishments of these troops went
down in history.

While promoting the demonstration of Japanese American loyalty
through segregated combat units, Masaoka advocated excluding from the
community any Japanese and Japanese Americans whom he and his followers deemed dangerous to their cause. While conducting a remarkable
propaganda campaign of loyalty to the white majority, he worked relent-
lessly to purge some of his countrymen who retained too much of their
Japanese-ness.

What we discover in the relationship Masaoka developed with the
U.S. government is a common tactic of those in power: use one enemy to
control another enemy — what might be called the "divide and conquer"
method. To divide a community, the U.S. government would make use of
the diversity, disagreements, and generation gap within that community,
arbitrarily appointing those supportive of the government as leaders of the

community. They would then communicate with that community only through this "puppet" liaison. The community would then splinter, weakened by confusion. At the same time, assimilation to white society would accelerate, and at last the community would disappear. This dividing then "whitening" of ethnic minorities is a familiar practice and has historically been the U.S. government's first step toward achieving its long-range intention of eliminating an ethnic group.

In the fall of 1941, just before the outbreak of the war, when conflict between Japan and the U.S. seemed unavoidable, Curtis Munson finalized his report on the investigation of the Japanese American community commissioned by the U.S. government. The report suggested dividing *issei* from *nisei*:

> The loyal Japanese citizens should be encouraged.... The Nisei should work with and among white persons, and be made to feel he is welcome on a basis of equality.... Put responsibility for behavior of Issei and Nisei on the leaders of Nisei groups such as the Japanese American Citizens League.... The aim of this will be to squeeze control from the hands of the Japanese Nationals into the hands of the loyal Nisei who are American citizens. It is the aim that the Nisei should police themselves, and as a result police their parents. (qtd. in Weglyn, 1996, p. 51)

"Squeeze control from the hands of Japanese Nationals"— those people the report targeted for exclusion from the Japanese American community as dangerous elements were *issei*, Masaoka's parents' generation, who had been born in Japan, and *kibei nisei*, members of his own generation who were born in the United States, educated at elementary and secondary schools in Japan, and who had returned to the U.S. Inside the Japanese American community there were many conflicts, including one between *issei* and *nisei* over generational change and another between *kibei nisei* and *jun nisei*, who did not know Japan at all, over who would succeed to power. The U.S. government was aware of these various conflicts and ready to take advantage of the ones that would benefit their interests.

It is no coincidence that the history of Japanese Americans in the

U.S. bears some resemblance to the history of Native Americans. Similar strands that allowed the government to take advantage of internal division within and among tribes, such as forced Anglicizing and English-only education intent on the extinction of a culture, run through both historical accounts. Some incarceration camps for Japanese Americans were even built on or near Indian reservations. Inmates at Poston in Arizona were used as laborers to build adobe schools for Native Americans (*Hokubei Mainichi*, March 14, 2008). Dillon Myer, director of the War Relocation Authority, was eventually promoted to director of the Bureau of Indian Affairs. Lucy W. Adams, who had been in charge of progressive education for the Navajos, became the first director of the Education and Recreation Department of the WRA (M. Mizuno, n.d., p. 278). In view of all of these "coincidences," how can anyone deny the U.S. government's intention? Japanese Americans and Native Americans, non-Christian and non-white "aliens," were in the same boat: *jamamono* [in the way].

In an oral interview, Ken Takatsui, a *kibei nisei* who was sent to a prison camp at a converted Navajo reservation boarding school for failing to pledge his loyalty to the U.S., waxed eloquently about his identification with the Native Americans:

> If these walls [of the boarding school] could speak, what sadness, grief, and tears were shed by these hapless little children who must have cried for their mothers and fathers! These people had experienced this self-same relocation ... as we the NIKKEIS had been forced to endure. They too were being scattered all over the country ... to be obliterated as a people.... Chief Sitting Bull was right. He said, "RedSkin speak with straight tongue, paleface, him speak with forked tongue.... We were also DESICCATED. This was our "TRAIL OF TEARS." This was our DIASPORA! (*Oral and Documentary History*, 2000, pg. 17)

Japanese American Community
and the Various Types of *Kibei Nisei*

On the power of language to unify, Park (1922) notes that "in America, ... it is language and tradition, rather than political allegiance that unites the foreign populations. People who speak the same language find it convenient to live together" (p. 5). Riggins (1992) observes that "shared language is a strong source of social solidarity. Language loyalty is also correlated with ethnic identity" (p. 281). Even today we can understand the necessity for this kind of social organization among Japanese in the U.S. in pre-war days, even in the face of Japanese linguistic diversity and the possibility of misunderstanding due to differences in dialect and nuance. In those closely knit communities, people "often quarreled bitterly among themselves, especially over economic matters, but when friction and dissension, whatever the cause, seemed in danger of being known to the outside, the leaders said, 'Let's forget it. After all, we are all Japanese together'" (*Impounded People*, 1946, p. 27).

Noboru Shirai, who was born and raised in Japan, explains how this friction divided the Japanese students at Stanford in the 1930s: The English-speaking *jun nisei* "faced the same devastating discrimination as we overseas Japanese did. As a result, they became very angry. Instead of venting their anger at their tormentors, they directed it at us Issei. Even though they tried to be quiet and polite in front of us, the Nisei could not contain their frustration. They blamed the Japanese for their suffering and condemned Japan in front of us" (2001, p. 16).

Even so, the *jun nisei* could not completely cut off their ties with the Japanese language or people because they still shared a great deal with the older generation. According to Kurashige (2000), JACL leaders took advantage of their Japanese-ness by rationalizing their "Americanism as being rooted in Japanese culture" (p. 1652). What is more, JACL elites, such as lawyers, dentists, medical doctors, and entrepreneurs, "relied upon the ethnic enclave for their businesses and practices and therefore had vested interests in enhancing and protecting" Japantowns such as Little Tokyo in Los Angeles (pp. 1636-1637).

Kibei nisei, American citizens, were born in the United States but for various reasons were sent to Japan when they were young. Most of the *kibei* attended elementary and middle school in Japan and then returned to the United States for high school and beyond. As children under their parents' control, going to Japan to be educated was not their own choice; therefore, when they came back to the United States, the *kibei* were forced into a very difficult position within the Japanese American community. Although technically American citizens, they were to some degree handicapped in their command of the language and culture of American society.

Emotionally, the *kibei* were Japanese, but their complicated situation made their relationship with parents, siblings, and *jun nisei*, as well as their lives in the United States, difficult. According to one U.S. government report, the *kibei* were like fair-weather friends in choosing between Japanese and American ways: "Some Nisei claimed that the Kibei were like bats in the old folktale of the war between mammals and birds; whichever side was winning would be joined by the bats" (*Impounded People*, 1946, p. 31).

However, JACL members too "differed significantly from the bulk of their own generation. They were overwhelmingly male … and were about a decade older than the majority of their peers in the second generation" (Kurashige, 2000, p. 1636). Furthermore, "they were almost twice as likely to have attended college and to be in management positions than most of the Nisei men their age" (p. 1636). The conflict between *kibei* and *jun nisei*, especially elite JACL members, was almost inevitable due to factors such as age, social background, and class hierachy, all of which the Japanese community emphasized.

The Japanese language and culture that the *kibei* brought back to the U.S. was welcomed not only as a means of facilitating communication with *issei* but also of maintaining a Japanese American community in which the Japanese language was still dominant, and the generally older Japanese-speaking *kibei nisei* were expected to do more for the future of the community than the *jun nisei*.

According to the San Francisco *Nichibei* (May 20, 1936):

As more energetic *kibei* youth come back to the U.S., completely different types of Japanese magazines and books begin to sell well in book shops. In the past, general-interest Japanese magazines were popular, but these days, political and economic review magazines like *Chuou Koron* and *Kaizo* are selling very well.... This is due to the *kibei* youth, who welcome new knowledge, as well as philosophical and intellectual writing, enthusiastically.... If this trend continues, Japanese bookshops and newspapers will be able to continue doing business for at least fifty years.... Needless to say, the reading capability of the *kibei* far outstrips that of the *issei*; therefore, this [the return of the *kibei*] is the first step forward in cultural progress from the perspective of ethnic development.

As such, the preservation of Japanese culture was seen as identical to the progress of the Japanese American communities, and it was widely believed that "the existence of *kibei* Japanese American citizens enriched the communities in which they lived" (*Nichibei*, June 14, 1936). In some ways, the future of the Japanese American community depended on the preservation of the Japanese language combined with the U.S. citizenship of the *kibei*, providing a kind of U.S.-Japan bridge. In fact, in May 1941, a column in the *Utah Nippo* suggested that *kibei nisei* should prove their citizenship and loyalty to the U.S. by leading it from a country of "masked justice" to a country of true "liberty and justice for all" (T. Mizuno, 2005, p. 222).

The *kibei* formed organizations in each area they returned to. In San Francisco, for example, they formed organizations such as the *Dai Nippon Seinen-kai* (Youth Organization of Japan) and the San Francisco Student Organization to strengthen unity among Japanese speakers through various activities, such as speech contests and film festivals. However, the difficulties the *kibei* faced in their lives in the United States and the isolation and discrimination they were experiencing from U.S.-educated *nisei* continued to be problems. These problems illustrated the need to create an organization that would educate *kibei* to be good American citizens. The *issei* depended upon harmony among the *nisei* for the development and expansion of the foundation they had created, through considerable effort and hardship, to protect the rights and improve the welfare of Japanese American citizens in the future. Considering the hostile atmosphere developing around the entire Japanese American community, the JACL needed to encourage even the somewhat suspect *kibei nisei* to participate in their organization, thus expanding their reach.

Troubled by the inability of the two factions of *nisei* to get along with each other, the JACL used biculturalism to "manufacture consent" among different groups of Japanese Americans (Kurashige, 2000, pp. 1634, 1648). Some chapters of the JACL wanted to expand their influence in the Japanese American community by incorporating *kibei* as members and educating them to be good American citizens. One of them, the San Francisco chapter, was active in the expansion, and big headlines such as "Citizens League Urges Kibeis to Join Group" and "SF Chapter Bids for Local CL [Citizens League] Unity" appeared in the *Japanese American News* on June 24, 1936.

But for the *kibei nisei*, the process of joining the JACL did not go very smoothly. While the JACL urged that all *kibei* be admitted, some *kibei* started claiming that they needed their own independent chapter, a move that Saburo Kido, the national executive secretary of the JACL, strongly opposed, arguing that "the Kibei cannot be given an independent charter. Only one chapter will be recognized in any city" (*Japanese American News,* June 24, 1936).

At this point, dark clouds seemed to loom over the situation, but the San Francisco JACL and *kibei*, realizing their need to unify for a common purpose, agreed that the *kibei* could have their own independent department inside the San Francisco JACL chapter if the following conditions were met: (1) that at least one *kibei* citizen be named to the Board of Governors; (2) that as American citizens, *kibei* be given every consideration to carry out activities not specifically prohibited by the constitution of the Citizens League or by decision of the Board of Governors; and (3) that both the English and Japanese languages be permitted in general meetings of the Citizens League. At a special meeting, JACL Executive Secretary Kido voiced his approval of the proposal (*Japanese American News,* June 28, 1936). These three conditions illustrate the critical role that linguistic and cultural differences played in the unification and management of an organization such as the JACL. More specifically, the JACL's compromise demonstrates the political power of language in intraracial and intracultural negotiations.

One *kibei*, Minoru Kiyota (1997), described the difference in attitude toward assimilation between *kibei* and *nisei* as follows:

> The nisei tended to believe that successful assimilation was vital to their survival in American society, so most of them struggled to mold themselves after the patterns set by the dominant Anglo culture.... But we kibei ... still had a spiritual foothold in Japanese culture. On the one hand that foothold gave us a firmer sense of identity, but on the other it rendered some kibei less capable of fully assimilating into American culture — and also perhaps less motivated to do so. (p. 59)

According to a WRA report:

> [The *kibei*] by and large ... were predominantly Japanese in culture and outlook. Careful examination revealed, however, that this group also exhibited significant divergencies. There was no hard and fast correlation between political loyalty, cultural identification, or economic attainment. Politically, they ranged from the few who had assimilated the jingoism of Japanese militarism, to those who were equally vehement in their opposition. The great majority fell somewhere between. (*Community Government, 1946*, p. 15)

The values of some of the *kibei* went far beyond the boundaries of nation, culture, and race, appealing instead to universal causes such as Communism. For example, Karl Yoneda changed his first name from Goso to Karl to honor Karl Marx. According to Yuji Ichioka, "The global struggle against fascism had the highest priority. Everything else was secondary, so that[Yoneda] chose to cooperate with his own [U.S.] government, even though it stripped him of his rights" (qtd. in Yoneda, 1984, p. xvii).

The Rising Power of the JACL

Yoshio Nishikawa, a *kibei nisei* who was sent to the Fort Lincoln Internment Camp for Enemy Aliens in Bismarck, was born in San Francisco in 1915 and went to Japan with his parents when he was five years old. Sadly, just after their arrival in Japan, his parents died. He returned to the United States when he was fifteen years old and later joined the JACL. According to him:

> There were *kibei* in the JACL. They asked me to become a member since I was a Japanese American, so I did. I don't think the Japanese speakers were disliked. I'm a *kibei* but I joined the *nisei* in a lot of activities ... and I spoke English a little. They probably liked those of us who spoke both languages; that's why they included *kibei* as members, I feel. The more members, the better, they thought. It was advantageous for them to use bilinguals like me for recruiting members.

Tsutomu Umezu, who later in his life became president of *Nichibei Jiji Shinbun,* the San Francisco English-Japanese newspaper, was born in 1919 in Sacramento, California. He went to Japan in 1924 and returned to the U.S. in 1937. Umezu, who had organized the *kibei nisei* youth association in Sacramento, was invited to join the JACL soon after his return to the U.S. Umezu recalls, "They said if I joined it would be to my benefit in many ways, so why not? The leader [of the JACL], who was much older than we were, thought we were stupid, as our English was not good ... and [was] really high-handed. Looking down on us, he tried to force us to join. I expected that he would do it in a more friendly way ... that's why I quit."

Building upon the foundation of the Japanese American community that the *issei*'s many years of hardship had set in place, the *kibei nisei* and the *jun nisei* were just beginning to gain momentum when war was declared on December 7, 1941. At the outbreak of the war, all *issei* leaders (representatives of Japanese American associations, such as prefectural associations, the press, Japanese language school teachers, and Shinto and Buddhist priests and monks) were immediately rounded up by the FBI, resulting in a power vacuum in the community. Those who quickly filled the vacuum were members of the JACL, who had already been collaborating with the government, utilizing their English ability and intelligence to communicate with the U.S. government.

At this point, the friction between the JACL and the Japanese American community, which had previously been smoldering as a result of the generation gap, became even more heated. Now that Japan and the United States were enemies, the concept of "patriotism," as defined by the JACL, clearly had the political intention of ousting the *issei*. Thus, the combination of U.S. citizenship and the English language all at once became a concrete and powerful weapon possessed only by American-born *nisei*. Ultimately, their citizenship became a "pass" that in itself proved their "loyalty to the United States," and their ability to communicate in English facilitated and validated their self-expression to the U.S. government.

Masaoka (1987) wrote that as the government gradually came to recognize and condone the activity of the JACL, emphasizing that they were an organization made up of U.S. citizens, the JACL's political power became a threat to many *issei*, causing them to become unfriendly (p. 59). The *issei*, aliens with no U.S. citizenship and unable to express themselves easily in English, had no way out. With the onset of the war, the delicate balance between the centrifugal force of the *issei*'s ethnic pride and the centripetal force of the *nisei*-led assimilation to the United States was lost amidst a loud outcry, and relations between the two groups quickly became worse. At the same time, a strong rivalry and friction emerged between *jun nisei* such as Masaoka and his supporters and the somewhat older *kibei nisei* with citizenship, a rivalry that would ruthlessly corrode Japanese American society for decades to come.

Suspicion Toward Japanese-Speaking *Kibei Nisei*

Presented in the fall of 1941, the State Department's Munson Report noted that many *issei* would become American citizens if allowed to do so, adding that they were loyal, good neighbors who expected to die here (Weglyn, 1996, p. 44). U.S. Attorney General Francis Biddle said that he intended to see that civil liberties in this country were protected: "[The] scapegoat may be someone who speaks with a foreign accent, or it may be a labor union which stands up for what it believes to be its rights. That sort of psychology is the very essence of totalitarianism.... Civil liberties are the essence of the democracy we are pledged to protect" (*Impounded People*, 1946, p. 9). Even after Pearl Harbor, he never wavered in his conviction: "For the Bill of Rights protects not only American citizens but all human beings who live on our American soil, under our American flag. The rights of the Anglo-Saxons, of Jews, of Catholics, of Negros, of Slaves, Indians — all are alike before the law" (p. 10).

The atmosphere of hysteria and suspicion was truly a tragedy of human rights brought on by the media and politicians who repeatedly made statements such as, "It is not only possible but probable that the Pacific Coast will be bombed.... We can lose this war, we can lose this war" (*Impounded People*, 1946, p. 16). War hysteria had begun to further divide the Japanese American community.

A bigger tragedy, however, was the deliberate manipulation of public opinion in which Japanese Americans lost their place in American society. Whereas before the war, liberal magazines such as *The New Republic* and *The Nation* had demonstrated a strong sense of mission in protecting minorities from war hysteria, after the war started, these publications were forced to backpedal on their critical function as watchdogs of government policy. As defenders of national interest, they had to give their full support to the great cause of war: the defeat of fascism and defense of democracy (T. Mizuno, 2005, p. 394). America's absolutism in the fight against "fascism" gave way to domestic relativism in the fight against racial discrimination.

Because of the threat that they might engage in intelligence or subversive activities in conspiracy with the enemy, English-speaking Japanese Americans regarded their fellow Japanese-speaking compatriots as a dangerous element. The Japanese language had always provided those who spoke it with a means of cultivating bonds with their *issei* parents and Japan. However, once Japan became an enemy of the United States, those with Japanese language proficiency, including those who used Japanese to maintain strong bonds with their parents or relatives in Japan, were deemed "suspects" by Masaoka and his supporters. These suspects were *issei* and *kibei nisei*.

Similarly, in the Munson Report the *kibei* were considered the most dangerous element of all. The report claims that if *kibei* were removed, ninety to ninety-eight percent of the *nisei* would be loyal to the United States (Weglyn, 1996, p. 43), but if Japan were to conduct intelligence on the West Coast, "they may get some helpers from certain Kibei" (p. 47). On the other hand, the Report also said that many *kibei* "come back [from Japan] with added loyalty to the United States. In fact, it is a saying that all a Nisei needs is a trip to Japan to make a loyal American out of him," alluding to the fact that in Japan the Japanese Americans were treated as boorish foreigners, which made them feel further alienated and resulted in stronger ties to the U.S. when they returned (p. 42).

Indeed, some *kibei* fiercely opposed Japan's fascism and militarism after they came back from Japan. Karl Yoneda, a Communist, believed that "Japanese Americans should first work to defeat fascism in Japan and Germany and then to address the wrongs inflicted on them by the U.S. government" (Niiya, 2001, p. 425). After being incarcerated at the Manzanar camp in California, Yoneda was trained for military intelligence service and engaged in propaganda work with other *kibei* in Asia (Yoneda, 1984, pp. 151-154).

Masaoka and his supporters considered the Japanese-speaking *kibei*, their rivals of the same generation, as "disloyal" from the very beginning, casting suspicious eyes upon them even before the war broke out. By March 1940, JACL leaders had had several meetings with Army and Navy intelligence personnel and had offered their full cooperation. Distancing themselves from the groups led by *issei*, they declared that they were not under the influence of Japan. They even thought that "many *kibei* had become irresponsible drifters and playboys" because "American dollars (sent from the U.S. to support them in Japan) when converted to Japanese yen permitted almost luxurious living" (Joe Masaoka, JACL Colorado memo, March 28, 1945).

After the war broke out, an anti-Axis committee was organized in a JACL chapter; in order to prove the JACL's loyalty and communicate its intention of completely defeating Japan, some members even proposed an "Earmark a Bomb for Tokyo" campaign, in which each chapter would buy a bomb to drop on Tokyo as testimony to the fact that they wanted to see

Japan defeated. Some even suggested painting the message, "Courtesy of the JACL!" on each bomb (JACL report, January 23, 1942).

Furthermore, the JACL conducted a survey of *kibei*, checking on their religion, education, military experience (in Japan and the U.S.), hobbies, and organizations they belonged to and keeping track of those with and without dual citizenship. They forced *kibei* to cooperate with the survey by threatening to report them to the authorities if they refused to do so. As a matter of fact, the JACL reported the names of uncooperative *issei* and *kibei* to the FBI and were requested by the Navy to report on the living situations of those listed in the Japanese directory on such matters as whether they had lifestyles that exceeded their income, whether they had received funds from Japan for espionage, and whether, in the "general public opinion," they should be trusted (Lim Report, 1990, pp. 37-40). Masaoka himself admitted that he had cooperated with the FBI to the best of his ability (Masaoka, 1987, p. 73).

In May 1942, the JACL first recommended to the Navy that *kibei* should be segregated from loyal *nisei*. This recommendation came just as the eviction order was issued and all Japanese had been gathered into temporary detention centers. In a letter addressed to War Relocation Agency Director Milton Eisenhower, dated June 6, 1942, Masaoka, together with Ken Matsumoto and George Inagaki, provided a detailed definition of the *kibei*. They used WRA letterhead for this letter, a fact that would seem to confirm the long-held suspicion of the Japanese American community that Masaoka and his followers were actually employed by the agency.

In the letter, the JACL leaders defined *kibei* as follows:

> ...in the case of families, if the husband is Kibei and the wife Nisei, the family should be considered Kibei, and if the husband is Nisei, and the wife Kibei, the family should be considered Nisei. Inasmuch as the parents sent the child to Japan[,] in most cases the parents should be held suspect, regardless of the number of other children which they may not have sent to Japan for study.... If the child in question is 16 years of age or more, he is entitled to elect whether he chooses to be placed in the same classification as his parents or not, provided that his parents are

declared suspect. If the child is under 16, he assumes the status of his parents, but on becoming of age may have the privilege of election. (Lim Report, 1990, p. 60)

The letter ends with an unambiguous statement of the JACL's position: "Incidentally, we are in unanimous agreement as to the principle of segregation" (p. 60).

At this point, the government was hesitant to adopt Masaoka's proposal to segregate *kibei* based on a definition that reflected Japanese family values (which bestowed absolute authority on a husband or father) because of the difficulty they anticipated in implementing such a segregation.

However, events soon came to pass that would change the situation. In the late autumn of 1942, Masaoka heard reports of Japanese Americans who, after being moved from the temporary detention centers to the incarceration camps, started "uprisings" at the Manzanar and Poston camps, demanding better living conditions. Hearing this, Masaoka immediately wrote to WRA Director Dillon Myer and advised segregating those who were "disloyal" (Lim Report, 1990, p. 94), since most of the leaders involved in the uprisings were anti-JACL or antigovernment *issei* or *kibei nisei*.

The JACL first offered to inform on those regarded as detrimental to the WRA's efforts. Later, it recommended segregation, calling first for "the immediate apprehension and removal of known troublemakers"; second, for "the segregation of those who desired repatriation to Japan"; and third, for "placing trained investigators within the centers to ferret out those who were disloyal" (Lim Report, 1990, pp. 94-95).

Masaoka himself put it this way: "Loyalty to the United States was not the main issue at that point," as "they were looking for a way to halt intimidation of the peaceful evacuees and violence against certain JACL leaders so the people could live without fear while waiting to be relocated or simply sitting out the war" (1987, p. 131).

Inside the camps, the English language had political power as well. Of course, in the residential blocks, Japanese-speaking *issei* and *kibei nisei* were influential because of age, and "the Issei conception had become crystallized in all centers in the often repeated phrase: 'We are all Japanese together'" (*Impounded People*, 1946, p. 81). But the real power was in the hands of those who were able to officially negotiate with the authorities, the English-speaking *jun nisei*, so the voices of Japanese speakers did not easily reach the authorities.

According to Noboru Shirai (2001), "The worst antagonism [at Tule Lake camp] was between the Issei and Nisei" (p. 74). Mainly due to the language difference, the two groups disagreed on many issues, such as whether to broadcast rebuttals to Japanese war propaganda and which language would be used to emcee entertainment shows (p. 76). Shirai observes that "the Issei and Nisei were behaving like oil and water, never to mix" (p. 78).

In his April 6, 1942, letter to WRA Director Eisenhower, Masaoka demanded preference for English-speaking *nisei* for leadership roles: "We recommend that *issei* be removed from public office; only *nisei* be permitted to vote and hold office of any sort and to have interaction with white Americans" (Drinnon, 1987, pp. 67-68). As a result, for the first time, English-speaking *nisei* were appointed to government jobs in the camps, and they applied themselves to the work earnestly, taking it as a unique opportunity to prove their abilities. Was it a sign of American democracy finally taking effect for those of "alien citizenship" who previously could not find employment, especially government jobs, outside their own ethnic community? All in all, it must have been easy for English-speaking *nisei* with some education to negotiate with administrators at a time when "government employees stationed in remote areas of California were considered third-rate," since "during the war there was a shortage of first-rate administrators" and "there were more highly qualified managers among the incarcerated Japanese than among their administrators" (Shirai, 2001, p. 72).

On the other hand, jobs for alien *issei* or non-English-speaking *kibei nisei* were limited to camp-supervised construction or farm work and cooking, dishwashing, and cleaning, none of which required English ability. *Kibei nisei* Yoshio Nishikawa worked as a cook, Masashi Nagai at the canteen on the nightshift, and Tadahiko Okamoto as a garbage collector. Quite a few of the elders, particularly *kibei nisei*, must have been humiliated by the way the young English-speaking *nisei* ostentatiously displayed their new authority. As it became clear that those with English language ability possessed political power, the radical implications of the Japanese language deepened, as if to counterbalance the English.

The Loyalty Questions —
A Test of Allegiance for Japanese Americans

In February 1943, the U.S. government asked a series of loyalty questions to inmates for 1) recruiting male *nisei* volunteers for Japanese American military units and 2) providing release permits for other inmates.

The most controversial questions were number 27, "Are you willing to serve in the armed forces of the U.S. on combat duty, wherever ordered?" and number 28, "Will you swear unqualified allegiance to the U.S., and foreswear allegiance to the Japanese Emperor and to any other foreign government, power, or organization and faithfully defend the U.S. from any or all attack by foreign or domestic forces?" An explicit confession of "disloyalty" in the form of answering "no, no" to these questions was exactly what Masaoka expected from the *kibei*, having insisted from the very beginning that dangerous elements should be segregated.

Some of the *kibei nisei* educated in Japan did answer "no, no" to the questions, playing into Masaoka's scheme to cause the "disloyal" to surface like invisible ink coming into view. In May 1943, Masaoka recommended to the U.S. government that these "disloyals" should be segregated and that the government should make no more efforts on their behalf. He thus completely turned his back on his countrymen, abandoning them to their fate.

Why did Masaoka and his supporters hate the *kibei* through and through? Since the JACL was from the very start a group that had promoted Anglo-Americanization through assimilation, one can easily guess that they hated the concept of "Japan" that the *kibei* had brought back to the U.S. with them. On the level of family dynamics, it was as if "they endeavored to save a sinking boat by reducing its load, and this came in the form of jettisoning some of their brothers — the inept *kibei nisei*, who were handicapped from the standpoint of living in the U.S. With the sense of superiority enjoyed by those who live on Main Street [i.e., English speakers], English-speaking brothers perhaps could not bear to coexist with the *kibei* — their dirty 'half brothers'" (Yamashiro, 1995, p. 107). Even now, so many years after the war, it has been reported that some English-speaking *jun nisei* still brand *kibei* as defective citizens (Nozaki, 2007, p. 60).

Viewed from the longer perspective of the Japanese American community's future, Masaoka's real intention becomes visible: he and his supporters were afraid that Japanese-accented English and the Japanese spirit and values embedded in *kibei* would remain in the Japanese American community in the future if *kibei* of the same generation, or a little older, were allowed to remain, so they tried to eliminate them completely. Perhaps they wanted to segregate *kibei* by labeling them "disloyal" in order to remove all Japanese things that could be "a blot" on the community or provide a source of shame. Frank Chin's (1991) dramatic interpretation of Masaoka's letter to WRA Director Eisenhower puts this sense of shame in perspective:

> Masaoka, straight-faced, patriotic, and macabre, assured Eisenhower twice that 50 percent of the Issei would die as a result of the conditions of their old age, compounded by the evacuation and violent adjustment to the extremes of desert summers and winters; their deaths would make it easier to eliminate the Oriental sounds, thoughts, and mannerisms in the remaining Nisei. (p. 59)

Issei of advanced years, whom the JACL said should "be branded and stamped and put under the supervision of the Federal Government" (JACL Proceedings, March 8-10, 1942), would die soon. It was just a matter of time. But what about *kibei* of the same generation as Masaoka? The future of the Japanese American community fifty years hence was in the hands of Masaoka and his supporters. They felt that they had to eliminate the "nuisances." First, segregate them as "disloyal," then ultimately repatriate them to Japan; above all, drive them out of the U.S. Those American citizens whose fate it had been to learn the Japanese language and culture were forced into a tight corner by their fellow Japanese Americans.

One day fifty-three years after the war, with a bitterness that obviously sprang from the bottom of his heart, one former Bismarck internee who had been a member of *Hokoku Seinen-dan*, remarked, "I will never forgive the JACL!"

CHAPTER THREE

DOES DUTY TO COUNTRY
GO BEYOND ONE'S FAMILY TIES?

Inu [Informants]

Our bloodlines and ancestry do not determine what we are or who we will become. What better determines the sum of our existence is the social context in which we are placed.

The U.S. authorities assumed that Japanese and Japanese Americans were allied in a close network of enemy aliens and that their imputed racial characteristics — dishonesty, deceit and hypocrisy (TenBroek, Barnhart, & Matson, 1958, p. 315) — would never be diluted or diminished, even after years of socialization in the U.S. So the authorities carried out their forced removal and incarceration indiscriminately, without regard for the many years that the Japanese and Japanese Americans had spent in this country.

However, individual histories show us that in daily life even members of the same family had different lifestyles, striving to find their own place on the spectrum of Japanese language/culture and English language/ American culture. An individual's position on the spectrum depended, to a large degree, on the family environment in which one was raised, the sense of values one inherited from one's parents, and one's own life experiences. Once an individual found his or her position on the spectrum, it would never be a fixed point but would keep moving in one direction or another as time passed. Some positions on the spectrum, of course, opposed each other — even in the same family.

When there is a great difference in power at opposite ends of the spectrum, it is no surprise that informants, known in Japanese as *inu* (literally:

"dogs"), emerged. In their quest for success and power, these *inu* felt it necessary to betray other members of their own community "for the sake of the community."

At their January 30, 1942, meeting, the JACL adopted a proposal for "voluntary evacuation" on the grounds that it would be a "loyal" act contributing to the security and welfare of the nation (Lim Report, 1990, p. 28). As the "voluntary evacuation" became a forced removal, the JACL continued to cooperate with the government.

The JACL worked remarkably hard to facilitate the removal, from providing interpretation/translation services to preparing food and documents. Since the JACL already had such a close relationship with the government through its cooperation on intelligence activities before the war, those involved in the JACL were given privileged positions and preferred treatment at the temporary detention centers, which prompted hostility from others.

According to Noboru Shirai (1981), who was sent to Walerga detention center, a converted migratory worker camp near Sacramento, the sight of those JACL members — sitting in wicker chairs, arrogantly smoking cigars that could never be purchased inside the centers — deeply angered their fellow Japanese, who were having a difficult time in rustic accommodations that did not even have chairs. Further, JACL members went to great lengths to denigrate themselves in the eyes of the whites but were very arrogant to their own countrymen (p. 61).[12] While inspecting people's belongings, the Japanese Americans in charge scrutinized their countrymen so severely that a resentful murmuring, "*Nihonjin doshi de sonogurai no koto wa yurushitemo iinoni*" [Among Japanese, these little things could be overlooked], was frequently heard (Memorandum to Inspector Gurnea, March 30, 1943).

JACL members also had a major role in constructing the incarcera-

---

12. "Regardless of how subservient the committee members were to the Caucasian administrators, they knew their status in the center was high. They became arrogant and haughty towards other Japanese. Sitting smugly in their rattan chairs, they smoked cigars not available to others in the center. This rubbed raw the nerves of the people who had to live without a stick of furniture in the one-room cells of the honeycomb" (Shirai, 2001, pp. 46-47).

tion camps they were sent to after the detention centers. The motive for this move was the expectation that the government would cooperate with them in handling future issues if they obediently followed orders now. After the war, Mike Masaoka (1987) wrote that he was certain that JACL contacts with the FBI and other government officials had done much to ease the plight of many members of the community (p. 73).

In March 1942, the JACL began an official advisory relationship with the War Relocation Authority (WRA). In exchange for his advisory role, Masaoka had the freedom to travel around the United States. He visited the incarceration camps, where he checked up on conditions and called on his countrymen to collaborate with the U.S. government. Informers in the camps reported on anti-government activities and gossip to the JACL headquarters, U.S. Naval Intelligence, and the FBI. Tokutaro Slocum,[13] a member of the JACL Anti-Axis Committee, took pride in the fact that he had handed over forty Japanese Americans to the FBI (Lim Report, 1990, p. 72).

Harry Ueno, a *kibei nisei* from Hawaii, organized about 1,500 Japanese Americans working in the mess hall of the Manzanar camp into a union and tried to stop the black-market sales of government food supplies. When I interviewed him, he said in a casual but provocative tone, "Probably some *inu* ratted on me, and thanks to them, I experienced eight

---

13. Slocum was described as a person "whose face was oriental but whose testimony was reminiscent of corned beef and cabbage and the baseball bleachers. Examples: 'By crackle, you've got me over a barrel, yeah, by golly'" (*Chicago Daily Tribune*, July 2, 1943). Slocum's first language must have been Japanese because he was *issei* and settled in North Dakota with his parents when he was only ten. He was later adopted by the Slocum family of Minot. Thus his family background, his intellectual ability (which earned him entrance to the University of Minnesota and Columbia Law School), and his service with the Marine Corps in World War I won him citizenship and must have given him easy access to total assimilation into mainstream white society, culminating in his being called a "superpatriot" (Niiya, 2001, p. 367). Further, as a very strong-willed and capable person with knowledge of the law, Slocum led a one-man crusade to establish naturalization rights for *issei* war veterans (including himself) and, as an official lobbyist of the JACL in 1934, worked hard to help pass the NYE-LEA bill, which enabled some World War I veterans to be naturalized in 1935 (Niiya, 2001, p. 368). Slocum, an *issei*, and Mike Masaoka, a *nisei*, shared a similar view of Japanese American integration.

prisons and camps without any trial."

Ueno's fellow protestor from that time, Joe Kurihara,[14] was a *jun nisei*, an English speaker who had also served in World War I. Having grown up in Hawaii where racial discrimination was not as harsh as it was on the mainland, Kurihara could not understand the *nisei*'s passive and negative attitude toward white society on the mainland (Nozaki, 2007, p. 170). Having insisted at JACL meetings that all of the Japanese American communities could change government policy by protesting as a single body against evacuation and by rejecting the JACL, he described the passive attitude of the JACL as "an already cooked goose": "These boys claiming to be the leaders of the Nisei were a bunch of spineless Americans. Here I decided to fight them and crush them in whatever camp I happened to find them. I vowed that they would never again be permitted to disgrace the name of the Nisei as long as I was about," he said, venting his anger (Weglyn, 1996, p. 122).

After the JACL resolved to adopt the Japanese American *nisei* volunteer system at the November 24, 1942, JACL convention, criticism of the *inu* became more severe. In fact, some people in the incarceration camps, especially the Japanese-speaking *kibei*, rivals of the English-speaking *nisei*, tried to apply sanctions against the *inu* through violent means.

At Poston camp, warnings to the *inu* "became conspicuous":

> A dog-faced man appeared on the post...; a cartoon of a dog and a real dog-bone bearing the message, "This is for dogs," on the police station wall; a dog with a wienie suspended in front of it on the block 19 post, and a Japanese boy chasing a dog on the block 35 banner. (Thomas & Nishimoto, 1946, p. 48)

---

14. "Joseph Yoshisuke Kurihara ... was almost fifty years old at the time of evacuation. He had achieved a high measure of success in business and commercial activities in southern California.... Prior to evacuation ... he had no interest in and no connection with Japan. ... He was known to be a firm advocate of democratic principles.... When evacuation came, Kurihara gave vehement expression to the embitterment he felt at his 'betrayal' by America and, correspondingly, began to voice pro-Japan sentiments.... Warm and friendly in manner, but self-assertive. Proud of his honesty and integrity and regarded by others as a man of his word. A devout Catholic" (Thomas & Nishimoto, 1946, pp. 363-364).

At Tule Lake camp, in northern California, the reputed *inu* were made to sit at a table marked "seat for *inus*" and nobody dared talk to them (Shirai, 1981, p. 126).[15]

Some inmates even "bow-wowed" when they passed *inus'* rooms, and in one camp someone built a monument marked with Mike Masaoka's name, on which they urinated every morning and evening, as if to wreak some kind of vengeance on him (Harry Ueno, personal correspondence, December 20, 1996). This behavior was even seen at prison camps such as the one at Moab, Utah, where only "troublemakers" were sent. At Moab, a prisoner put a picture of a dog right next to the bedside of a person he suspected; the suspect was of mixed blood, Japanese and white (Embrey, Hansen, and Mitson, 1986, p. 82).

However, rather than show anger, the JACL welcomed the attacks against them because they helped them to identify and rid themselves of troublemakers (*Rafu Shimpo* [Los Angeles], July 15, 1995). Citing the hatred and violence sustained by their Japanese countrymen inside the camps, Masaoka contended that the decline in moral standards in the camps, such as the intimidation of *inu* and riots, was due to the unfair treatment of the *nisei*, which disqualified them from serving in the war. "Rescue *nisei* out of the unhealthy community; segregate those who are 'disloyal' and release those who are 'loyal' from the incarceration camps as soon as possible. The visibility of Japanese American soldiers will be good publicity to turn around public opinion, facilitating the release and relocation of Japanese and Japanese Americans to the Midwest; then, it might be possible to close the incarceration camps sooner...," thought Masaoka. By way of accepting Masaoka's suggestion, the Department of War announced the formation of a special all-Japanese American unit on January 28, 1943, and the next day announced the registration program for both recruitment to military service and leave clearance.

People were confused by the significance of the words "permission to volunteer" and by the content of the questionnaire. They asked, "Why do

---

15. "At mealtimes, [one] family had to sit at a separate table marked *inu*. When they walked through the camp, even their acquaintances avoided coming face to face with them. They were treated like outcasts" (Shirai, 2001, p. 97).

we, who've been detained in camps despite having American citizenship, have to apply to volunteer? Why do *issei* have to take the risk of becoming stateless by taking an oath of loyalty to the United States?" Criticism of *inu* grew even stronger.

Among the holdings at the Bancroft Library at the University of California, Berkeley, are microfilms of papers found at Tule Lake that bear criticisms of the *inu*. Making fun of the *inu* traitors, on one paper are the words, "I'm The White Dog — Sad Jap," in English. On another is a hand-drawn picture of a square Christian-style gravestone inscribed with a name and "FEB 1943, Tule Lake," and topped with a cross marked "*inu*" in *katakana*, probably drawn with strong hatred, a desire to kill.

According to Tsutomu Umezu, a *kibei nisei* who rejected loyalty registration at Tule Lake:

> ... the JACL held a dance party in a neighboring hall while we were seriously preparing for registration, wondering how we could do it. They asked people from Hawaii to be bodyguards in case *kibei nisei* should attack them. Although we never dreamed of attacking or hitting them, they actually feared that we would. They were really scared of *kibei* because we were supposed to be unpredictable. At the same time, they looked down on us as inferior because they thought we couldn't speak English.

Umezu said this sarcastically, with a slight curl to his lips.

Family and Loyalty

In reality, being released to the "outside" world full of strong anti-Japan sentiment was regarded as a kind of punishment by the general inmates. They had a ready-made excuse in suggesting that they had been sent to the camps on the grounds of national security and thus these camps were the safest places for them until the end of the war. They felt that these "relocation centers" were the only places where they could make the effort to become "perfect Americans" until the anti-Japanese sentiment in white communities died down.

At the time of loyalty registration, no one was informed that only the "disloyals" would be segregated. However, on May 10, Secretary of War Henry Stimson indeed suggested to the president that the "disloyals" be segregated, and on July 15 it was announced that Tule Lake would become a segregation camp for disloyals. Facing the limited options — become an Army volunteer, be released, or be interned and remain at the center — people thought hard about the future of their families. They were scared that their families would be separated.

And once disgraced and demoralized by the United States, the problem of how to conduct themselves and make decisions loomed large: "By what rules should we live in these camps?" some people asked. According to Shirai (2001):

> The camp was part of America, and yet it lacked the elements that made it an American society. It was a Japanese society all right, and yet it was not Japan. We in the camp were not living for the benefit of America, and yet we were not living for the benefit of Japan either. Our affiliations had been stripped from us to the point where we asked ourselves why we were living at all. Could it be that we were living just for our families or just for ourselves? (p. 79)

Ultimately, when under such pressure to make a decision, people naturally chose their families.

Masashi Nagai, a *kibei nisei* born in 1922, still remembers his mother's excited voice during the camp years:

> Half-jokingly, Mother said she was lucky to be sent to the camp because for the very first time we lived together under the same roof. We had lived together only four or five years in America when Father was still alive. I went to Japan with Mother when I was five; immediately after that, Mother went back to the United States, and we were separated for twelve years in Japan and the United States. Even after I returned to the United States, Mother was a live-in housemaid and I worked as a live-in house-boy in different houses. Poor things, we were.

The oldest son, he was scared of being drafted by either Japan or the United States.

Even among *jun nisei*, who had been brought up in the strong Japanese culture of their parents, there were some who shared Nagai's feelings about being drafted. As they were expected to be the main source of support for their families, some of them answered the loyalty questions in a way that would ensure that they would be deemed "disloyal" and thus preserve the family:

> I owe a lot to my father. Everything I am I owe to him. All through his life he was working for me.... We are taught that if you go out to war you should go out with the idea that you are never coming back. That's the Japanese way of looking at it ... the men go out prepared to die.... I listen to white American boys talk. They look at it differently.... In order to go out prepared and willing to die, expecting to die, you have to believe in what you are fighting for. If I am going to end the family line, if my father is going to lose his only son, it should be for some cause we respect.... I would have been willing to go out forever before evacuation.... I know my father is planning to return to Japan. I know he expects me to say "no," so there will no possibility that the family will be separated. (Thomas & Nishimoto, 1946, p. 95)

In general, Japanese people thought that once a man was drafted he would certainly be killed, and many *nisei* carried with them the same Japanese fatalistic mentality of "devote yourself to the country and fight until you are killed." This attitude is demonstrated in the story of a *nisei* soldier who fought in World War I; he wrote down his honest feelings about an incident in which a lieutenant asked the soldiers in his command to take out insurance: "It is the tenet of *Bushido* not to bother about money matters, as the soldier's fate and fame is death on the fighting lines, but my duty is to support my parents at home, so, that they might realize something after my death, I wrote ten thousand dollars' insurance. The lieutenant seemed surprised to see it, and he may have thought that I was a miser even after death" (Park, 1922, p. 166).

Sons bore responsibility to their parents even after death. Because of
the forced removal and incarceration, the *issei* had already lost everything
they had earned through many years of toil and sacrifice; on top of their
expulsion and imprisonment, it was unbearable to them to think that their
sons would be taken by the military, especially since they had only ten or
fifteen years of life remaining (Thomas & Nishimoto, 1946, p. 94).

According to Confucian values, not only should children obey parents,
but wives should obey husbands. One Tule Lake pilgrim explained to me
her dilemma in answering the loyalty questions: "In those days, there was
almost no conversation between Japanese men and their wives, so they
didn't talk to each other before answering the questions. So most wives
did not know how our husbands answered the questions. However, even
if we wives answered 'yes' to the questions, if our husbands answered 'no,'
we obeyed them without talking back because we thought of children and
financial matters."

Families Divided in the Camps

Although some parts of camp life, particularly the hard decisions about
loyalty, in fact brought families together, other aspects of camp life actually separated families. The inmates did not have to work hard, and food
and some clothing were provided, which freed parents from many of their
obligations in bringing up children. *Issei* women used their leisure time
for knitting, sewing, and handiwork. *Issei* men played *go* or *shogi*. At night
there were free English classes, so, for the very first time, *issei* could learn
English reading and writing (Drinnon, 1987, p. 76).

Adults, many of whom had worked themselves to the bone to make a
living in the U.S., could take a break for the very first time since arriving in
this country. They absorbed themselves in studying English and pursuing
hobbies; as a result of this and their lightened duties in the area of food
and clothing, they kept a loose rein on their children. Children led lives
that were fairly independent of their parents, picking up a rather carefree
lifestyle. Many returned to their rooms in family quarters only to sleep.

Motomu Akashi, the son of Sanae Akashi, one of the leaders of *Sokuji*

Kikoku Hoshi-dan (Volunteers for the Immediate Return to the Homeland to Serve) at Tule Lake Segregation Center for "disloyals," had no idea of his father's activities. As if shocked by his own words, Motomu said, "I didn't know at all what my father was doing outside in those days ... because he was not at home the whole day and did not talk to us at all. Our family went out to work or spend time with friends, each going their own separate way. And now I read in the history books what my father was doing when he was out of the house those days. That really astonishes me."

According to Shirai (2001), there were many complaints about extramarital affairs and illicit relationships in the camps: "Loud marital disputes between husbands and wives were common. There was so much freedom in the personal relationships between men and women that many were involved in love triangles and even quadrangles. Extramarital love affairs were a major source of fighting" (p. 80). In quite a few of the marriages between *issei* husbands and *nisei* wives there was a considerable age difference, even as much as a generation, meaning that some husbands were old enough to have been their wives' fathers (p. 98).

Many of these marriages were beset by domestic problems and infidelity, all of which exerted a strong negative influence upon the *nisei* children (TenBroek et al., 1958, p. 278). The environment that these children were born and brought up in was completely different from what their parents had experienced. Furthermore, due to the language barrier, both parents and children had difficulty in communicating affection and building emotional bonds, and the breakdown of the family that *issei* lamented as a weakening of "fragile parental bonds" (Shirai, 1981, p. 13) became even more clear as families were faced with loyalty registration.

When discussing loyalty registration with me, Masashi Nagai raised his voice in complaint: "Incarcerated in such a place for such a long time, people became more and more distrustful. Even if they told others they had answered 'yes,' they might have actually answered 'no.' They did not always tell others the truth ... [you] never know."

The distrust was the same even inside families. When parents and children disagreed about whether to be "loyal" or "disloyal," either was allowed to change to "disloyal" and thus accompany those who were identified to be segregated. However, there were some children who answered "yes" secretly, choosing to be released and in effect "shaking off" their parents. More daughters did this than sons.

More daughters chose to depart than sons probably because, according to traditional Japanese family values, women were expected to leave their families when they got married, whereas men, especially first sons, were expected to take the major responsibility for the care of their parents. But it might also have been because the cherished American notion of freedom was much more attractive to the daughters than their Japanese duty to maintain the family, which would compel them to obey and care for their fathers, husbands, and sons.

Manipulation of Japanese Identity

Masaoka's loyalty registration scheme forced his countrymen to pit their loyalty to a country against their family bonds. According to Ichiro T., a *kibei nisei* who saw Mike Masaoka visiting the Topaz camp in Utah several times, "Since Masaoka was educated in the United States, his Japanese traditional family values must have been diminished. In his mind, since parents (*issei*) had their individual rights, children (*nisei*) should have their own rights, too."

Although they were American citizens, *nisei* were forced into camps; even so, they were eager to prove their loyalty to the state, going so far as to beg for government permission to let them prove it and by applying to the Army as volunteers. In some way, these selfless acts must have been a way of repaying an obligation to the country (the United States) that had fostered them and, more importantly, a way for them to redeem the honor of their *issei* parents (Shishido, 1998, p.195). But what was most ironic was the way in which Masaoka was able to convert the same Japanese sense of values — obligation and honor to parents and country and even shame (values that he otherwise regarded as obstacles for Anglo-Americanizing Japanese Americans) — into representing an act of loyalty to the United States.

Masaoka's skillful manipulation of Japanese culture in his political dealings could be best observed in his success at getting many Japanese Americans to serve in the war, leaving their parents and brothers behind as a form of security in the incarceration camps. Masaoka had already proposed this model to the U.S. government in his concept of "parents as hostages" in the forced removal of spring 1942.

It was Masaoka who had put forth the idea of organizing *kamikaze* battalions made up of *nisei* volunteers for the most dangerous missions in exchange for not sending Japanese Americans to incarceration camps. At that time, he suggested that in order to prove their loyalty, the *nisei* should offer their families, particularly their *issei* parents, as "hostages" to the government. According to Masaoka (1987), "I *tried to impress* on them the faith we had in the loyalty of the parent generation. Let them stay in their homes, I urged, and we Nisei will volunteer for a combat battalion to fight against the Japanese. We'll vouch for their loyalty by our willingness to fight and die for our country if necessary, and they in turn would serve as hostages to guarantee our loyalty" (p. 80; emphasis added).

What Masaoka said appears to refer to strong bonds between parents and children. However, to a person raised in the context of Japanese parent-child bonds, what he said does not seem like parent-child loyalty. To be sure, to let their children die for the United States might be proof of Japanese parents' loyalty to the United States because there is an assumption that parents would allow their children to die.

Parents serving as "hostages to guarantee our loyalty" — did Masaoka mean that if children failed to prove their loyalty to the United States they would be abandoning their parents to their own fate or allowing them to be killed? Would these children not be insisting on their *own* rights, even taking advantage of the parents' love for their children rather than children's love of their parents, resulting in a kind of abandonment of the parents? Ultimately, the concept of holding parents hostage, a kind of collateral for loyalty, should be brought up *by* the parents, never something children should force their parents to do. The parent-child relationship that Masaoka tried to impress on the government may have had an "Oriental" flavor on the outside, but it was, in essence, representative of an individualistic American relationship: parents are parents; children are children.

The U.S. military officials turned down Masaoka's proposal, claiming that concepts such as "suicide" and "hostages" did not represent American

values (Lim Report, 1990, p. 24). However, at loyalty registration, the "suicide" and "hostage" issues resurfaced when it became clear that to apply to
join Japanese American troops meant to apply for "suicide," with a "go for
broke" rallying slogan, leaving only "hostages" in the incarceration camps.

Suicide is another Japanese cultural construct that Masaoka unconsciously manipulated. This suicide construct was sometimes attributed to
the soldiers' "samurai spirit" (Kiyota, 1997, p. 240). Minoru Kiyota called
this "samurai spirit" a romantic notion that reveals a total lack of understanding of Japanese Americans; the tears of Japanese American *nisei* units
returning victorious to the United States "were by no means the tears of
Japanese samurai" (pp. 240-241), but were instead the tears of American
soldiers who barely recognized the "samurai spirit."

Caught between American and Japanese family values, the "hostages"
suffered. The authorities judged Japanese families by American family
value standards and prohibited Japanese parents from exerting a "bad
influence" over their children at loyalty registration. Around the time of
registration, the Planning Board, which was organized mostly by *issei* to
negotiate with the authorities at Tule Lake, attempted to stem the anti-
registration tide. They prepared a statement urging "careful thought"
about the registration decision, particularly by those who wished to
remain in the United States. The *issei* statement, however, was withheld by
the authorities because of their objections to the following sentence in the
statement: "Parents should act as consultants to their children" (Thomas
& Nishimoto, 1946, p. 76).

The U.S. government reacted to this *issei* statement by requiring that
before being permitted to leave, those who had answered "yes, yes" to the
loyalty interrogation must answer a final question: "Would you under any
circumstances act contrary to the dictates of your parents?" (Weglyn, 1996,
p.199). The WRA did not want to contradict their conditional acceptance
of *nisei*, an acceptance based on the ability of children to go against their
parents' wishes.

As such, the forced removal, incarceration, loyalty registration interrogation, and Anglo-Americanization of those with Japanese ancestry, all of
which Masaoka supported, were brought together by the U.S. government
in a concerted effort to destroy Japanese hierarchical family relationships

based on Confucian values.

Masaoka (1987) himself admitted that he and his generation of *nisei* were "the products of an educational system that promoted Americanism by rejecting one's ancestral heritage" (p. 75; 1988, p. 66). He also said that he had never been to the land of his ancestry, "did not speak its language, and knew almost nothing of its culture" (1987, p. 239). Masaoka's mother did not understand English well, and it is said that she spoke only broken English when she was naturalized as a citizen in 1954 (1988, p. 305)[16] but that she could somehow communicate with Masaoka. "Even if we could not communicate easily with Mother, neither did we argue with her," said Masaoka, emphasizing "the Japanese style family relationship" (1987, p. 36), but had his mother ever been able to speak her mind clearly enough to Masaoka for him to oppose or disobey her?

Tsutomu Umezu, a *kibei nisei*, said that he thinks that these difficult family relationships are the reason that *kibei* tend to be viewed as violent:

> The *kibei* were unpopular even among *issei*. Many *kibei* had been sent back to Japan because they were a burden to their parents in the United States. When these *kibei* finally came back to the United States, there had been a thirteen- or fourteen-year interval, during which their brothers or sisters had been born. The *kibei* did not understand what those siblings were talking about ... they could not communicate with their siblings. Besides, the *kibei* had spent the most sensitive period of their lives away from their parents ... they [felt] they were not accepted by their parents. What's worse, looking into the future, they could never see themselves being accepted into the world of *nisei*. What could the *kibei* count on? Nothing. How frustrating! To hell with us!

Kenji Takeuchi was sent to his mother's parents in Kumamoto, Japan, to be educated when he was five years old. He attended junior high school

---

16. An extended account of his mother's naturalization experience is included only in the Japanese edition of his book (1988); it does not appear in the English edition (1987).

in Seoul, then under Japanese occupation, and moved to Tokyo by himself. He confessed that he had had a lonely childhood:

> What hurt me the most was that I had been separated from Mother. Still small and young, I felt abandoned.... When I came back at age eighteen, I practiced calling them "Father and Mother," so I wouldn't be so distant from them. But I had never really had any love from Father and Mother. I relied on the idea that my parents' love for me was something like the love I had received from my grandparents. Because of this, I fear that I am somehow psychologically warped.

All things considered, the loyalty question was nothing more than a painful dilemma tearing at the hearts of *kibei* who had taken on Japanese values, even though their family bonds were very likely to be weak.

Kenji Takeuchi was the only one in his family who answered "disloyal" at the loyalty registration, as if to sever his bonds with family.

> My father had been teaching Japanese and *kendo* [Japanese fencing] at a Japanese language school just before the war, so he was sent to the camp for enemy aliens in Crystal City, Texas, when the war broke out. It had already been decided that Mother would be sent to Crystal City from the Topaz camp. My younger brother, who had gone to Japan with me, had come back to the United States earlier than I had and was released after answering "yes, yes" to the loyalty oath. He had not graduated from Japanese junior high school, so he had easily adjusted to life here in the U.S. My other brothers were with Mother. My second brother, who was about twelve years old, then took care of the other three brothers. After making sure that they could join their parents, I decided to [answer no and] go to Tule Lake. Of course, it was scary to take the more difficult path on my own and answer "no, no." But I was firm in my belief. My answering "no, no" was a way to remain constant in my belief, so I had to stay with it. Mother understood me. As a human being ... this

unwavering conviction is what I believe in…. I remember seeing my mother off as she was leaving for Crystal City when I went to Tule Lake. And that was the last time I saw her….

For Takeuchi, was loyalty to country really thicker than blood, as in the case of Masaoka?

CHAPTER FOUR

U.S. CITIZENSHIP AND *BUSHIDO*

I Cannot Shoot a Japanese Soldier!

Kibei nisei Tadahiko Okamoto, who had once been a member of *Sokuji Kikoku Hoshi-dan* [Volunteers for the Immediate Return to the Homeland to Serve], the parent group of *Hokoku Seinen-dan* [Patriotic Young Men's Group to Serve the Homeland], the Japanese youth group at Tule Lake Segregation Center, recalled sullenly:

> I intended to join the U.S. military at any time if they called me up. I had to do my duty as an American citizen. But there's a big difference between going to war after being called up and being asked to take a loyalty oath. In fact, no one could perform their duty without giving an oath. To the loyalty questions, I could not, in good conscience, answer "yes, yes." So I wrote "no, no," and as a consequence I could not join the military. Among the *kibei*, those without principles wrote "yes, yes." They were smart. It was not to evade the draft that I wrote "no, no." It was because I was educated in Japan, had principles, and had the feeling that once we undertake something, we have to follow it through to the very end — to death even — so I thought, in light of that fact, that I could not turn the muzzle of a gun toward Japan. I really felt that I could not shoot a Japanese soldier.

Okamoto regretted being labeled as "disloyal" for the rest of his life because he felt that he had not fulfilled his duty as an American citizen, but when asked, he said that he regarded the loyalty questions and registration as inconsequential. "Why was I 'disloyal'? Why didn't I choose the honor

of being in the Japanese American regimental combat team?" He regretted the way that Japanese martial educational values had permeated his
behavior and the strong sense of conscience that those values had instilled
in him. Torn between conflicting cultures, he spent his life exhausted by
the inner struggle between the Japanese values unconsciously imprinted
upon him in his youth and his sense of duty as an American citizen, which,
instead of being valued, had been trampled upon in a test asking him to
denounce his past in the name of "loyalty."

Okamoto was born in 1921 and held dual Japanese American citizenship from birth. He said that he had never thought of renouncing Japanese
citizenship and that he would hold it dear until the end of his life, as he
was born into it. In fact, Japan passed a law enabling those born prior to
December 1924 to renounce their Japanese nationality by application,
stipulating that a child born in the U.S. of Japanese parents would not be
eligible for Japanese nationality unless the parents submitted a birth certificate to the Japanese consulate within fourteen days of the birth. Many
people were not able to meet this deadline.

In reality, after 1924 the number of people holding dual citizenship
actually decreased, with two-thirds of the children born to Japanese
parents in the U.S. after 1924 retaining only U.S. citizenship. According
to a survey carried out by the War Relocation Authority in 1943, fifteen
to twenty-five percent of all Japanese Americans held dual citizenship
(TenBroek et al., 1958, p. 273).

However, because it was assumed that all *kibei nisei* had dual citizenship, mainstream U.S. society looked upon them with distrust and prejudice, and this was one reason that the Japanese American Citizens League
pressed its members to renounce their Japanese nationality in the 1930s.
The JACL advocated renunciation because the mainstream white community thought those with dual citizenship had loyalty only to Japan,
ignoring the fact that their U.S. citizenship might actually signify loyalty
to the United States.

In his comments about Japanese Americans during the war, Mike
Masaoka (1987) said, "For most Nisei there was no question of divided
loyalty" (p. 56). Did the *nisei* mentioned in Masaoka's term, "most Nisei,"
include *kibei nisei*, whom he detested? Did *kibei nisei*, particularly those

with dual citizenship, really have dual loyalties? If someone thought, "Japan will win," did that indicate his loyalty only to Japan? Wasn't what distinquished *kibei* from other *nisei* simply the fact that the foundation of their own being had been cultivated in Japan and that they possessed the memory of two worlds — Japan and the United States — which they happened to have experienced because of their family situations?[17]

As human beings, we cannot choose our parents; neither can we choose the language, culture, and sense of values we inherit from our parents nor our place of birth nor the family circumstances we are born into. In Okamoto's case, his father died when he was four. Because it was so difficult to make a living in the U.S., his mother immediately took him to Japan, left him in the care of her husband's grandparents, and returned to the States. In 1939, he failed the entrance exam to high school (under the old Japanese system of education) and returned to the United States, as he had no other place to go. His desire to see his mother, from whom he had been separated for fourteen years, provided an added incentive for his move.

When World War II broke out, Okamoto was attending high school in the United States, optimistically thinking that he would go back to Japan after learning English. He said that he most certainly felt a sense of loyalty to Japan in those days. "When I heard about Pearl Harbor, I felt that I was in the wrong place." This feeling was a consequence of his formative years and education in Japan due to his family situation; it was not a simple matter of choice.

Much later, in February 1943, the reason that Okamoto could not simply answer "yes, yes" to the loyalty oath questions at the Topaz camp in Utah was not that his name was registered with the Japanese family registry office. It was really because he could not, with his own hand, deny the core of his personality (what he called his "conscience"), that is, the twenty-two years of life he had lived up until then, the heart and mind cultivated by the education he had received during the most sensitive

---

17. Sachiko Takita (2007) views the experience of the *kibei* as "the memory of a diaspora that transcends more than two national and cultural frameworks" (p. 340) but does not belong to "a proper community of memory" (p. 280).

period of his youth, and the honest vacillation between cultural loyalties that shook him to the core.

Nationality and citizenship are not usually large factors in the formation of character or in the creation of one's core personality and identity. Instead, they are only symbols attached to a person by virtue of where she or he was born and raised. But wartime thinking converted the benign notion of "citizenship" into the armor and helmet of "loyalty," unwittingly forcing people who had experienced very different lives in Japan and the United States to make a political choice whether or not to be loyal to the United States. It asked these people to suppress their emotionally fraught hesistance and to cut off a sense of the past that had been woven into the fabric of their minds through myriad personal experiences. It crushed people's dreams as well as their very human attempts to recapture, in the flow of time, two worlds separated by the Pacific yet which nevertheless coexisted within their souls.[18] Despite this dilemma of honestly conflicted feeling — being unable to wholeheartedly answer "yes, yes" to the questions about loyalty to the United States — those who had problems deciding were dealt with in a politically cut-and-dried manner. In wartime, "no" indicated "disloyalty" to the United States, and "disloyalty" to the United States could only mean "loyalty" to Japan.

Human nature, which includes mixed feelings that cannot be explained

---

18. "In one center where the composing of three-line poems called Senryu, flourished, an Issei put into a poem what he and thousands of others felt about it:

> Balancing the war news
> With his own future
> Dilemma of Dilemmas!" (Impounded People, 1946, p. 154)

According to the same WRA report, the *issei* shared sentiments similar to those of the *kibei*. A young Japanese-born, American-educated block manager called the culture of the relocation centers "California Japanese culture" (p. 150). He observed that the Japan they had left twenty, thirty, or forty years ago had been "more a memory than a reality. The reality of which they bore the marks in the seams of their faces" (p. 151) was more from their experiences in California than those they had in Japan. Indeed, "the Issei world was not a Japanese world" (p. 151); however, "from the deepgoing and pervasive insecurity arising out of denial of citizenship to the little daily frustrations of being unable to communicate with children, the fact of being Japanese was central and inescapable" (p. 151). The meaning of being Japanese "was not to be explained in the simple concepts of loyalty and disloyalty used by nations at war" (p. 152).

in black-and-white terms, was first ignored by the U.S. government then later manipulated through convenient labels such as "disloyal/loyal," "anti-U.S.," and "pro-Japan." In the case of one *jun nisei*, the government's convenience brought tragedy through labels progressing from "native alien" to "friendly alien" to "alien enemy" (Akashi, 2005, p. 130).

Of this conflicted experience, Teruo H., a *jun nisei* who answered "yes, yes" to the loyalty questions and joined the U.S. Army after being released from camp, said:

> I hated the camp and just wanted to get out. I joined the Army purely for economic reasons. I had to have some sort of job, eat, and survive outside the camp. Loyalty is not so profound as people think. Of course, at school we pledged allegiance, placing our hands over our hearts. You know that kids just say words by rote, without knowing their meaning. Loyalty is simply something like that.

He further admitted that he detested the *kibei*. "They were just violent," he claimed. Ichiro T., one of those *kibei* labeled "violent" (who also answered "no, no" to the loyalty questions), similarly noted, "Loyalty to Japan was not all that romantic a notion, either."

The Twelve Thousand "Disloyals"

On February 10, 1943, the U.S. government began a program of loyalty questioning and registration to screen those over seventeen years old at ten incarceration camps in the United States. As a result of the loyalty examination, sixty-six thousand, or eighty-four percent, of the seventy-eight thousand examinees pledged unconditional loyalty to the United States (Thomas & Nishimoto, 1946, p. 62). The "disloyals" numbered twelve thousand and were made up of both *issei* and *nisei*. Most of the *issei* men and women unhesitatingly proclaimed loyalty to the United States by answering "yes, yes" to the questions. In those days, the *issei* had lived in the United States, on average, thirty-five years (MacWilliams, 1944, p. 3). Thus, they had lived far longer in the United States than they had lived in

Japan. Circumstances of their daily lives in the United States were severe, but their lives in Japan had been so much worse that they had no time for entertaining any sweet, unrealistic nostalgia about Japan, even though they would not say they liked America (Yamashiro, 1995, p. 76). In fact, some were "thorough believers in democracy, care[d] very little about the hallowed traditions of their homeland, and laugh[ed] at the Imperial rule founded on a myth" (Park, 1922, p. 154). Even so, they were proud that their children had been born citizens of a major world power, the U.S. Investing their hopes for the future in their children, they were probably ready to work hard and live out their lives in the country where their children were born and grew up.

The resolve of these *issei* — aliens who were not permitted to become naturalized — could be summed up in the words, "I cannot do such a stupid thing as leave behind the base I have built up here, even if Japan and the United States go to war" (Otani, 1983, p. 59). This resolve was based on practicality, not sentiment. They did not feel that their children "fighting for the United States" as American citizens would force them to make the heartbreaking choice of cutting off their ties to their Japanese homeland or living in the United States (Otani, p. 60). In sharp contrast to the *issei* response was the reaction of young *nisei*, who were American citizens. In every camp, many more *nisei* men were considered "disloyal" than *issei*. Seven thousand people — nearly twenty percent of the forty thousand *nisei* over the age of seventeen subject to loyalty registration — revealed themselves to be "disloyal."

Strictly speaking, the determination of "disloyalty" was made on the basis of answers to Question 28: "Will you swear unqualified allegiance to the United States and foreswear allegiance to the Japanese Emperor?" Those who answered "no," did not answer the question, or rejected the registration altogether were regarded as "disloyal." Those who answered "no" to Question 28 usually answered "no" to Question 27 as well ("Are you willing to serve in the armed forces of the United States?"), so they were called "No No Boys."[19]

---

19. The reference to "allegiance to the Japanese Emperor" was an indication of the emphasis which the government placed on the dual nationality held by many *nisei* (Collins, 1985, p.24).

However, among those regarded as "disloyal," some answered "yes, no" or "no, yes" to the questions. Furthermore, those who answered "yes, yes" and applied for repatriation before July 1, 1943, but did not cancel the application afterwards, were also sent to Tule Lake Segregation Center for "disloyals." As such, the center brought together people with a variety of different attitudes, including both the "loyal" and "disloyal." But from this time onward, the abhorrent word "disloyal" began to take on a life of its own, and for many years, even up to the present day, Tule Lake has been regarded as a badge of dishonor in Japanese American society.

Kibei Nisei "Disloyals" and Bushido

Out of the seven thousand *nisei* "No No Boys," twenty-six hundred were *jun nisei* who had never lived in Japan. The remaining forty-four hundred were *kibei*, comprising a little less than twenty-five percent of the *kibei* population of approximately nineteen thousand.

According to research conducted by Yoko Murakawa and Teruko Kumei (1992), *kibei* who had lived in Japan for more than five years had a much greater likelihood of answering "no, no." The rate was also much higher among those who had completed their highest level of education in Japan rather than in the United States: the higher the level of education (e.g., college), the more likely they were to say "no, no." In contrast, the higher the level of education achieved in the United States, the lower the rate of answering "no, no" on the questionnaire. As such, the inmates' answers were naturally affected by the difference in their ability to interpret information and make a judgment in a situation in which they had to consider national power and the complications of war (pp. 26-27).

These contrasting results in the research may be explained if we consider the strong linkages between education and "loyalty" in the nationalistic and militaristic education that *kibei* received in Japan. U.S. officials suspected that the longer the period and the higher the level of education in Japan, the more deferential to the Emperor and the more patriotic a young man would become; consequently, he could be expected to become a more Japan-oriented "no, no boy." Another strong influence in their labeling the *kibei* as "violent" was the authoritarian Japanese military education that *kibei* were supposed to have received.

On the other hand, however, Norihiko Kuwayama (1996) suggests that the higher the educational background and sense of pride a person has, the more vulnerable he will be to teasing because of difference, and the more unadaptable he will be to the new environment of a foreign culture (p. 51). For example, those who were arrested in the Manzanar incident of 1942 were all *kibei,* except for Joe Kurihara, and half of them were college graduates (Nozaki, 2007, p. 170). So then, was the "no, no" orientation of the *kibei* an expression of a sense of loyalty to Japan directly tied to their having had a Japanese education? Or do we here see an ironic paradox? Wasn't their ethnic pride, heightened through higher education in which they rejected assimilation by the U.S. "Anglo" mold, deeply related to their answering "no, no"?

Another paradox involving the *kibei's* ethnic pride and education is revealed in a consistently biased interpretation of *bushido* (often trans- lated as "*samurai* spirit" but really a concept that is rather ambiguous and subject to misinterpretation). When the peacetime draft bill passed in 1940, Secretary Tsukamoto of the JACL urged Japanese Americans "to be loyal citizens in accord with the Japanese spirit that we are always taught" (Otani, 1983, p. 55). The "Japanese spirit" to which he referred must have been what could be found in traditional Japanese attitudes such as "do not resist authority," "devote oneself to the Emperor," and "*shikata ga nai*" [it can't be helped].

Mike Masaoka praised this Japanese spirit, referring to *bushido* in an anecdote about his meeting with Japanese Ambassador Yoshizaburo Nomura, who met Masaoka in Salt Lake City, Utah, in February 1941. As Masaoka (1987) puts it, Nomura advised, "Masaoka-san, you are right. Whatever the circumstances, you must be loyal to your country. That is *bushido*, the way of the *samurai*" (p.53). And even after the war, in prais- ing Masaoka at the San Francisco peace treaty conference, Shigeru Yoshida claimed that "Japanese-Americans ... acted as Japan would have expected them to act, as Americans and not as Japanese in the tradition of the *samurai* code, which demanded absolute loyalty to one's 'lords' regardless of one's origins" (p. 250).

In this way, *bushido* was used to justify the actions of Masaoka and other members of the JACL; they did not protest but instead cooperated with the injustices of the U.S. government. The *jun nisei* of the JACL, whose objective was the Anglo-Americanization of Japanese Americans, brought up the very thing they were trying to deny as they faced incarceration and, as such, spoke out of both sides of their mouths. They used Japanese cultural values opportunistically to persuade the Japanese American communities, elicit their cooperation with the U.S. government, and win favor among the Americans.

What was the true nature of the "way of the warrior" (*bushido*) that Masaoka and his followers took such pride in? *Bushido*, a philosophy born of the Sengoku era of civil war (1467-1568), is thought to have developed rapidly, with various refinements, in the Meiji Period (1868-1912), which marked the end of Japanese national isolation. In this new context, it was valued both from the standpoint of emphasizing Japan's unique traditions and from that of introducing the Western system of values (Saeki, 2004, p. 29).

In Japan, the sense of crisis at the incursion of the Western powers into East Asia heightened around 1887, accompanied by a surge in nationalism. Against this backdrop of opposition to the Europeanization of Japan, *bushido* came to be lionized as the foundation upon which a Japan confident in its role as leader of Asia could counter global rule by the Western nations (Saeki, 2004, p. 252).

On the other hand, *bushido*'s spirit of self-restraint and asceticism found points of commonality with Christianity, as evidenced in the 1899 publication in the United States of Inazo Nitobe's *Bushido — The Soul of Japan*, which argued that whatever exists in Western culture can be found in Japan as well. Nitobe was a Christian believer who based his thought about Japanese culture upon the Western viewpoint. The *bushido* that he wrote of was an entirely new concept of the "way of the warrior" — one based upon the Western ideal of chivalry and therefore detached from the history of *bushido* in Japan (Saeki, 2004, pp. 253, 262).

The question of the accuracy of Nitobe's definition of *bushido* aside, there can be no doubt that the concept of *bushido* was employed opportunistically as an easy-to-grasp characterization of Japanese culture. For the English-speaking Japanese Americans, the *yang* (positive side) of *bushido* — the precept of loyalty to one's lords even to the point of sacrificing one's own life — formed the backbone of their loyalty to the United States. On the other hand, the *yin* (negative side) of *bushido*, as it might have been interpreted by the Japanese-speaking Japanese Americans, held that the loyal acts of the subject could consist of "deriding those who sacrifice their own principles for their wayward lord and correcting the mistake (or fault) of the lord at all costs in cases where the lord and the subject (citizen) differ" (Nitobe, 1995, pp. 84-85). However, English-speaking Japanese and the JACL consciously or unconsciously ignored this competing aspect. Somehow they could not view answering "no, no" as an attempt to use the *bushido* spirit to justify correcting the mistakes of the government out of loyalty to and trust for the United States. On the contrary, they regarded it as evidence of loyalty to the enemy, Japan.

In his autobiography, Masaoka (1987) later defended himself, explaining, "We were told this was a matter of military necessity and we had no way of disputing that contention, nor could we risk the possibility of bloodshed if we stood on our rights and resisted military orders" (p. 364). In addition, he noted that he regarded evacuation and incarceration as different issues and even stated, "My worst mistake was believing in the absolute integrity of the Constitution" (p. 365).

Thinking expansively about "believing in the absolute integrity of the Constitution," we might allow that "to correct the mistake of the lord at all costs" would be consistent with the democratic rights of U.S. citizens. In this context, to explain his wartime actions, a friend of Harry Ueno's said, "I know I am powerless and unimportant, but I am determined to fight, even risking my life, when directly insulted [by the government]" (Embrey et al., 1986, p. 40). In statements like these, we can see that those who received their higher education in Japan might actually have had a better understanding of the two sides of *bushido* beliefs as represented in the different ways they came to be enacted in two cultures: on the one hand, the *yang* of the sincerity and honor of the samurai, and on the other, the inspiring and far-reaching fundamental principles of freedom, equality, and justice represented in the *yin* of dissent guaranteed by the U.S. Constitution. Could the case be made that the conflict of these two beliefs is what led some to protest resolutely against the United States and become "No No Boys"?

The *nisei* who answered "no, no" to the loyalty questions may have put too much faith in the integrity of the Constitution, as did Masaoka, a faith that actually prevented them from tolerating the U.S. government's act of depriving citizens of their rights.

This was especially true of the *kibei* who had attended institutions of higher education in the U.S. Some *kibei* who became "disloyal" trouble-makers and later took leadership positions in the so-called "pro-Japan" radical groups were graduates of Stanford University, Tokyo University (Akashi, 2005, p. 117), and the University of California — Berkeley and Davis. One *kibei*, who was reputed to have studied at Tokyo University, had the leadership skills to become secretary-treasurer of the Western Fishermen Union of the American Federation of Labor in southern California, the first Japanese American to hold an AFL position. As if to underscore the relationship of U.S. higher education to philosophical resistance, *kibei nisei* Masao Kawate, himself a graduate of UC Berkeley, emphasized in a 1944 letter to the Spanish Embassy that even though he had been through twelve years of education in this country, including university, he was still considered a traitor and thus had answered "no, no" (Personal correspondence, private collection of Haruo Kawate).

The tragedy was that these contradictory manipulations of traditional Japanese culture pushed the "no-nos" into a corner.

Loyalty Registration and Confusion

On January 29, 1943, the *Topaz Times News Daily* distributed an extra at Topaz camp in Utah, which had a population of approximately eighty-two hundred. The extra, with the headline "TO RECRUIT NISEI," was about a press release that Secretary of War Henry L. Stimson had issued on January 28:

> The War Department announced today that plans have been completed for the "admission" of a substantial number of American citizens of Japanese ancestry to the Army of the United States. This action was taken following study by the War Department of "many earnest requests" by loyal American citi-

zens of Japanese extraction for the organization of a special unit of the Army in which they could have their share in the fight against the nation's enemies.

Furthermore, Secretary Stimson expressed the principles behind his statement in the department announcement: "It is the inherent right of every faithful citizen, regardless of ancestry, to bear arms in the nation's battle" and "loyalty to country is a voice that must be heard, and I am glad that I am now *able to give* active proof that this basic American belief is not a casualty of war. However, if the government has suspicions about a volunteer's loyalty to the US, that volunteer *will not be approved*" (emphasis added).[20]

It should be clarified here that the aforementioned "many earnest requests by loyal American citizens of Japanese ancestry" consisted mainly of a proposal to the government made by the JACL, through Mike Masaoka, exaggerating the number of JACL members by as many as ten times (Lim Report, 1990, p. 65). Masashi Nagai, a "No No Boy," had his own reaction: "'We will let you join if you volunteer' is very different from, 'I will go as required by the government,' since I thought that's the only way I could go — if they called me up, I would have to go."

Tadahiko Okamoto, a close friend of Nagai, had a very different experience. He was called up for service a year before the Japan-U.S. war broke

---

20. This part of the statement has been translated back into English from the original Japanese section of the newspaper in order to reproduce what Japanese speakers at the camp would have seen and reacted to. "Unknown to local administrators, a counter-propaganda effort had also been published in the Japanese-language sections of the newspaper (*Topaz Times*) ... two editors decided to add a pro-Japanese spin to the news, urging readers to declare loyalty to Japan instead of to the United States" (Lyon, 2012, p. 88). Scholars, including Thomas and Nishimoto (1946), "have noted significant discrepancies betweeen" the English and Japanese versions (p. vii) and commented that they "had to be on constant guard against linguistic and cultural distortion both in recording and in interpreting observations" (p. x). Furthermore, they note that an official Japanese translation of the speech prepared by the War Department to recruit volunteers "reached most centers too late to be of any use. In at least two projects [camps] it was not used on the grounds that it failed to convey the meaning of the English version. Thus, many Issei were not exposed to the propagandic effects of the speech" (Thomas & Nishimoto, p. 59).

out. Okamoto registered and received a classification of 1A (eligible), but as soon as the war broke out, he was switched to 4F (ineligible due to physical disability). "I still have the card where they switched me from 1A to 4F," he said with annoyance. He could not believe that his own government would consider his race a legal form of physical disabilty. Later, *nisei* were categorized as 4C (enemy aliens).

If enlistment could be considered a form of loyalty, Okamoto's loyalty to the United States had already been denied by the State. Even as late as 1997, at age seventy-six, Okamoto was still worried and haunted by the question. "Why did I have to volunteer again to have them acknowledge my loyalty?"

When the problematic loyalty registration started on February 10, 1943, heated debate arose in the incarceration camps. Wherever people gathered, either in the common laundry area or mess halls, the subject of loyalty registration dominated the conversation.

Nisei registration in the Army was voluntary. Therefore, not cooperating with the registration was by definition not a criminal act. Due to their own misunderstanding and inefficiency, however, the WRA issued conflicting sets of instructions one after another, which confused people. There was so much confusion that, finally, on Friday, February 26, 1943, two weeks after the registration started, WRA Director Dillon Myer commented that he was "greatly surprised and disappointed" to learn that registration was not compulsory (Drinnon, 1987, p. 93).

At the Topaz camp, at the start of registration on February 10, *issei*, *nisei*, and especially *kibei*, respectively, held meetings attended by eight or nine hundred people to discuss the complicated situation of "being allowed to volunteer." *Issei* assumed a firm attitude and resolved, with great deliberation in the name of the residents' conference, to urge the authorities to reconsider (*Topaz Times* [Japanese edition], February 11, 1943).

Kibei nisei heatedly discussed this at citizens meetings held in the mess halls of each residential block and split into two groups: one planning to first register and then protest, the other to first protest, demanding citizens' rights, and then register. The latter group was somewhat dominant. The *kibei* were "over the barrel. They had a loud meeting ... and were very belligerent in their attitudes. People got reckless in their speeches, stating frequent willingess to be jailed in actual violation of any act, only to get their 'rights' now, since this was the 'last chance'" (Government report in the private collection of Harry Ueno, p. 55).

Frequently, speakers would be caught up in a sharp outburst of emotion. Some spoke to the audience in tears. For example, "one twenty year old kibei, very eloquent and sincere, deploring the lack of unity among niseis in a common front for a common cause, declared he would commit *harakiri* in front of the assemblage and die as a martyr to the nisei cause if the group could not agree on an answer. He had already bade farewell to his family this noon before [he] came to the meeting, put his room and things in order and had offered his sacrifice before the Buddhist altar. With tears streaming down his face he begged for a serious consideration of the body to unite. His confidence, sincerity and determination brought the united stand to fight for our rights now" (Government report in the private collection of Harry Ueno, p. 59). Ichiro T. was another speaker at the meeting "with tears streaming down his face." In the report, he is called the "loudest Kibei" and got "the prize" for the best "weep act."

One of the meetings, at which a resolution was adopted, was like a "near-riot" and went on from 2:30 to 10:00 p.m. nonstop, without even a supper break. Here and there, men were heard to shout such things as, "Those from Japan can never say yes!" "Yes is unpatriotic!" and "Be dignified, answering 'no, no' consistently!" "Though no vote was taken, it was impressed that no registration was to be done, since the resolution stated expressly that all registration will be held up until a satisfactory answer was received on the resolution" (Government report in the private collection of Harry Ueno, p. 56).

Although Topaz was "the most orderly and conservative" camp, perhaps due to the turmoil it went through, the government had even considered converting Topaz, rather than Tule Lake, into a segregation center (*Nikkei West*, February 10, 2013). Remembering those days of his youth, Ichiro T., regarded as the "boss of No Nos" at Topaz, spoke emphatically when I interviewed him in Japan:

> We are American citizens, with citizenship, but have been
> imprisoned in concentration camps. We should answer "no, no"

and make a protest against the government.

If we wish to be loyal [to the country], we cannot be dutiful [to our parents]. If we wish to be dutiful, we cannot be loyal. If we swear loyalty to Japan, our parents in the States will be unhappy. If we try to be dutiful to our parents, we cannot be loyal to Japan. We are all torn between loyalty and duty. This is not politics, though. We have to live and survive. Can we swear loyalty to the United States, where we are treated as alien enemies? Can we shoot our brothers, relatives, and friends in Japan?

Yes, I made speeches at several meetings. To those meetings, *issei* also came, trying to understand the feelings and thoughts of their sons. I called out to them, "If you agree with me, come with me."

It wasn't as if I was valiantly pledging loyalty to Japan for the sake of appearance. I was just a realist. I could neither pledge loyalty to the United States, nor did I want to become a soldier...that's all. I did not have any political intentions at all. I just thought realistically about which side I should be on. Since the questions were very political, I could only answer that way. The United States, from the very start, had no right to ask such questions of their citizens. But at the same time, they could not help asking such questions. They wanted to screen [the citizens]. The primary issue in my consciousness was not the Japanese Emperor; it was just that I would rather not fight against my former classmates in Japan.

Jiro T., Ichiro's younger brother, is a *kibei nisei* as well. He followed his brother's comments with these words: "What he says is correct — on the surface, but his real intention is ... he was educated in Japan as well... so he could not write 'yes.' Well ... that could involve the issue of loyalty/disloyalty, I guess."

Jiro T., who turned seventeen during the loyalty registration, intended to answer "yes, yes" so he would be able to leave the camp earlier. He was dreaming of entering college. Throughout the night before the registration, his older brother tried to persuade him:

"What are you going to do?" he asked. I told him that I would answer "yes, yes," which made him angry. I was listening to him crying. My brother became a so-called leader, opposing the registration from the beginning. He did so publicly, so he said it would look strange if his brother answered "yes, yes" and said that I should go along with him for appearance's sake. Another thing he pointed out was that I had received a Japanese education, and that appealed to me the most. I was a young military aspirant, raised in a militaristic Japan. I could understand that.

Kibei Nisei Without Japanese Nationality

Jiro T., however, could never have become the imperial military man he wanted to be in Japan. He did not have Japanese nationality.

In reality, many parents may simply, but unintentionally, had forgotten to submit birth certificates for various reasons because they were busy making ends meet. Actually, many *kibei nisei* did not realize that they did not have Japanese nationality until they applied for Japanese higher education after years of difficult study and enduring the unaccustomed lifestyle and unfamiliar language in Japan. Masashi Nagai found out that he possessed only U.S. citizenship when he learned that his monthly tuition for the local school was more than that of his classmates, since he was not considered a resident.

> My parents were farmers working on a farm on the outskirts of Sacramento, where there were only two families living nearby. It took a whole day to get to the Japanese consulate in San Francisco, which might be the reason they forgot to submit the birth certificate. Or they might have thought it unnecessary.

Jiro T., an applicant for admission to the Japanese Naval Academy in Fukuoka, was another who discovered that he did not have Japanese nationality.

> In those days, for those living in the countryside, one way to become a success in life was to go into the Army or Navy. My

teacher said he could check my family register, as I was born in the United States. Of course I thought I had Japanese nationality. He checked it but could find no record of my registration. He said I was an American, which disappointed me. An American could not apply for the Japanese Navy. It was so shocking that I deliberately avoided answering questions on tests so as to lower my scores … though I had maintained the top ranking in my class up until then.

Kenji Takeuchi, who later opened the Japanese language school (*Dai Toa Juku*) in the Tule Lake Segregation Center, also found he did not have Japanese nationality when he graduated from Kokushikan Junior High School. Takeuchi, born in 1920 before the enactment of the Immigration Law of 1924, should have been legally acknowledged as a Japanese citizen, since his father was Japanese, regardless of whether or not his parents registered his birth, but:

A general from the Army General Staff department came to our school. At graduation, he told me to bring a copy of my family register. I immediately inquired at my town office in the country. They said they could not issue a copy because I had only American citizenship, not Japanese. I had not known this at all up until then. Two hundred and fifty students graduated. I was graduating with the best grades. The best in military training. But they said, "No, we cannot issue a military training certificate. We will not issue a certificate stating that you received Japanese military training because you are an American." On graduation day, I received a graduation diploma. When handing out the military training certificate, they called each student's name. The students were all called and stood up, except me. "Ah, this won't do," I thought. Without a military training certificate, I could not advance to higher education.

Not knowing what to do, Takeuchi returned to California in 1938, where his parents lived.

These *kibei* boys had gone to Japan with their mothers when they were still young and had lived separately from their parents afterwards. Takeuchi went to Japan in 1925, when he was five; Nagai, in 1926 at age four, when his father died. The T. brothers went to Japan in 1934, when Ichiro, born in 1922, was twelve and Jiro, born in 1926, was eight years old. Leaving the children with their grandparents, the mothers of these boys returned to the United States. In Japan, the boys studied desperately, as if to distract themselves from their loneliness for their families. They were raised by their grandparents in their parents' hometowns in an unfamiliar country. When these boys' dreams were cruelly shattered because of their lack of citizenship, their sense of disappointment was devastating.

Quite a few of these young men had to return to the United States due to hardships or troubles in their lives in Japan. Ichiro T., who was lucky enough to have dual citizenship, said that he had experienced conflict in junior high school, where he was the *kendo* club president. Angry at the situation, Ichiro defiantly declared that he was an American and came back to the United States with his brother Jiro in 1940.

Resistance and Disappointment of the *Kibei*

In pre-war Japan, many young Japanese American *nisei* who arrived there from the U.S. were received coldly. They were teased as "emigrant" children and criticized because they were materialistic, would "chew gum on the streets," and "speak a loud mix of Japanese and English" (Tomita, 1995, p. 12). Because of their difference in habits and culture, as well as for many other reasons, quite a few *nisei* felt rejected by the Japanese and found that they really had no place in Japan. Thus, many *kibei nisei* had very positive feelings about the United States when they returned, now that they knew of the miserable conditions in Japan. As the Munson Report, issued just before the outbreak of the war, noted, "A Japanese trip was necessary to have *nisei* make a pledge of allegiance to the United States" (Weglyn, 1996, p. 42). *Kibei nisei* were proud of being American citizens and had big expectations of their lives in America. Their American citizenship was a symbol of "a dream and a chance at life" unobtainable in Japan.

However, what awaited them in the U.S. was another life of hardship, not to mention racial discrimination, further discrimination based on their inability to speak English, and (most humiliating) even discrimination from the *jun nisei*, who were Japanese Americans just like themselves.

How embarassing it must have been for teenagers to study in the same classroom as elementary school children! Jiro T., who re-entered an elementary school to learn English after coming back to the United States, said he was mortified because his younger brothers and sisters were in a class above him: "I was at the head of my class in junior high school in Japan, but here, because I could not speak English at all ... [things were different. However, in] subjects like arithmetic, teachers asked me questions."

He kept studying as if driven by shame. Though gifted, he could not display his abilities because of his poor command of English.

After ten months in school, Kenji Takeuchi received his graduation certificate from elementary school, then, because of his age, he was urged to leave. "In Japan I understood everything and could have done a very good job, but here, I could not understand what they were talking about."

Word has it that of Japanese Americans, the *kibei* showed the most active resistance and hostility to the registration program (Weglyn, 1996), probably because their U.S. citizenship had become their greatest comfort and hope in the midst of a harsh life in Japan; then once again in the United States, their motivation to return to Japan was low. But the demoralizing process of forced removal, incarceration, and loyalty registration put them on edge.

"First, I felt like I was kicked out of Japan," Kenji Takeuchi explained. "Then, when I came to the United States, they treated me as an enemy alien. This was overwhelming to me. I never thought of sacrificing my life for Japan; instead, I wanted to live as a human being and as an American citizen. They didn't give me a chance. They were arrogant. I guess I did it [answered 'no, no'] out of stubbornness."

Ichiro T. recalled his participation in a speech contest at the San Francisco Buddhist Youth Organization before being forcibly removed:

> The subject of my speech was "a *nisei*'s duty attendant upon the world situation." I concluded my speech in this way: "The soil of America has nurtured Japanese Americans, so it is our

duty to be good American citizens willing to become part of the soil of America." But then they put us in the camp. "This is no joke," I told the FBI. I came from Japan and just when I was about to start my life as a loyal American citizen, it turned out like this. The war changed the situation, but why did they have to put us in a camp? That was the breaking point. I guess, in part, I must have acted out of the impulsiveness of youth.

Masashi Nagai does not recall actually answering "no, no" to Questions 27 and 28. "A *nisei* officer in charge asked me, 'Yes or no?' and I replied hesitatingly that I had studied in Japan for various reasons. I was reluctant to say anything one way or the other. Then he asked me if my answer was 'no, no.' All I remember is that I said I would not sign. And then he said that if I did not sign, my answers would be recorded as 'no, no.'"

Of those labeled "No No Boys," there were a variety of types. To be sure, for many, the stance contained an element of the desperate "so what?" attitude of youth who had suddenly lost their place and direction in the world. That was not something they chose of their own volition but rather was an outcome of the dilemma and anguish they experienced as a consequence of stepping, quite by the chance of their lives, into two different worlds: Japan and America.

I asked Susumu Kako, who had been sent as far as the Fort Lincoln Internment Camp for Enemy Aliens in North Dakota on charges of being a "pro-Japanese militarist," whether he would still have answered "no, no" if he had not been taken to Japan at the age of five and attended school there. I also commented that he might not have been stigmatized by the Japanese American community as a result after the war. He rolled his eyes and replied, "*Shikata ga nai desho* [We could do nothing about it]. There was no choice. It all happened because of our parents' family situations. And it's pointless to hold a grudge against one's parents."

Born in 1917, Susumu Kako went to Japan with his parents when he was five years old. "They got a telegram that my dad's mother was sick. Dad said it was okay even if he could not go back to Japan, but Mom said we had to, and we did. My mother did not feel that she could save face without doing so, I think."

Susumu Kako, who had completed advanced coursework in elementary school in the pre-war school system in Japan, left his mother in Japan and came back to the United States with his father in about 1932, at the age of fifteen or sixteen. Having attended school in the United States for less than one year, he started working full time to help his father with strawberry farming. When he arrived at the camp, he was already married with children. When he answered "no, no" to the loyalty questions, what ran through his mind were thoughts of his family, anger against America, and consideration for his father, who wished to return to Japan. "I answered 'no, no' of my own will. I couldn't stand the fact that they put people with U.S. citizenship into such places as the camps. Besides, we had received a Japanese education."

Having "received a Japanese education" meant an inclination, bond, and attachment toward Japan that prevented these men from taking action against that country. At the same time, it also entailed a sense of opposition and desperation because of a sense that citizenship would be meaningless in a country that did not trust them. Feelings such as these were based on the values of family and state, centered on loyalty and filial piety, that they had been taught in Japanese schools. Ultimately, these feelings formed the spiritual foothold of the *kibei*, a foothold that gave them a sense of identity much deeper (Kiyota, 1997, p. 59) and more pronounced than the imitation of white Americans promoted by Masaoka and the JACL.

Yoshio Nishikawa, who was also sent to the Fort Lincoln Internment Camp for Enemy Aliens, had been born in the U.S. but raised in Japan by his paternal grandparents after the death of his parents in Japan. He reports that he was "reserved and became timid, feeling like a nuisance or a troublemaker in Japan," so at the age of fifteen, he came back to the United States and renounced his Japanese citizenship. It may have been the case that the bond he felt with Japan was not strong enough for him to cling to his citizenship, for he no longer had anyone to love or depend on in Japan. But even so, he answered "no, no" to the loyalty questions.

"Those educated in Japan, even for a short period of time, could not answer 'yes' to those questions," Nishikawa explained. Immediately after the registration, he was summoned and urged to change his answers to "yes." "They said that [if I answered 'yes'] they would let me out soon. I could become an interpreter and be sent to the Philippines, they said."

The "no, no" answer of Nishikawa, who had clearly and deliberately renounced his Japanese nationality, should never have been interpreted as having any relevance to, much less any devotion to, Japanese militarism or loyalty to Japan.

Spread of the Registration Refusal Movement

In February 1943, Tule Lake was thrown into uproar and confusion, with inmates splitting into several groups: those in favor of "yes" answers and those in favor of "no" answers to the registration, as well as those who found it difficult to make a decision at all. Registration was to take place simultaneously in all blocks on the morning of February 10. While inmates at other camps were carefully informed about the registration through events such as administration-sponsored Q & A workshops and indeed most people were judged "loyal," at Tule Lake the registration "was handled in a manner almost guaranteed to create misunderstanding and antagonism." The camp residents had no time to ponder the questions; they had only one informational meeting at which the form was given to them in English, the possible answers were read only in English, and the inmates were not permitted to ask additional questions (Takei & Tachibana, 2001, p. 14).

On the third day after registration began, a movement to stop the inmates from registering arose in some blocks. Before long, the "refusal of registration" movement spread throughout the entire camp. Based on the assumption that refusal of registration was the work of pro-Japan agitators, the authorities began to identify, arrest, and transfer individuals they considered "dangerous."

On the evening of February 22, the Tule Lake *kibei* held a mass meeting at Block 4 to confirm their absolute refusal of registration. They also attended other block meetings and called for refusal of registration.

The University of California–Berkeley's Bancroft Library preserves a copy of the original resolution in Japanese, but the first thing one notices about it are the words, "THE GOD DAMNED BASTARD WHO WROTE THIS SHOULD BE SHOT," scribbled across the statement in English capital letters.

Here is a translation of the full text of the resolution:

> "We, as U.S. citizens residing in Tule Lake Relocation Center, shall make the following statement and resolve as loyal citizens of the United States to perform our duty and protect the spirit of democracy established by the Constitution of the United States.
>
> ### Statement
>
> 1. We Japanese American citizens of the United States are required to pledge unconditional loyalty to the state under our government.
>
> 2. We are loyal and duly cooperative in spite of the extraordinary orders of the U.S. military authorities.
>
> 3. We feel that we offered our utmost cooperation regarding evacuation.
>
> 4. We have temporarily ceded the privileges of that citizenship that we possessed, as well as many of our rights.
>
> 5. The U.S. government failed to protect people's assets in federal banks.
>
> 6. We lost family, property, jobs, and freedom of action and tolerated separation from many friends and the loss of all things precious to us without complaining.
>
> 7. We request that mass evacuations and internments of citizens without examination be prevented in the future.
>
> 8. We possess citizenship in one nation only – the United States. A loyal and good citizen of one ethnicity should not be treated differently from one with another ethnicity.
>
> 9. We are convinced that the above-mentioned actions have constituted a violation of our rights.
>
> 10. We believe sincerely and truthfully in the spirit of freedom of assembly, religion, and language, as embodied in the Constitution and its amendments.

Resolution

1. We petition that those whose identities are certified by the Secretary of War Henry L. Stimson after a thorough investigation by the U.S. Army Intelligence Bureau, the Federal Special Political Police, or other U.S. authorities should have absolute freedom of movement and freedom to choose to return to their homes (present address).

2. We request that President Roosevelt exercise his kind offices to bestow upon us all of our legal rights as American citizens and the rights provided for by the U.S. Constitution and to guarantee the above.

3. We request that the safety and protection of issei be guaranteed.

4. We petition President Roosevelt to exercise his kind offices so that American society might come to hold a favorable impression of these good and loyal citizens.

5. We request that issei who are not regarded as disloyal by the U.S. government be classified as pro-U.S. aliens.

6. We urge the U.S. government to give heed to and incorporate nisei soldiers into general army forces rather than organizing a separate Japanese American combat force, on the grounds that it would benefit the great nation of the United States. Japanese American soldiers could learn from the deep friendships cultivated among soldiers sharing a common effort, and the endeavor would be of educational benefit to American society.

7. The United States, which perceives itself to be fighting for the four great freedoms embodied in the Atlantic Charter, should apply these principles of democracy to us who live within the United States.

8. If government representatives, or hopefully the President of the United States, provide us with satisfactory answers to those questions, we believe we shall be able to fight for the country without fear or concern in connection with the guarantee of our rights in the future.

In the event that we are not given satisfactory answers,
we take it that our rights provided for by the Constitution
are not being protected and understand that there is no
reason for us to register without being provided with any
information we should have regarding our citizenship.

Further, we pass a resolution respectfully calling for an immediate response to these questions."

It was certainly *kibei nisei* who wrote these statements, in Japanese,
with an outpouring of passionate confidence in the ideals of democracy
and citizenship — rights guaranteed under the Constitution.

Although he was unaware of the resolution, Tsutomu Umezu most
certainly rejected the idea of loyalty registration based on his independent
understanding of the following statement in the resolution: "... there is no
reason for us to register without being provided with any information we
should have regarding our citizenship."

There were about fifteen thousand people held in Tule Lake. More than
thirty-two hundred, about one-third of those over seventeen years old and
thus eligible for registration, rejected loyalty registration altogether or submitted applications for repatriation and did not register. Of those, fourteen hundred were American citizens (*nisei*) and eighteen hundred were
Japanese. Together, they constituted twenty-five percent of the fifty-seven
hundred eligible *nisei* and thirty-six percent of the five thousand *issei*.

Umezu, born in 1919, was involved in the *San-en Kai*, a Tule Lake camp
group whose name was derived from the famous "see no evil, hear no evil,
speak no evil" monkeys of Nikko Toshogu Shrine. This group advocated
self-restraint among residents to avoid being deluded by or repeating
rumors inside the camp. "It was a liberal group that would gather and talk
about all kinds of things," Umezu recalls.

There were about eight hundred members and about ten
leaders. We did not promote it intensely and, in the beginning, it
was a small group. Then people started talking about the loyalty
registration. Of course, we were willing to think about and discuss it. Early on, we never thought of campaigning throughout
the camp. The issues were directly related to the residents and

we had a lot more things coming up, such as whether we should hold a demonstration or not. A demonstration would be outrageous, we thought.

We had a heated discussion about why we had to go through such a thing [the registration]. Our freedom had already been constrained, they put us in the internment camp without answering any questions, they put us here as "Japanese" although we are Americans — why do we have to undergo this kind of registration? It was a big question. We wanted to present the questions to the authorities ... to those in charge ... though we were not in a position to ask directly. So we went to the council representing the center residents and asked them to ask the questions. They said that they could not. We said that we had a problem with the way they arbitrarily decided, and they said they could not. We said that it was our wish, as residents, and asked them to take the risk of talking with the authorities themselves. They said no. We continued to plead with them to just try. At that point we thought we should pool our efforts, and we held meetings in groups. We got more and more agitated and angry.

Some of the *San-en Kai* members were radical ... or violent. They insisted on beating up those who did not listen to them. It is really the worst to have to resort to violence. Rather, most of us thought that we should never fight back against whatever they did. "If the authorities say they are going to hit you, run. Don't resist them, but continue with your struggle calmly." As a matter of fact, however, thousands of people gathered in a kind of anti-loyalty registration demonstration. People had nothing to do inside the camp, so they gathered together just for fun. It wasn't a real demonstration, though. If we had demonstated, the military would have been left in an awkward position, forced to act. The authorities probably thought, "Why are you making a fuss? Why don't you register, loyal or disloyal? Express your opinion!" We did not think that way. We thought, "Why do we have to do this?" Before we came to the camp, or at the time we were evacuated, if they had told us about it, the situation would have been different. But they pointed guns at us, saying that they would protect us and put us in the camps.

We pleaded with the authorites but were getting nowhere. Then our leaders went from block to block telling people not to register. "Let's reject it in order to clarify our intent. The situation will never get as bad as you fear, even if you do not register," they said. If only a few people rejected it, those people might be imprisoned, but if thousands of people rejected the registration, the authorities would not be able handle it. Saying this, the leaders told the people not to register. They wrote letters to the councils of nine other camps, asking them to urge people not to register. The only response came from someplace like Arkansas, saying it was a great idea and that they would campaign. We thought, "What can they be thinking?" Probably they thought, "What is the point of talking about it now?" In Arkansas, however, it did not develop into a campaign because only a few people agreed. The authorities were not able to take a strong attitude toward us to suppress us, either. We did not register, and at the same time we neither demonstrated nor resisted. For the authorities, we must have been very hard to control.

According to published accounts, early in the morning of February 22, a siren sounded, which announced the emergency closing of the high schools. Then mess hall gongs in each block rang to call residents to meetings. "Petitions for refusal to register were widely circulated, under conditions of maximum social pressure, e.g., at meal time, when all residents were assembled and nonsigners could be readily identified" (Thomas & Nishimoto, 1946, p. 78). Groups such as the *nisei* council and *issei* planning department, who were authorized to negotiate with the director of the camp, demanded the authorities to stop the white and *nisei* teachers from pressuring the inmates to change their answers from "no" to "yes," but the authorities refused (p. 78).

Umezu continued:

Under pressure from a lot of people who had a lot to say, we dissolved the council, which had existed in name only and had been unable to negotiate with the authorities, but this made the authorities angry. They said, "Who will represent the residents in negotiating with the authorities? There are nearly twenty disgraceful men who broke up the residents' representative group. We have to punish them. Otherwise, Tule Lake will never settle down!" And they decided to arrest us.

We had spies among the authorities. Some of them were *jun nisei* women who worked in the main office. They leaked information to us regarding police movements and so forth. They shared what they knew without reservation. While we were sleeping, the police came to arrest us, saying, "Get up." We had been informed of the coming raid beforehand, so we were prepared, sleeping in our overcoats with toothbrush, toothpaste, vitamins, and underwear in the pockets. When they came, they were surprised at how well prepared we were.... We already knew they were coming, and we were ready.

According to Mamoru Tanimoto, "The WRA came up and brought half a dozen Dodge trucks; called out our names. We were all ready, had our suitcases all packed, ready to go" (*Nichibei Times*, January 1, 2009).

One of those arrested that night was Masao Kawate, who was born in Lockeford, near Stockton, California, in 1913, had lived in Japan from age five to fifteen, and had graduated from the University of California–Berkeley in 1941. He was a teacher at Tri-State High School at Tule Lake. According to his diary:

> Ever since this problem arose, I had thought that there was sure to be big reaction to it, so I submitted my resignation to the school around the second of the month, and while I was waiting to see what would happen, the afternoon of March 5th arrived. A notice came saying that I was to come in for interrogation. I packed up all of my baggage that night so that I would be ready to go to the "isolation" camp the following day. That night I was invited to have a last dinner with Mr. Yamashiro.

On the following day, the 6th, I was treated to a farewell meal by Mr. Tanaka and Mr. Masuda. With that, all preparations were completed, and together with 13 others, I joined the assembly at Block 11 at 1:00 p.m. To send-off of cries of "banzai," we left for the interrogation site. The people who had come to see us off accompanied us as far as the interrogation site. At the interrogation, two were released, but a total of 12 people were accepted as resistors without incident. Around three o'clock we were herded into Army trucks and, in high spirits, bid farewell to the relocation center where we had lived for the past seven months, leaving behind the lingering cries of "banzai" from those who had come to see us off. The fact that all were in high spirits and seemed to be enjoying themselves was evidence that all were conscious of the fact that they were doing what was right, with great fortitude. In fact, I too was extremely pleased.

Kibei Who Were Arrested

At first scheduled to finish on March 2, the registration that had started on February 10 was extended until March 10. Nearly a hundred *kibei* who were arrested on March 17 because they rejected loyalty registration were moved to a Civilian Conservation Corps (CCC) camp in Merryl, Oregon, approximately fourteen miles northwest of Tule Lake, where they were interrogated.

The CCC camp, which had previously been a residential camp for laborers involved in federal economic development projects during the Depression, became a virtual prison managed by the War Relocation Authority and supported in part by Army collaboration. Mail was censored at the camp and family visits were not allowed. Among the 130 people already imprisoned there was Teruyoshi H., a member of *San-en Kai*.

Teruyoshi H.'s interrogation, as witnessed and recorded by an interpreter, went as follows:

Q: How old are you?
A: *Twenty-two.*

Q: Were you born in this country?
A: *Yes. I was born in Sacramento, California.*

Q: Have you been to Japan?
A: *Yes, I have.*

Q: How old were you when you went to Japan?
A: *Two years old.*

Q: How long did you stay there?
A: *Seventeen years.*

Q: Did you go to school there?
A: *Yes.*

Q: Did you go to school in this country?
A: *No.*

Q: What kind of work did you do before the evacuation?
A: *Laundry.*

Q: Where do your parents live?
A: *Japan.*

Q: What is your block number?
A: *24.*

Q: Did you have Tojo's pictures on the walls of your barrack? And Japanese mottoes?
A: *Yes.*

Q: Do you know that WRA said everyone must register?
A: *Yes.*

Q: Why didn't you want to register?
A: *I feel that I'm American citizen — and then after being brought to the camp, I felt I had lost my citizenship. When we were put into camp, they said it was for our protection, and now when feelings of people are stronger, why do they want us to go out on indefinite leave? Why are they practically forcing me out of camp?*

Q: When you registered for indefinite leave, it didn't mean you have to go out.

A: *If that is so, it wouldn't be necessary to register if it wasn't compulsory to leave the center.*

Q: WRA wanted everyone to register for leave clearance so that everyone could be cleared at the same time. Clearance takes quite a long time, and sometimes a job cannot be held until it is finished, as long as a month. So they decided to register everyone and clear all of the people, so if they found a job or decided to leave, they could do it in a short time. Indefinite leave is voluntary, however. Internal security people say you are an active agitator and caused a lot of trouble.

A: *No, never tried to influence anyone else.*

Q: Do you know Nakamura, Block 48?
A: *No.*

Q: Do you know Yamahata?
A: *No.*

Q: Do you know Yoshida, Block 44?
A: *No.*

Q: Do you feel that you would ever want to register?
A: *No.*

The lawyer in charge of the interrogation wrote in his remarks that the man's attitude was "very defiant and that he showed a definite loyalty to Japan" by the fact that he had Tojo's photo displayed. The lawyer added that Teruyoshi H. should be held in prison at Moab, Utah (WRA report, March 18, 1943).

Umezu, a good friend of Teruyoshi's, said:

His nickname was *bonbon* [young master]. He was a handsome man with chiseled features. He was, however, short tempered, aggressive, misleading, and had been treated badly by the white people. He was confined for twenty-four hours in a guard room, hit and tortured. I guess that made him hostile to the whites. They said he posted Tojo's photo in the room, but Tojo was the only thing we knew about Japan. We just happened to be in such a situation. To look at it in philosophical terms, being judged loyal or disloyal to the U.S. or Japan just for that reason made no sense.

Teruyoshi H. and Umezu came to share the same fate.

The authorities continued interrogating the *kibei*, trying to find the agitators who were instigating the campaign against registration. Reasons for refusal of registration varied, however, ranging from those who were exempted from registration due to having served in the military before forced removal, to those who rejected it because they could not understand the meaning of registration, to married couples who wished to stay in the camp as long as the war went on, to those who said they wanted to obtain immediate release by answering "yes, yes" but insisted on attaining all the same rights as white Americans before their release in exchange for registration (WRA report, March 18, 1943).

In his diary, Masao Kawate vividly recorded his feelings about the interrogation:

> What kinds of things was I asked? They asked, "Why won't you register?" I did not see any need to sign something when I didn't understand its true nature. In the light of my past record, it was an insult to ask me whether I was loyal or disloyal to the United States. It was absolutely impossible for me to swear loyalty to the United States. "Did you attend meetings of the *kibei* youth group?" they asked. "How many times? Did you go to block meetings? Have you spoken before large groups of people?"
>
> "I went to the meetings, but I didn't take part in any movement in particular," I answered. I plainly stated that it was meaningless to question me any further, that it was just a waste of time, so the whole thing was over with relatively quickly. Actually, there was no room for argument. After 15 or 20 minutes, we arrived at the new camp and joined the other 80-odd people. We all received numbers; mine was No. 90. From this day

forward, we were referred to by our numbers. The entirety of the supplies that were allotted to us consisted of two sheets, one pillow cover, four blankets, one mattress and a canvas bed. The barrack was a row house without partitions, walls, or ceilings. Over 30 people slept in a single barrack.

Later, Kawate explained his feelings about his situation in a letter (December 2, 1958) to Mr. Wayne Collins:

The evacuation was very severe shock to me even more than the declaration of war itself because I never thought that would be possible constitutionally. I was more than willing to go to the war against Japan if called upon, but when all of us were forced to be evacuated and put into the camp I was so shocked and disillusioned with the American democracy that I changed my mind and decided to resist getting into the military service.

It was this attitude that had decided the course of my life in the relocation center throughout the war. So when those questionaires on loyalty were passed on to us in late 1942, I decided not to answer them because I believed that filling [out] the questionaire would mean getting us into the military service. (I had been classified 2-B before evacuation, which was later changed to 4-F.) Rumours to this effect were quite widespread in the camp then and meetings were held almost every day by radical groups, although I never took any active part in it.

There were many *Nisei* who took the same attitude as I did and when we were were given the last chance to fill in the questionaire we (about 15 persons all [of] whom were evacuated from Placer County, California) went to the center's administration office together. As it so happened that I was one of the oldest among the group and I walked in front of the group I was mistaken to be the responsible ring leader. It was for this reason, I think, that I was sent to the segregation camp. As I said above, I had never taken any active part in this movement; I was rather strongly influenced by it instead.

Under question now was the right of the War Relocation Authority to treat people who had not committed crimes as "prisoners" and insinuate that they would suffer fines and penalties, although the WRA actually lacked any authority to implement criminal punishment. After the interrogation, most of the men were released and went back to Tule Lake, but some of the young men, including Kawate, Teruyoshi H., Umezu, and Takatsui, were transferred to other camps as "prisoners of the WRA" on the grounds that they had violated the WRA's rules for maintaining order.

Umezu was arrested and sent with fifteen or sixteen other leaders of the *San-en Kai* group to Klamath Falls county jail in southern Oregon, just across the border from Tule Lake. After two weeks imprisonment, during which the men were plagued by bedbugs, they were transferred to the Meryle CCC camp, where they joined other *kibei* and *jun nisei.*

According to Kawate's diary, arrest warrants and litigation papers were formally handed to seventeen of these men, including himself, on March 21, 1943. At this time it was determined that the trial would be held at Tule Lake that same day and that the project director, a man named Coverley, would officiate. According to Kentaro Takatsui (*Oral and Documentary History,* 2000), the trial was a "kangaroo court" administered by a "kangaroo judge" (p. 6).

Kawate's account continues:

> I myself was being sued for the crime of refusing to register. That day after lunch, just after one o'clock, we gathered all of our baggage and set out for the trial in Army trucks, leaving the CCC camp as a group of nine. Approximately 30 minutes later, we again arrived at a relocation center. It was certain that our punishment would be determined at this trial, but what kind of trial would it be? Was the WRA of a mind to render a fair and conscientious judgment? Where would we be sent as a result of the ruling? Some might be allowed to return home, but would the remaining majority be sent to yet another camp somewhere? Would they be sentenced to a punishment of several months, or several years? While hoping in our hearts to be allowed to return home, as we passed through the front gate, jostling about

in the truck, we thought that such an outcome was probably impossible.

Umezu remembered his trial very well:

They held the trial in a high school auditorium. There were prosecutors, a judge, and lawyers, but the lawyers in this case were not real lawyers. Instead, high school principals and military men played the roles. But at least there was an interpreter at the trial.

I told the interpreter to translate what I said literally. He said he would. I said, "This trial is nonsense," and asked him to translate it; I went on, "because you, the judge and the others, are holding this trial just as a formality on the assumption that we will be found guilty. Such a trial is meaningless! You know from the outset what the sentence will be." I told the interpeter, who was older than me, to translate it, just as I said it. He said he could not. I said, "You can do it, so why don't you try?" He translated about eighty percent of what I said. Then the judge got angry, stood up, and shouted, "You JAP!"

He was fuming, getting emotional, banging on the table. I pretended not to see him. I didn't care if he was angry or not. I was the second or third to undergo trial. At the beginning, we were all obedient as we received our sentences. Then I said it all was nonsense, so the judge got angry. But it really *was* nonsense, since we had no right to appeal to a higher court. They just did what they wanted to do. What a ridiculous trial, I thought. But later, one of the prosecutors came across the room to me and said in a low voice that I had done well, probably meaning something like, "Don't forget your *yamato damashii*" [native Japanese spirit]. Not everyone felt the same way. Interesting, isn't it?

Masao Kawate was tried at the "Caucasian dining hall" and was the first to be put on trial, with only Caucasians as witnesses.

First Mr. O'Brian, the attorney for the prosecution, read the written complaint and asked whether there were any objections. I answered that I had no objections. Thereupon the presiding judge handed down the sentence of two months in prison and suspension of clothing allowance. To this, too, I clearly stated that I had no objections. And with that alone, the trial ended. It was truly cut-and-dried. In the first place, could you really call such a thing a trial or a court? In spite of myself, I had to wonder. But I ended up being surprised at and satisfied with the light sentence of two months. To explain the legal details, the prosecutor held that I had violated the rules of the WRA by refusing to register as ordered to by the WRA. So, was I guilty or not guilty? Of course, it was decided that I was guilty. Because I was found guilty, they sentenced me to two months in an isolation camp in accordance with the law and WRA rules, and I was asked if I had any objections. Because it was handled in this summary manner, I had neither the opportunity nor the time to defend my own position. I had been planning since yesterday to grandly launch into a polemic, but I realized that it would be of no use at all. I was kept secluded in another room until the trials of the other 14 were completed. All of us agreed that this had not been a real trial when all was finished. Still, we all were surprised at how light the sentence was.[21]

The offenses that Umezu and the others were charged with were as follows: failing to conform to the orders issued by the camp's director of registration, agitating others, disturbing the order, and interfering with the authority of the WRA, a federal organization. The Japanese Americans observing the trial in the gallery were impressed by the polite manners of the accused youth, who were never intimidated, even before the judge.

---

21. Kawate's trial at the "Caucasian recreation hall" is also introduced in Drinnon (1987, p. 96). I have translated the passages included here from his diary, written in Japanese, in possession of his son, Haruo Kawate. Slight differences between Drinnon's account and my translation are noted.

From California to Moab, Utah

On Wednesday, March 31, the trial ended around 8:30 p.m. While waiting for the trial to end, Kawate ate a dinner of meatballs and rice in the waiting room. He observed in his diary, "After the trial, everyone who came to see the 'criminals' was talking happily because they thought that now that the sentence had been decided, they would be able to meet again in a short time. But it became clear later that their expectations were to be betrayed."

Umezu was sentenced to the maximum six months imprisonment. He was put on a military truck with fifteen fellow *San-en Kai* members, including Teruyoshi H. With no warm clothes to protect them from the cold air, they left Tule Lake that night. They waited until dawn at Dorris, on the California-Oregon border, and were then put on a train heading for Salt Lake City, Utah. Arriving at Salt Lake City, they were taken south in a truck and placed in a CCC camp somewhere in the highlands. Their final destination was the Moab CCC camp in southeast Utah, close to the Colorado border.

Kawate described the trip as follows:

March 31

Around 8:50, we all were crammed into a boxlike baggage truck, and the lock fell into place with a "Ga-chan!" We set out with a "*banzai*" send-off from the crowd of people waiting outside. I peered out the small peephole to see whether we were turning right or left after the gate. As it turned out, we turned left. We all were of the opinion then that we would either be transferred to the prison at Alturas or we would be sent to another CCC camp to serve out the remainder of our sentence there. When we asked where they were taking us, they wouldn't speak a word of truth; they only answered that they didn't know. When the truck picked up speed on a national highway, we started singing, "Behold, the day breaks on the Eastern Seas...," to allay our boredom. When we had been driving along for more than an hour, we arrived at Alturas, but there was no indication that we were going to the prison. They just fueled the truck with gasoline, and we started off again. East, west, south, north? In which direction were we headed in the pitch-dark night? Boxed inside the truck, we had no idea which way we were headed. After leaving Alturas, we just kept driving through what seemed to be a hilly area. As time passed, it kept getting colder and colder. Our bodies were tired, and we began to feel sleepy, but it was impossible to sleep in the truck, which zoomed along through the night.

April 1

At a little before two the next morning, the truck stopped suddenly. Looking out through a small hole, we saw that we were at a train stop surrounded by a dozen or so houses. "Oh, so we are being sent somewhere else by train," we thought. But then, where on earth are we now? We thought surely that we must have already left California behind and were perhaps over a hundred miles into Nevada at this point. After a while, the external lock was removed, the door opened, and we were allowed to get out of the truck. First we all had to relieve ourselves. But it was so incredibly cold outside!

After a while, we learned our present location and where we were headed. We had arrived at a small town called Doyle at the California-Nevada border. The railway belonged to the Union Pacific Company, and it would travel through the city of Reno and continue on to the east. The guard spoke for the first time, telling us that we would board the train here and be taken to a special segregation camp in a relocation center in the state of Utah. They said that the train was to depart at around 2:50. We still had a little time, and it was cold, so we asked them to let us wait in the waiting room at the train station, but they wouldn't grant our request, saying that there were no soldiers to guard us, or something to that effect. We were awfully upset about that. There was nothing else to do, so we just got back into the truck.

It was so cold that we could hardly bear to just sit there. It had all
happened suddenly, with no advance notice, so half of us hadn't
come prepared with warm clothing, and the cold was hard to
bear. I was lucky because I had come with an overcoat.

The men were told not to make any noise and to converse only in
English so that there would not be any trouble with nearby residents
(Drinnon, 1987, p. 96).

Kawate continues:

If the train had arrived on schedule, we might have been able
to stand it, but we were made to wait a whole five hours, and
we were at the limits of our endurance. American trains were
known throughout the world for leaving and arriving late, even
in peacetime, so, needless to say, the situation was even worse
during the war. It was 6:50 by the time we were finally able to
board the train.

Even though it was warm inside the train, anyone who is not
accustomed to train travel will find it hard to sleep on a train,
and after all, I was unable to sleep at all. After being jostled
around in the truck, we were all hungry, but we were not able
to eat breakfast until after ten o'clock. We were Japanese, and we
were in a group, so there was nothing we could do about it. Still,
the meal that finally came was a feast, so we were happy. For
the first time in four or five months we were able to taste eggs,
bacon, and real butter. There were so many soldiers in the train
that it was fair to say that they made up half of the passengers.
And the sight of two military policemen (one Navy and the
other Army) patrolling the aisles gave testament to the fact that
it was wartime. The soldiers on board were all using their one
or two weeks of leave to travel within the United States. Many
of them were drunk on alcohol, and, characteristic of American
military men, they were disorderly and disheveled. It was impossible to sleep even if you were drowsy.

When I looked out the window at the passing scenery, I saw

nothing but the vast deserts of Nevada and Utah, with only sagebrush for ground cover. Whatever hills there were were all bald of vegetation. Here and there, one might spot a stream or some horses and cattle, as well as human residences.... The one thing I had been looking forward to was seeing the famous Salt Lake, but because the train was running late, it was already pitch black by the time the train passed by there. Moreover, the window blinds had to be lowered for military reasons, so we were unable to see a thing. It was 10:30 at night when we arrived at Salt Lake City Station.... We had to wait there for about an hour to transfer to the next train.

April 2

The train arrived at the Thompson Village stop at around seven the next morning.

From here we boarded a truck that had come to meet us and headed toward the Moab CCC camp. The morning air was cold, so they gave us each one blanket, but we still found it unbearably cold. However, we arrived safely at the camp in just thirty minutes. We were disappointed when we ended up at an old CCC camp. We had heard that a new segregation camp had been built in Utah, so we had imagined that the camp we would be staying in would be a fine one. But both the buildings and the facilities were inferior to those at the Tule Lake CCC camp, so we were truly disgusted. But when we entered the camp, we learned for the first time that for us it would be just a temporary segregation camp and that we would be transferred to the state of Arizona before long.[22]

---

22. Kawate's diary entries of the journey from California to Moab are also introduced in Richard Drinnon's *Keeper of Concentration Camps: Dillon S. Myer and American Racism* (1987, pp. 96-97). The above is my direct translation from Kawate's diary in Japanese; there are minor differences between Drinnon's translation and my own. For example, Drinnon emphasizes that Kawate understood the political motivations behind the transfer: "Tracing the steps that were taken to handle us, I can say that there is not a speck of doubt that the whole scheme was carefully planned beforehand" (p. 97).

In those days, the population of Moab was about twelve hundred. The camp was fourteen miles away from town, in the "middle of nowhere," far from human civilization, culture, and any other sign of life. In a photo captioned, "The Dalton Wells CCC Camp, 1940," about twenty dark buildings seem to float in the vast desert with only low shrubs dotting the landscape. Beginning in January 1943, about fifty-four so-called "traitors" were sent there from the various incarceration camps, escorted by military guards.

Previously, from 1935 to 1942, the Moab camp had been a CCC camp where more than two hundred young men lived while engaging in land improvement projects. It had been neglected for a while, and the facility had become a ruin, badly in need of repair. On December 10, 1942, it became a secret "prison" to enforce criminal penalties on those who did not obey the WRA. "The locals were told that between 25 and 50 men would be placed there with Army Military Police for guards 24 hours a day. Later up to 200 plus might be put in the camp.... Future possibilities were that they might work on range projects and that their families might join them: things never really considered but a nice pap for the locals" (*The Zephyr*, July 1989). The government never meant for these special prisoners to perform work or have their families join them.

Knowing full well that the acts of Umezu and others were not subject to penalty as subversive acts against the state, the WRA could only segregate them for being "trouble-makers." These "criminals" were arrested without warrants and segregated without formal trials.

On January 11, 1943, the first group from southern California, called the "Manzanar Sixteen," arrived; on February 18, the "Gila Thirteen" arrived from Arizona; on February 13, ten more came from Manzanar; and on April 2, 1943, the "Tule Fifteen" arrived from northern California. In a picture that looks for all the world like a school picture, the fifteen young men from Tule Lake appear in three orderly rows. Kawate stands teacherlike in the last row and Umezu appears in the center of the middle row, his face a picture of the clash of youthful energy with the bitterness and fatigue of a long, difficult journey.

In April 1943, Umezu and Teruyoshi H. met Harry Ueno and Joe Kurihara, who had been sent to Moab from Manzanar camp for causing a "riot" in December 1942. In this group was also Tsutomu Higashi, a *kibei nisei* who was eventually to become president of *Hokoku Seinen-dan* at Tule Lake Segregation Center.

From various accounts, we can piece together a picture of the prisoners' feelings about their arrival at the Moab camp. In a letter to Mrs. Kato, his friend at Manzanar, Higashi writes sarcastically about the experience: "From county jail, we rode the bus and was escorted by seven soldiers, so-called tour with government expense. It is a great success in life while we roar with laughter" (private collection of Harry Ueno).

Masao Kawate describes in detail the prisoners who came out to greet them and the complexity of their legal status as inmates:

> What struck us as most odd when we arrived at the camp was the group of people who came out to greet us. There were a dozen or so men who looked just like South Seas aborigines to me. Their hair was clipped short, and they were barefoot, wearing only trousers. They were so sunburned that one could hardly imagine them to be Japanese. They hung together in a group, and the only other people present were the exact opposite, dressed and behaving like gentlemen. This group exchanged no speech with the "barbarians" and would not even go near them. It was only later that we learned why the people at the camp had split into two groups.
>
> After a few days, I came to understand what manner of place the Moab Special Segregation Camp was. When our group of 15 from Tule Lake entered the camp, the people who were already there had all been transferred from the Gila and Manzanar relocation centers, and we learned the inside story by listening to them talk. At the time, the population of the camp was 16 from Gila, 18 from Manzanar, and we 15 from Tule Lake, for a total of 49 people. Several of the residents had already been living there for three or four months, but when we asked them about the reasons for their imprisonment, the Gila group said that it was likely because they had been active as officials of the youth group protesting the registration program, while the members

of the Manzanar group gave various reasons that could not
be summed up easily. Many of them had been responsible for
the Tayama Incident and the Gunfire Incident. In other words,
they had been interned for agitating or for interfering with the
Wartime Relocation Authority, but, in general, they were not
being held in the camp on account of being disloyal. We listened
carefully to what they had to say, but there did not seem to have
been clear evidence against them. They were what you might
call "suspects." In fact, there were many who were absolutely
innocent. Accordingly, some of them thought that they could be
transferred from here to another camp or to the outside. They
were saying that, depending upon how well they behaved inside
this camp, they might be allowed a transfer, with the permission
of Camp Director Myer.

Apart from the question of the sincerity of the camp director, the fact that they raised the possibility of another transfer
presented a major problem for those of us who were interned
in the camp for the first time. Yes, it's only human nature that
most men are driven by concern for their wives and children,
or at least by their desire for the company of women. This is all
the more true of those who are weak willed. Like those clois-
tered away from women in Buddhist monastic complexes such
as the famous Koyasan, men ruled by transient emotions could
not withstand long periods of life in this segregation camp and
would soon expose and succumb to their weaknesses. Forsaking
their original intentions, they would not stop to reflect on their
own behavior. Forgetting that we were all comrades, they would
begin scheming, thinking only of getting themselves out, and
they would not care whether they did so at the expense of others.
In a manner of speaking, these fellow prisoners are even worse
than dogs or cats. Even if those interned here do not think of
themselves as Japanese people, loyal to Japan, at least they should
serve their fellow Japanese.

If this is true, then it goes without saying that we should act
like Japanese every bit of the way in our internment. Even so,

some people cooperated with the WRA authorities by reporting on what others said or did, so that they themselves might escape from the camp. Even worse, they did menial tasks like laundry for the "white devils" (even their underwear) to gain their favor. Surely there is no one who could silently observe these events for very long. It is only natural that one would eventually have to speak out strongly in judgment of these men. It was no wonder, then, under the circumstances, that the group from Manzanar had split into two factions.

Adding to Kawate's commentary, Kentaro Takatsui offered his own grim but wry description of the Moab camp. Although the old, dilapidated, tar-papered barracks were larger than the barracks at Tule Lake, "sanitary facilities were cruder than crude. The outhouse was the worst. You sat on a wooden hole in a large group of twenty holes. The excrement was still underneath from the former occupants of the C.C.C. camp. No water flushed toilets. We figured that this was one of the methods being used by our Great White Father in Washington to DEHUMANIZE us" (*Oral and Documentary History*, 2000). In despair at this inhumane treatment, Ueno, Higashi, and nine others applied to renounce their U.S. citizenship on March 10 at the Moab prison camp. But their applications were not accepted.

According to Harry Ueno, whom I interviewed:

We were confined in an old building, under guard 24 hours. Special guards accompanied us even when we went to the dining room for meals, and mail delivery was totally prohibited for a time. After a while, we were allowed to receive mail, but each piece of mail was inspected. I did not have any hearing, though they said I was going to have one when I left Manzanar. I protested to Director [Raymond] Best. He said threateningly, "Nothing but sage grows here. Whatever happens to you, nobody would find out about it for a million years." Soon after that, two soldiers started practicing their marksmanship with my building as a target. Then I made up my mind. If I renounced my US citizenship and became an alien, international law would protect me.

On the night of April 13, soon after the arrival of Umezu and others, minor violence occurred among the prisoners, and one of the *kibei* was taken in as a ringleader on the following morning, the 14th. In addition to this unjust arrest, the prisoners were issued a general order that restricted the inmates of one barrack from visiting another barrack without first securing permission from the proper authorities. They were also prohibited from using the Japanese language at meetings with other prisoners. Those who disobeyed were to be imprisoned for three months. The authorities challenged the prisoners to come to the office with their baggage if they had complaints. To protest this order, twenty-one, including Umezu, Ueno, and Kawate, took up the authorities' challenge by marching to the administration building carrying their packed bags at 1:15 p.m. on April 14, 1943. As there was no room for more than seven prisoners in the county jail, most of them were sentenced to solitary confinement or confined to their rooms. Eight were given the maximum three months imprisonment, along with suspension of all wages, clothing allowances, unemployment compensation, welfare grants, or other pay priviliges to which they might have been entitled under instructions and regulations of the War Relocation Authority. Ueno, Teruyoshi H., and Higashi were among the eight; Masao Kawate and Tsutomu Umezu were given one month's imprisonment with similar suspensions (Memorandum to Project Director Best, April 19, 1943). But Umezu said that he never went to prison.

From Moab, Utah, to Winslow, Arizona

"Utah state seemed to have said something to the effect that they could not rent the camp for use by such troublesome Japs and we should get out of Moab. The federal government had no alternative but to look hard for another location," Umezu recalled with some amusement. About two weeks later, on April 27, Umezu was again transferred with Teruyoshi H. and Ueno. This time they were taken to Leupp prison camp, near Winslow, Arizona.

The transfer from Moab to Leupp took about eleven hours. Most of the men, including Umezu, were taken by Greyhound bus, but five men, including Ueno, Teruyoshi H., and Higashi, were transported in small boxes loaded on a truck carrier. According to Ueno:

[These boxes] measured 4 ft x 6 ft, with air holes at each corner. More miserable than pigs, and without speaking, we were put in these boxes, powerless before bayonets in the dark. We found this treatment offensive, but we were prisoners. The truck started, and we did not know where we were heading. Just as we would be on a small boat in a rough sea, we were tossed and jolted. The air was terrible, and dust blew in through a little gap in the back. I felt like vomiting. Roads in this area were not as good as in California — there were a lot of bumps. If I had thought about my discomfort, I wouldn't have been able to bear it for a moment. Our destination was more than 400 miles away. "I have to hold on," I told myself. "How can I let myself be defeated at this point? I am Japanese. Bear it! Bear it! It is easy to die. I have a wife and children. Physical pain is nothing. I have to overcome ... overcome." I just forced myself to concentrate on overcoming the suffering. It was so dusty that I put a handkerchief over my nose. We all lay there without exchanging words. Lying down or sitting, the terrible bumps made us feel like everything in our stomach was coming up.... They seemed to enjoy our pain, and I thought: "White devils ... they talk about justice, but their acts are just the opposite. They are demons, beasts. Japan must win ... we have reason enough here why we shouldn't lose." (Personal letter in Japanese, private collection of Harry Ueno)

From his words, it should be evident that Harry Ueno believed that American justice and democracy were full of hypocrisy. He called it a "cheap spirit," the kind of democracy that would be applied to a defeated nation. He cheered himself by identifying with Japan as it fought against the United States and telling himself that Japan (and he himself) must not lose.

Leupp prison was located along the banks of the Little Colorado River, which flows through the Painted Desert. It was built in 1923 as a boarding school to accommodate five hundred Navajo children. Umezu recalled:

> The land the federal government could use was an Indian reservation. They looked for an empty reservation without any Indians around and found a small one called Leupp, which was not even marked on the map back in those days. The boarding school was in the middle of a vast wasteland. It was a nice stone building that the government had built for re-educating Indian children. The dining room, for example, was really magnificent. I was shocked when I first saw it. It had served hundreds of people with lots of meat and had an array of splendid refrigerators, the likes of which were rarely seen in ordinary restaurants. There was so much food that we could not easily finish it. We were assigned individual rooms to use, and we were always playing baseball when we had free time.

Among the pictures Kawate kept from the Leupp camp is one of the mess hall. It clearly shows the enormous size of the hall, which dwarfed the three rows of tables where about twenty Japanese American men would eat, bathed in bright sunlight from several big windows. Ueno also recorded his impressions of the buildings at Leupp, comparing them with the ones at Manzanar: "They were built better. The mess hall was better, too" (Embrey et al., 1986, p. 76).

From May to July 1943, twenty-six new "troublemakers" joined the fifty at Leupp, sent from other incarceration camps such as Gila, Manzanar, Tule Lake, Topaz, Jerome, Rohwer, Heart Mountain, and Granada (Letter from Leupp Project Director Robertson to Mr. Myer, Director WRA, November 13, 1943). At Leupp, the more than seventy "troublemakers" were confined with about three times as many soldiers standing guard.

Four men, including Harry Ueno, were put into boxes again only thirty minutes after arriving at Leupp, for transport to a prison in Winslow, thirty miles from Leupp. According to Ueno:

There were only two bunks for 4 of us. The sheriff handed one blanket to each of us. Since Winslow is quite high, the nights were very cold. We spent four days there. Every meal that was served was covered with salt, hot chili or ketchup. Unless we washed the food, we wouldn't know what we were eating. Two young men wanted to go on a hunger strike, but I disagreed. I told them that we are not going to die like dogs in here. We answer for them. Our credibility as a leader of the free world is eroding now. ("I Am a Captive of the U.S. Government," unpublished)

At that point, Umezu noticed that the authorities were hesitant about shuttling troublemakers from one camp to another or to prison:

The U.S. government seemed to be avoiding the issue of confining *kibei nisei* altogether. They kept saying that it was an issue inside the camp. Americans in general had no idea about the loyalty registration. If they had decided to look into it, there might have been an uproar, as America had common sense, too. They worried about how to handle us, and I suppose the government had a hard time.

On June 15, 1943, Umezu was released from Leupp because of his health and moved to a hospital in Gila camp in Arizona. "When I saw women for the first time in the hospital after several months, I was about to faint," he laughed cheerfully, remembering those young days. The remaining men were all released from Leupp by the end of 1943. It was summer 1944 when Umezu returned to Tule Lake by train in a sleeping car.

In July 1943, Tule Lake became a segregation camp for those considered disloyal. "No No Boys" and others labeled "disloyal" had been gathered up and segregated there, safely away from other Japanese Americans. Then, on July 1, 1944, a bill enabling *nisei* to renounce their U.S. citizenship in time of war was signed by President Roosevelt. Those at Tule Lake who wanted to return to Japan organized *Sokoku Kennkyu Seinen-kai* (Youth Groups for Research on the Homeland) and *Sokuji Kikoku Hoshi-dan* (Volunteers for the Immediate Return to the Homeland to Serve). Inmates of Tule Lake were about to enter the turmoil of a citizenship renunciation movement.

The True Objective of Loyalty Registration

During the loyalty registration, *kibei* called upon English-speaking *nisei* to reject registration in an English document entitled, "Why Is It That You Should Not Register?"

Why you should not declare yourself in black and white by writing "yes" or "no" on your statement, Form 304 A, Selective Service.[23] Do you know that the Army, Navy, politicians and congressmen are trying to obtain proof that the Japanese are disloyal and no good? Do you know that the politicians and the American Legion are doing their best to enact new laws or amend the clauses in the Constitution, in order to cancel our citizenship...? Your fathers and mothers came to this country and labored arduously for years. By saving their money, they bought the properties and lands in your names. I am sure that you are aware of the fact that it is of no avail to throw away your properties, your lands and your farm equipment.... Congressmen and the Army are looking for evidence in your statement on Form 304A, stating "Yes" or "No," to enact new laws or amend clauses in the Constitution so that they can internationally confiscate your property.... "No" means that you are willing to denounce your privileges and rights as an American citizen, so they can define all of us as disloyal and cancel our citizenship, thus making us enemy aliens. Our properties will be classified as enemy alien properties, making it legal to confiscate them.... Your written statements of "Yes" or "No" will be used against you. Don't

---

23. The War Department's form for male *nisei* bore the Selective Service seal and was called, "Statement of United States Citizens of Japanese Ancestry," DDS Form 304-A. The WRA form was called, "Application for Leave Clearance," Form WRA-1126. Male *nisei* were required to answer an abbreviated version of the WRA questionaire at the same time they filled out the one for the Army. The fact that the Army questionnaire was voluntary while the WRA form was mandatory for all evacuees led to serious difficulties later in the program (Collins, 1985, p. 25).

write anything. Don't provide them with evidence.

Across the copy of this document in the UC Berkeley Bancroft Library were scrawled the words, "God Damned PRO-JAPS!"

To those who drafted this document, loyalty registration was a way of finding excuses to make people renounce their citizenship. By the time registration was enforced, the *kibei* believed that they had uncovered the underlying intention behind the introduction of Mike Masaoka's volunteer system, under which those of Japanese descent would prove their loyalty to the United States by begging the government to allow them to give up their lives.

From his words and actions, one might conclude that Masaoka's ultimate intent was to exclude from American society those of his countrymen who were unsuited to becoming fully Anglo-Americanized. And the situation developed just as Masaoka had expected.

In mid-April 1943, a *kibei* at the Moab prison camp who had applied to renounce his U.S. citizenship and repatriate to Japan was reported to have drawn his empty fist across his belly many times, implying *harakiri* (Memorandum to Project Director, April 19, 1943). The idea behind this gesture was that renouncing one's U.S. citizenship meant to give up on being an American, signifying one's "death" as an American citizen. As mentioned earlier in this chapter, in the ancient precepts of *bushido*, the way of the samurai warrior, if the loyal subject disagrees with his lord's opinion and cannot convince the lord, he must spill his own blood "as proof of the truthfulness of the words used to make a final appeal to the lord's wisdom and conscience" (Nitobe, 1995, pp. 84-85). This is why the *kibei* at Moab drew his fist across his belly. It was his way of protesting, with the symbolic taking of his own life, the absurdity of having been forced into an incarceration camp despite American citizenship, the unfairness of having been treated as a criminal simply because he exercised his American right to "freedom of speech."

In April 1997, Kenji Takeuchi, one of those who renounced his citizenship, proudly displayed his Receipt of Alien Registration to me, saying, "I always carry this with me."

Takeuchi, an American, registered as an alien when he renounced his

U.S. citizenship. The Tule Lake Immigration authorities issued to him Receipt #6158360. The credit-card-size document bears Takeuchi's signature, together with the print of his right forefinger. When affixing his signature to the document, Takeuchi added the words, "I am signing under protest, for [I] consider myself as an American citizen." [See photograph on pg. iii.]

CHAPTER FIVE

DEFEAT, BROKEN DREAMS,
AND AGAIN, *BUSHIDO*

Re-Segregation

In a firm voice, *kibei nisei* Tadahiko Okamoto pronounced, "America is not my home." He continued, "I cannot forget such memories as my grandmother taking me to a temple. Regardless of Japan's defeat, those things live on inside me. The Japanese way of life centers around things of the heart, so I give a lot of thought to human bonds, obligations, and responsibilities. We are different from the Americans. Japan may have been defeated, but it is still my home."

Yoshio Nishikawa's experience was only slightly different. Nishikawa, who was in charge of discipline and character development within the *Hokoku Seinen-dan* (Patriotic Young Men's Group to Serve the Homeland), graduated from high school in the United States, so he had no difficulty communicating in English. Whenever he hears Japanese, it reminds him of his elementary school days in Japan.

> I am getting old, as you see, but my childhood in Japan is burned into my memory. I have happy memories of it. In 1961, I went back to Japan for the very first time since the war and found that most of my elementary school classmates had been killed during wartime — actually, even before the start of the war with the U.S.
>
> I watch Japanese satellite television here in America. Yesterday, I saw a scene of people catching *ayu* [smelt or sweetfish] in the river. There was a river in our village, too, and we swam there from morning until evening during the summer holidays. There

were *ayu* in that river. The program yesterday reminded me of those days. When I was in the third or fourth grade, I put stones in the river to make a trap to catch the fish. They swam in under my feet (bare feet, they must have been) and I scooped one up with my hands. If anyone asks about my childhood, it is all about Japan. Childhood is the foundation of the man, I think. My grandfather, who was a school principal himself, was in charge of disciplining me. I think his discipline took root inside me naturally and I am very thankful for it.

Partially due to the complicated emotions and remembrances of childhood in Japan like Nishikawa's, more than a few inmates of Tule Lake wanted to go back to Japan. One of the documents from the war years that reflects this desire is the "Prospectus on the Re-Segregation Petition," written in 1944 at the Tule Lake Segregation Center. It reads as follows:[24]

What kind of thing is this re-segregation petition? Looking back, countless people, not only our representatives, but other fellow Japanese as well, have been arrested since the demonstration last November. Time has passed and we have felt anxiety, worry and indignation, yet we see no sign of any solution.

One of the reasons such a confusing scandal occurred was that the WRA classified the center, domestically and internationally, as a segregation camp for those disloyal to the United States, while in reality the detainees sent to the center were never thoroughly screened. In the course of all these changes in status, we regrettably have found ourselves varying widely in beliefs and positions. Accordingly, we who perceive ourselves as detainees, who have willingly undergone a procedure whereby our status was determined to be disloyal to the United States, called pure Japanese — no, rather, enemy alien — now petition for re-segregation. This we do, in part, to offer a solution to the authorities who have refused to release us on the grounds that we are dangerous and in part as a way

---

24. Author's translation from the original Japanese. Motomu Akashi's *Betrayed Trust* (2004) also has a translation (pp. 136-141).

of notifying both the U.S. and Japanese governments that we remain loyal to Japan, as pure Japanese, to the death, and to make preparations for the future by clarifying our legitimate reasons.

After further explanation, the petition moves to a list of principles:

* We sincerely hope that you will study the intent of this petition and determine your stance toward it in accordance with your own free will.

* We acknowledge the significance of this war and swear absolute loyalty to Japan and therefore declare that we cannot be loyal to the United States.

* We realize that we do not need [U.S.] citizenship and are willing to renounce it when the Citizenship Renunciation bill passes Congress in order to clarify our status as pure Japanese. Therefore, we demand that we be classified as alien enemy detainees and that we be treated in accordance with the Geneva Protocols.

* We wish to return to Japan immediately to attend to national concerns under this unprecedented situation, in accordance with national policy implemented during wartime, and, if possible, we would like to repay our debt of gratitude to the Emperor and the State.

* Even if it becomes impossible to return to Japan during the war, we would like to convey our wishes and thoughts to our country, Japan, by way of clarifying our allegiance.

* Even if an agreement is reached in the future, offering us a way to return to California or our previous addresses, we wish never to return. We will hold fast to residence in segregation centers during the war.

* Acting in accordance with the Japanese spirit, we will strive to discipline our minds and bodies in confinement, expecting to live up to our moral precepts as Japanese. Those who resist this movement, taking actions that are a disgrace to ordinary Japanese, will have to be expelled.

* For the above-mentioned reasons, we demand that the segregation center be true to its name, segregating the true
Japanese from the rest, and, hoping to see this realized as soon
as possible, we urgently petition the appropriate authorities.

The above-mentioned prospectus and the list of those wishing for re-segregation have already been transmitted to both
the U.S. and Japanese governments via the Spanish Embassy
as of May 30. Here, we again supply the final list, which we
wish to be delivered to the Japanese government. At the same
time, we would like to notify the U.S. State Department of our
views and stance, on which basis we expect them to make
their decisions; that is, we expect everyone to decide upon
a course of action in accordance with his own beliefs. We are
willing to return to Japan during the war, to devote ourselves
as citizens of the State and the Emperor; therefore, with conviction and demeanor, and careful attention to our children's
education, we are determined to discipline, control, and
restrain ourselves so that we may become active members of
society when we are given a chance to return to our country.

The total number of applicants for re-segregation has
reached 8,000.

Sanae Akashi, a "Hard-Liner"

Sanae Akashi is known for having started the above petition for re-
segregation of "genuine disloyals" at the Tule Lake Segregation Center in
early 1944. He is recorded in history as a leader of *Sokuji Kikoku Hoshi-
dan* [Volunteers for the Immediate Return to the Homeland to Serve], a
pressure group that was rumored to have used threats to incite the *nisei* to
renounce their U.S. citizenship and repatriate to Japan.

To learn more about his father, Sanae Akashi's son, Motomu Akashi
(born 1929) ordered all the government documents related to his father
from the National Archives, and it took about ten years for all of them to
be sent to him. Opening files up to eight inches thick, carefully turning
page after page, he discovered a story quite different from what appears in
the history books.

My father might not have been as much a hard-liner "No No" man as generally thought. He submitted a Request for Repatriation on July 15, 1943. Originally, Father had come to the United States believing in American democracy and he wanted to remain in the States. But the internment caused a complete about-face in him, and in my life, too.

Had they not been forced to choose either Japan or the U.S. in the loyalty questions, all the Japanese would have stayed in America. The *issei* had a strong attachment to America. They had left Japan in their earlier years, built up their lives here, and had finally begun to enjoy some stability in their livelihoods.

Those "pro-Japan" hard-liners such as Sanae Akashi and others had organized groups whose loyalty to Japan was obvious from their names: *Sokoku Kenkyu Seinen-dan* [Youth Groups for Research on the Homeland], *Sokuji Kikoku Hoshi-dan* [Volunteers for the Immediate Return to the Homeland to Serve], *Hokoku Seinen-dan* [Patriotic Young Men's Group to Serve the Homeland], and *Hokoku Joshi Seinen-dan* [Patriotic Young Women's Group to Serve the Homeland], whose purpose was to call for segregation camp inmates to renounce their U.S. citizenship and ask for repatriation to Japan. Although there were indeed some one-sided pro-Japan militants in these groups, there were many others who joined as a result of peer pressure from the militants and the indignities of incarceration. The groups as a whole have since been branded with a negative image in the pages of Japanese American history, where they are characterized as "violent underground organizations," "radical extreme rightists," or "militant pro-Japan groups." But rarely are the complicated histories of the individual members of these groups told.

Motomu Akashi continued:

My father tried as hard as he could to be an American. Take a look at this. This is a record of his university student registration at Berkeley. In 1917, he registered and studied in ROTC, an Army program. After completing this program and joining the Army, he could have become a second lieutenant. This was around the time of the First World War. Anyone who entered the Army, even a Japanese, could be naturalized as an American. I bet my father joined the Army program hoping to become an American someday.[25]

The loyal son talked excitedly about his father's unknown background, lamenting the fact that Sanae Akashi's name will go down in history only as "a hard-liner who swore loyalty to Japan."

Sanae Akashi was born in Saga Prefecture in Japan in 1893. After completing high school in Japan in 1912, he came to California as a foreign student. According to his son, Sanae had a profound belief in American democracy. After graduating from high school in Los Angeles, in 1915 he entered the University of California's Farm School (which was then part of the Berkeley campus but is now the University of California–Davis) and received his Bachelor of Science in Agriculture degree with a specialty in animal husbandry and poultry in 1918 (Akashi, 2004, p. 7).

Motomu recounts, "Father had been a Buddhist in Japan, but because the American family he worked for was Christian, he too became a Christian. He probably converted because he wanted to be an American. He surely and steadily prepared to be an American. But then they put him in a camp..., so it's certainly no accident that he was a Buddhist when he died."

After graduating from the University of California Farm School, Sanae Akashi joined Yamato Colony, a utopian Christian farming community of Japanese Americans founded by Kyutaro Abiko in Livingston, California, in 1906. Sanae worked in tomato and apricot production and at the same time helped countless Japanese Americans with their agricultural issues

---

25. In fact, Tokie Slocum, a Japanese national who served in the military during World War I and was proud of his connection with the FBI during World War II, actually became a naturalized citizen on the basis of a 1918 congressional act that made "any alien" veteran who served honorably in the war eligible for citizenship. Later, after *Toyota v. U.S.* ruled that Japanese *issei* war veterans were excluded from those eligible for naturalization in 1925 (Niiya, 2001, pp. 367-368), Slocum vigorously worked for the Nye-Lee Citizenship Act, passed by Congress in June 1935, which gave otherwise ineligible aliens a chance to obtain citizenship. Those who had served in the U.S. armed forces between April 6, 1917, and November 11, 1918, and had been honorably discharged could obtain citizenship under this act if they applied before the deadline of January 1, 1937 (Thomas & Nishomoto, 1946, p. 2).

as manager of the Japanese American Production Union. In the Yamato Colony, Sanae met Vivian, a *jun nisei,* and married her in 1926. They visited Japan on their honeymoon; this was Vivian's first visit to the country of her ancestors.

In 1934, the couple moved to Mount Eden in the East Bay area of the San Francisco suburbs, where Sanae worked as a teacher at Eden Gakuen, a Japanese language school. His house was close to the school. According to Motomu:

> He was the only teacher. He always talked about morality, discipline, the words of the Emperor, family and loyalty, and filial devotion to parents. He was a strong believer in *bushido.* My mother worked part time at a farm, since his teacher's salary was low. Father was strict at home: dinner was served exactly at six. We children had to be at the table before Father came and had to finish eating before he finished. He sometimes hit us children to discipline us. He hit fast, as he was skilled in *kendo.* As a teacher's family, we were very poor. I went to school wearing shoes with holes in them. My academic record was good, so when I was in the seventh grade I was given a special responsibility at school, which I shared with another Japanese American classmate with the same top ranking in our class. Our job was to direct traffic with a whistle to protect younger children on the way to school in the morning. This role was only given to a few specially selected students, and I was very proud of it. However, when the war broke out, I got hit by another student at school. When I was taken to the principal's office, Father came to get me. He asked me why I quarreled, and I answered, "Because they called me a *Jap!*" As far as I remember, all he said was, "Good."
>
> My father was a strict disciplinarian, but a very kind man, helping everyone in the community, as he was fluent in English. He spent his time helping the Japanese language school students and their families. Mother often complained about how he was always helping others instead of us.

When the war broke out, Sanae Akashi, the "good Samaritan" Japanese language teacher, was taken away by the FBI, but soon released.[26]

The Akashi family was sent to Tanforan Temporary Detention Center, where Sanae became a warden, in May 1942. Motomu recalled:

> Even at that time, the wealthy farmers of our neighborhood invited us to leave voluntarily before the forced removal started. Father declined, saying that he would like to be with his students and go to Tanforan with them. At Tanforan, he was called "*sensei*" [teacher] by everyone. All the *issei* leaders were arrested, and, as most of the remaining *issei* were uneducated farmers, unable to speak English, Father took care of them in many ways.

This caring father — as Motomu Akashi recalls — was a man who liked America very much, a man of character who took care of others, even before himself or his family.

In 1942, the family was moved from Tanforan to Topaz camp, Utah, where they were asked the loyalty questions.

> I remember that a lot of Father's students came to the barracks. They did not know what to do or how to answer, so they came for my father's advice. I heard him answer them, "You were born in America. You are American citizens. What you have to do is to love America and to fight for America. It is your country." And he suggested that they answer "yes, yes" to the questions. But according to Mother, Father himself wrote, "no, no."

Motomu Akashi showed me the copy of the "Application for War Relocation Center's Permission for Release" signed by Sanae Akashi on February 18, 1943. It had been altered and clearly showed even the U.S. government's confusion regarding the loyalty registration.

"I think that Father probably registered twice," Motomu said. "He

---

26. In his interrogation, Sanae answered the FBI that as a Christian he believed in God and would do what God wanted him to do, and that was to help his people, the Japanese in his community, to endure this war peacefully and quietly and obey the orders of the government (M. Akashi, 2005, p. 107).

might have answered 'no, no' to the first set of questions asked of the *nisei* men."

This was because, at the beginning, *nisei* women and *issei* men and women were all asked if they "would be willing to volunteer for the Army Nurse Corps or the WAAC" (Women's Army Auxiliary Corp; Question 27) and if they would "foreswear any form of allegiance or obedience to the Japanese Emperor" (Question 28). Question 28 troubled all those who were obliged to register. For *jun nisei* who had never thought of the Emperor or had no knowledge about Japan, the answer was neither "no" nor "yes" (Takezawa, 1994, p. 110), and the alien *issei* could only answer "yes" at risk of becoming stateless. The government, confused by the ensuing commotion and angry reaction of the people, made a change in Question 28 four days after the registration began, substituting, "Will you swear to abide by the laws of the United States and to take no action that would in any way interfere with the war effort of the United States?" for the original question directed to the *issei*, which made specific reference to the Emperor.

Motomu continued:

> In the copy of the questions I have at hand, Questions 27 and 28 are masked, hidden by paper. On top, new questions were typed. The first new question is, "If you are given an opportunity, will you be willing to apply for Army Nursing Troops or Army Women's Troops?" and the second one is, "Will you take an oath that you will comply with the law and will not take any action that will interfere with the war effort?" Father just drew a line through the first question, answering neither yes nor no because it was irrelevant. But to the second question, he answered "yes." His was *not* a "no, no" response.

Motomu Akashi frowned many times during the interview and finally said:

> The government acted in an arbitrary manner. They rearranged and changed things arbitrarily as it suited them. They

even turned those who fought for the United States during
World War I into enemy aliens. When Father applied for release
from Topaz in order to join my mother's relatives in the Granada
[Colorado] camp, he was permitted to go. But somehow he
was reassigned as a "no, no" respondent and was sent to Tule
Lake. The loyalty registration form was titled "Application for
Permission for Release," so Father might have misunderstood,
thinking he would be released no matter what answer he gave.

Among those segregated at Tule Lake as "no, no" respondents were
those who applied for repatriation to Japan prior to July 1, 1943, but who
did not cancel their applications afterwards, those who did not change
their "no" answers by July 1, and those who could not obtain permission
for release, even though they had changed their answers to "yes" or had
canceled their applications for repatriation.

Sanae Akashi applied for repatriation after July 1 and was somehow
classified as a "no, no" respondent, which automatically labeled him as
"disloyal." For this reason he was sent to Tule Lake Segregation Center
with his family.

Lawlessness at Tule Lake Segregation Center

One of the biggest problems with the Tule Lake Segregation Center was
that approximately eighteen thousand people were contained in a camp
that had a capacity of only fifteen thousand. The overcrowding caused
continual problems with living space and jobs. A total of 893 dark and
rough wooden barracks stood in rows equally spaced on a land area of
a bit more than one square mile. Each barrack was twenty feet wide, one
hundred feet long, and thirteen feet tall and was partitioned at intervals
of about twenty-three feet to provide living space for four families. There
were no ceilings or upper partitions in the barracks, so noise traveled freely
and the families had no privacy. Fourteen barracks plus a recreation hall,
mess hall, laundry and ironing room, and shower and toilet complex made
up one block, in which about two hundred fifty to three hundred people
lived. Nine blocks comprised a ward.

The camp was fortified by a chain-link and barbed-wire fence eight feet tall. Nineteen watchtowers were spaced every four to five hundred yards along it. The barracks had been constructed to house an entire battalion, thirty-one officers and nine hundred enlisted men, a number that was eventually increased to twelve hundred soldiers. A half-dozen tanks were lined up in the military area in full view of the residents (Shirai, 2001, p. 227; Thomas & Nishimoto, 1946, p. 106).

The situation was further complicated by the fact that the center was supposed to segregate and contain only "disloyals," but in actuality, about six thousand loyalists were mixed in among them. Some who had answered "yes" to the loyalty questions but desired repatriation to Japan were sent to Tule Lake; others, who did not want to start a new life in an unfamiliar part of the U.S., exposed to discrimination and hostility, decided to become "disloyals" to avoid release. And among those who said "yes" to the oath of loyalty but at the same time did not want to be relocated to other camps were many who strongly opposed the Tule Lake camp becoming a segregation center for "disloyals."

According to a memorandum from Corlies Carter to Kenneth Harkness and Harvey Coverley, dated July 22, 1943, the feeling of evacuees was described as follows:

> Evacuees express their resentment not on a political basis but on a personal and family basis.... The people who will be moved from the center are those who are earmarked as loyal Americans. The converse is true, that those individuals marked disloyal will have the greater stability of staying in their present homes.... Segregation, therefore, places a premium upon "disloyalty...." During the evacuation, I urged cooperation with the government. During registration I urged cooperation and was called "inu" [rat, informant]. If the government forces me to leave Tule Lake, even with bayonets, I'll scream my disloyalty at the front gate and threaten sabotage....

A government informant, the Reverend D. Kitagawa, reported in an account recorded by the War Relocation Authority ("Passive Resistance") "the whole thing [has] closely to do with ... human nature. ... Let it never be forgotten that we are dealing with families and not troops. ... Segregation on the basis of that registration ... is as far as evacuees are concerned of utter nonsense."

The Tule Lake camp was already a flashpoint at the time it became a segregation center for "disloyals." It was in a state of near anarchy from summer into autumn of 1943, with people continuously moving in and out. Those who had been interned in Tule Lake from the beginning moved about freely without permission, and the confusion and shortage of housing made everyone ill-tempered. New arrivals "had been told prior to departure from the other camps to leave their furniture and other things behind because [they] would not be needed at Tule Lake. A number of them had done so and found that [the departing evacuees] had taken everything movable with them. They were herded into vacant and dirty recreation halls that were not prepared" (Shirai, 2001, pp. 227-228). To make matters worse, those in charge of housing abandoned their duties, and nobody stepped up to fill their positions. The confusion and disorder made most feel that the situation was getting out of control.

Unlike other camps, where people from the same hometown were gathered together, Tule Lake housed people from ten other camps, so differences in place of origin and economic level tended to cause friction. Those from urban areas who had had a lot of contact with white people were called "Levi's"; those who came from agricultural areas, where the Japanese had survived by helping each other, were called "corduroys." Those from California, who had experienced a great deal of racial discrimination and social segregation already, were looked down upon as being rough and were called "Cali-kuro-chan" [Cal niggers]. According to Shirai (2001), "The social behavior of the Californians was viewed by Northerners as 'barbarous' and strange. They had dark skin, used slang, danced the jitterbug, and the boys wore zoot-suits" (p. 223):

> We Californians could not contain our frustration. We did not like playing second fiddle to the Japanese from Oregon and Washington.... We hurled jeers and taunts at the Northerners, and they returned them. Since the Japanese from Washington

and Oregon were generally lighter skinned, thanks to geography and the weather, and their demeanor was more subservient to the Caucasians, we called them "T.B. Lilly" [tuberculosis lilies]. This made them so mad, they couldn't keep quiet. (Shirai, 2001, p. 58)

Even many years later, Mitsuo Aoyama, who was sent from Seattle to Tule Lake and remained there until repatriation, proudly recalled, "Those of us from Seattle were quiet. I think it was the *kibei* from California who were violent."

Motomu Akashi spoke in a more envious and irritated tone about this seemingly class-based friction:

Wealthy families who had been successful in agriculture before evacuation had a good life even in the center. They could buy everything they wanted by direct mail. The family of a neighborhood friend, who had been sent to the center at the same time as us, had been running a large farm. They always had new shoes and new jackets. I could never afford such things just by working at the mess hall and getting paid sixteen dollars a month.

According to one *issei* author, interviewed by Kaname Saruya, a third of the people thought that meals at the center were worse than meals at their homes, a third thought they were the same, and a third thought that they were better than meals had been at home. This division by thirds roughly parallels the social/economic class hierarchy in the pre-war Japanese American community (Takeshita & Saruya, 1983, p. 38).

As if to exacerbate these economic disparities, even such luxury goods as candy, ice cream, cake, silk, and wool products were sold in the camp. Stores selling such luxuries often became targets for attack since they were regarded as dens for *inu*.

Besides these sociological/geographical/economic differences that caused tension among inmates, there were cultural differences as well. The *kibei*, who had previously been "disapproved by the majority of the Nisei in the [nine other] centers because of their imperfect English and lack of familiarity with American ways and etiquette ... now found themselves in a majority ... [and] took as license the designation of the center as a place where people could live like Japanese":

> Young men moved in groups, bursting in on dances of Nisei, breaking up the dances, and denouncing the style of dancing as 'not Japanese.' Others appeared in women's shower rooms, announcing that 'This is Japan and here men and women bathe together.' Still others slapped and insulted Nisei girls serving as clerks in the housing office.... As a Nisei girl said shortly after her arrival in Tule Lake: "Anything can happen in this dump. It's almost as bad as being in Germany. You wonder why you were born. No fooling, these guys have no respect for women, and boy, do they believe in Gestapo methods." (*Impounded People*, 1946, p. 136)

However, just after the Tule Lake camp became a segregation center for disloyals, there was still a feeling among the inmates that they should take action against the authorities. At this critical juncture in wartime America, a feeling of camaraderie and spirit of social cohesion brought together people from different backgrounds, people who had either chosen to be "disloyal" for various reasons or had been unfairly labeled so. In this situation, Japan, as represented by their use of the Japanese language, together with their respect for the idea of the "Emperor," became a symbol for "disloyals" who tried to defend their identity as a protest group. For someone taking on the label of "Japanese" under such circumstances, "the suffering and the shame became a badge of honor and self-esteem" (Takei, 2005, p. 92).

The authorities did not take kindly to inmates' attempts to unify and take action. For example, a simple request for improvements in living conditions in November 1943, which had been triggered by a fatal traffic accident in October, is described as a "riot" in the history books. On November 2, when WRA Director Dillon Myer visited Tule Lake, four to five thousand people gathered for negotiations with the authorities. The sight of them must have been terrifying for the outnumbered whites, almost as if they had fallen captive to Japanese soldiers in an enemy zone.

This so-called "riot," however, was an important occasion for the inmates to show the authorities the power that they possessed as a united group. In his speech, a minister who was a member of the negotiating committee called on people to behave honorably as Japanese. Propelled by the mass psychology of nearly ten thousand people mobilized under the banner of "Japan" to act with one mind, events culminated in a ceremony marking *Meiji Setsu*, Emperor Meiji's birthday, which was held at ten in the morning on November 3 in the central plaza amphitheater. The Rising Sun flag was hoisted front and center in the hall, and yellow and white chrysanthemums were arranged on both sides of the flag. The ceremony began with the crowd singing *Kimigayo* (the Japanese national anthem) and proceeded with a reading of the "Rescript on Education" (a document setting forth Imperial doctrine on education), followed by palace worship facing east, a silent prayer for the Imperial troops, and three *banzai* cheers for the Empire of Japan at the end.

The more momentum the crowd gained from revering these symbols of the Emperor and the "Japanese polity," the more the authorities tried to evade the people's demands for negotiation, as if to dampen their spirit and moderate their sentiments. The authorities suddenly assumed a position of strong opposition, rejecting the negotiators as true representatives of the people just before the talks were to take place, with the result that no progress at all was made.

On the evening of November 4, the day after the *Meiji Setsu*, Army troops were sent in to put down the "riot." Martial law was proclaimed, and Japanese Americans were sent to the stockade for punishment one after another. Under these circumstances, the Japanese language rapidly lost its collective power to unite, and people rapidly decided to keep a safe distance from politics inside the camp. Ultimately, both sides discovered that when the Japanese language was used as a means of communication, the images of Japan embodied in that language brought people into unconscious conflict with each other, inciting struggle and unrest within the camp.

Suspicion, Betrayal, and Slander

As the negotiations with the authorities came to a deadlock and control over the protest activities was tightened, the inmates, bored with monotonous camp life and the lack of any productive activity, turned their dissatisfaction, irritation, and anger toward their fellow Japanese. Factional conflicts took place among the inmates over their approval or disapproval of taking a strong stand toward the authorities and leadership. Eventually, the relationships among the inmates themselves began to affect their daily lives more than their relationship with the unreliable authorities.

Many people suffered from the double fear that the *inu* supplying information to the authorities might pass on unfavorable rumors about them, or that they themselves might be subject to hostility or violence if they were suspected of being an *inu*. One inmate put it this way: "If you are good to people, you'll get put in the stockade. If you cooperate with the authorities, you'll be called *inu*. So I'm going to play baseball" (Thomas & Nishimoto, 1946, p. 246). Many people thus decided not to take sides, just "sitting on the fence" to pass the time and to help ensure their eventual freedom. Their slogan (and excuse) was, "Let's wait until the war ends, and we will find a way." At various times, people grew suspicious of, fought with, and even expressed hate for each other. As splinter groups surfaced among inmates, violence erupted among the Japanese Americans. The segregation center was a world where "you don't need a knife to hurt people when a word will suffice" (Saki, 1999, p. 73).

Sanae Akashi thought that "it was embarrassing and dishonorable for the Japanese to fight other Japanese, especially in front of white administrators, and said it was inexcusable for Japanese to inform on Japanese, especially to the WRA authorities or to the Army" (Akashi, 2005, p. 111), but he himself seemed to have taken part in various betrayals and reports, as the following story illustrates.

On March 3, 1944, a Japanese letter was delivered to Tule Lake Project Director Raymond Best. The letter had been translated from Japanese into English by an *issei* or *kibei nisei* who was obviously not a native speaker of English. It reads as follows:

When person go to work for agricultural job this man to tell person not go to work however he do not like your policy. We want job but we can he gived tell black mail for person family. He is always to instigate people. The man work in kitchen then he tell many person for (present or actual keep) then he rebel you. Please take him way far other camp or to arrest if you do not we can go work really trouble start in block that we ask for your please. (WRA Internal Security Case Report, March 10, 1944)

As we learn from a more accurate translation, a fellow Japanese had made the following accusation against Akashi: "When people are about to go to work in the fields, Sanae Akashi tells them not to go. He always watches and threatens them. Unless they take him to some other camp far away or arrest him, there will be problems."

But on the same day, another anonymous letter was sent by mail to Project Director Best. This one was written in the perfect English of a native speaker:

We investigated and found out that Sanae Akashi had contended that each family should have only one of the family members work in order to share work with other families who do not have work and to give other families a chance to earn income. He is just trying to help people in the block as much as possible.

In fact, the WRA had hired "30 spies, or confidential informers, who infiltrated meetings, recorded incriminating opinions in boiler rooms, latrines, laundries, mess halls and other places to eavesdrop on dissenters," to help with employment issues and to "perform intelligence work which is to be used only for the advantage and benefit of the colony" (Takei, 2005, p. 83). The second letter must have come from one of these informants. In response to the complaints and reports, in late March, the WRA embarked on a policy of limiting employment to two persons per family (Thomas & Nishimoto, 1946, p. 238).

When I interviewed him, Motomu Akashi spoke proudly of his father, showing me copies of the English-language letters containing widely contradictory remarks and insisting:

> I don't know the identity of the *inu* who was working as an informant. My father did the right thing. People did not have much work in the camp, so Father made an effort to get everybody a job. He was as kind as ever, helping others. To be sure, Father was stubborn, short-tempered, and argumentative, but he was a man of principle. Once he made up his mind, he lived up to it. He thought Japanese should be Japanese forever and that Americans should be Americans. He did not like things halfway at all ...; in that sense, he was really a very rigid person.

However, generally speaking, a "man of principle" is easily misunderstood and invites antipathy. A U.S. Department of Interior report entitled, "Community Analysis," dated April 17, 1944, claims that Akashi "shouted his sentiments for an hour, and the author who checked later found that the residents regarded him as an immoderate and bumptious middle-aged man whose reputation for lack of restraint on all issues was well-known long before evacuation" (pp. 24-25).

The Repatriation Movement

It was in early February 1944 that Sanae Akashi, a man who had previously kept a low profile, appeared on the stage of internal camp politics as the lead petitioner of a letter demanding permission to conduct a signature campaign for those wishing to repatriate to Japan as soon as possible. It was addressed to the U.S. Attorney General and the Spanish Embassy in Washington, D.C.

The application procedure for repatriation via the State Department began on June 1, 1942, immediately after incarceration started. However, wartime exchange ships actually traveled between the U.S. and Japan only twice, in the summers of 1942 and 1943. As the tide of war was turning against it in 1943, Japan had no opportunity to send out a third ship.

As a prisoner, Akashi probably had no knowledge at all about the difficult war situation in Japan. He blamed the cancellation of the third exchange ship on the WRA's miscounting of those wishing to repatriate, which he thought must have confused the Japanese government. He believed that Japan would dispatch a ship if they knew that a sufficient number of Japanese desired repatriation, and to prove this, he would make a list of people prepared to repatriate. Later, during the hearing, John Burling, of the Department of Justice, taunted Akashi, saying, "The reason there is no boat is that the Japanese government does not want you.... They wanted only the people they asked for and they didn't ask for you or you wouldn't be here" (Hearing Report for Sanae Akashi, Calendar D-13, December 12, 1944).

For Motomu, this other face of his tall and robust father, who was always willing to help people, remains a mystery forever.

> He had made such an effort to be an American. Why did he want repatriation? It was probably because, as a Japanese, he could not honestly say he had no desire to repatriate.... I believe that he also had found out that he had a house and land in Japan when he went back in 1927 on his honeymoon.
>
> I had no idea what Father was doing in camp when we were living there. He worked in the mess hall doing dishes and rarely stayed at home. He didn't have any secret meetings at home, and there was no trouble in our block. Only in the past decade have I come to realize he was involved in politics inside the camp. I think that when he first began to call for re-segregation of "disloyals"... it was because he hated the trouble inside the camp.... He wanted peace.

"Genuine disloyals," who thought that the disturbance at Tule Lake was due to the authorities' failure to clearly separate the loyalists from "disloyals," demanded a peace under which they could live separately from the others. To accomplish this, Akashi made requests, first on March 10, 1944, together with thirty-nine other re-segregationists, to Secretary of State Cordell Hull and subsequently on May 30, 1944, to the Honorable

Francisco De Amat, Vice Consul of Spain in San Francisco, urging the Japanese government to consider resumption of the exchange ships. His letter read:

> It is intolerable for us to remain entirely indifferent while our mother country is at war.... Because our every act shall really affect the greatest influences to our mother country, our actions must always be so that the honor of Japanese subjects shall not be disgraced. Accordingly, we must keep away from such shameful behaviors [as] that of fighting among brothers, and to bring about mutual understanding.... The resegregees, if granted to live in a separately established area, will guarantee full cooperation with center officials in keeping peace and harmony within that area. (Petition of the Re-Segregation Committee, May 30, 1944, signed by Akashi, Ono, Matsuda, Miyamoto, and Shishido)

Meanwhile various rumors were circulating around the camp, such as that the U.S. authorities supported re-segregation and that an exchange ship would be dispatched in the near future. Secretary of War Stimson declared a military draft for Japanese Americans on January 20, 1944. After his declaration, the campaign for repatriation gained momentum very quickly, and Akashi and his fellows proclaimed that persons signing the petition would have priority to board the exchange ship. Furthermore, "rumors were prevalent that the Japanese government was negotiating for an exchange ship" (Thomas & Nishimoto, 1946, p. 230).

Sanae Akashi's name will be remembered in history for the "Petition for Re-Segregation," which was signed on April 7-9, 1944, by sixty-five hundred camp inmates desiring re-segregation, then submitted to the Spanish Embassy in Washington, D.C., on April 24, 1944. A portion of the text reads as follows:

> We ... residents of Tule Lake Relocation Center, true to our Imperial Government, respectfully implore your Excellency to communicate to our government that we, the signees, wish immediate repatriation. When our wish comes true, we will rally around the flag of our country in its unprecedented dif-

ficulties, offer all our life and property to follow the national
policy of the war regime, and return the favors bestowed by
our Emperor and our country if such a thing could ever be
possible.

In the ensuing months, Akashi continued to petition several U.S. government agencies for both re-segregation of the Tule Lake camp and repatriation to Japan on an exchange ship. From April to July 1944, he petitioned the Secretary of State, the Secretary of the Interior, WRA Director
Dillon Myer, Tule Lake Project Director Raymond Best, and Assistant
Director Harry Black, but it was all in vain (Akashi, 2005, p. 115).

Meanwhile, it was impossible for demoralized camp inmates to make
plans for their futures while surrounded by barbed wire; the forced removal and incarceration had completely deprived these inmates of their livelihoods in the United States. The greater their previous expectations had
been for a successful life in the United States, the more these *issei* and *kibei
nisei* found the vectors of their dreams turning toward the negative and
the more their disappointment in a hypocritical America (which *claimed*
to be a democratic country) turned to anger and despair. Sanae Akashi was
perhaps one such person who began to lose all hope.

In this small, artificial Japanese community isolated from the outside
world, *issei* and *kibei nisei* whose feelings had been hurt by America's
betrayal sought ways of healing themselves. "Is there anything that could
save us from the uncertainty and emptiness of the incarceration camp and
the chaos of life with nowhere to go, cut off from both our past and future in
the United States?" they asked themselves. "If there is something, what is it?"

Could these *issei* and *kibei nisei* have had recollections of the distant past and homeland that they had forced beyond the reach of active
memory? Did they ever feel nostalgia for the land and time that connected
them with their ancestors, where they had been raised? Feeling betrayed
by America, many people might have seen nowhere else to turn but their
"home" in Japan, across the vast Pacific. In many cases, their sole reason
for desiring repatriation may have been that life in Japan did not seem
worse than the one they faced in the United States.

After having been shuttled from prison to prison, Harry Ueno, a *kibei
nisei*, wrote a series of letters from prison that formed a kind of diary, for

he could never send them. Ueno's letters reveal complicated and painful feelings toward his compatriots and family:

> Even if we fight against them [the U.S. government, all we will get] is hardships unknown to others. It will stymie our well-being as long as we live. Instead, even though it may be offensive to us, we should be patient and have the repatriation campaign carried out as soon as possible. That is the only way we can endure this. We should give careful thought to how meaningless it would be to suffer and kill ourselves in prison during a war, when we don't even know when that war will be over.

This sentiment wasn't limited only to *issei* and *kibei nisei*. At the end of a note written in English at Leupp prison camp, Arizona, on June 1, 1943, even *jun nisei* Joe Kurihara, who had served in World War I, remarked:

> In the face of what has been done to us must we continue to submit ourselves to further insults? No! Then let us proclaim ourselves Japs. Yes, Japs! I repeat, What is there for us to be ashamed of being Jap? To be born a Jap is the greatest blessing God has bestow[ed] on us. To live as Japs is the greatest pride we can enjoy in life. And to die as Jap under the protection of the Japanese Flag which has weathered through many national storms without a defeat for 2600 years is the greatest honor a man can ever hope to cherish. I in the name of the Niseis proclaim ourselves Japs, 100 percent Japs, now tomorrow and forever. Tenno Heika Banzai! Banzai! Banzai! Dainippon Teikoku Banzai! Banzai! Banzai! (Correspondence in private collection of Harry Ueno)

"An important foundation for creating one's human identity is a consciousness of one's mission, role, and responsibility in society" (Kajita, 1997, p. 148). For many who felt betrayed by American justice, losing their mission and role in the United States as well as their identity, Japan may have been just about the only thing left that they could rely on. This was a time when a country could provide its people with a sense of cultural belonging. In the heat of their anger at the U.S., some of them must have thought, "We are Japanese. Japan would never abandon us Japanese. We have to represent the values and generosity of the Japanese." When these Japanese and Japanese Americans, who had committed no hostile acts during their life in the U.S., declared their wish to repay the Emperor and the country for its support in statements such as the "Petition for Resegration," could it just have been to find a legitimate reason for returning to Japan, justifying their feelings of frustration and disappointment in the United States, rather than out of a political intention to be "anti-U.S.," "non-U.S.," or "pro-Japan"? Having nearly been disowned by the U.S., they sought identity and belonging from Japan.

"How to die with dignity" was the only discussion among *kibei* who were arrested and put in the "bullpen," the stockade (Takita-Ishii, 2005, p. 169). Compelled by the feeling that they would like to expunge the "shame" of having separated from their ancestral land (Tana, 1989, p. 190), where people were determined to protect their nation to the death, might these displaced people not have felt an irrepressible desire for self-preservation, to provide proof of their own existence by reconfirming the essence of Japanese culture concentrated within themselves? Did they really wish Japan would win? Did they really believe Japan would win? Even if they wished Japan would win the war, wasn't it because they regarded Japanese success as the best outcome for their future in the United States? According to *Impounded People* (1946):

> If Japan had emerged as a strong nation, either through victory or negotiated peace, then the Japanese minority in the United States would have a strong nation at its back. Japan could protect their interests here as she had never done before.... The whole accumulation of discriminations which has handicapped them might be eliminated.... A strong Japan would mean greater security for the Japanese in the United States. (p. 153)

Before the war, the *kibei* were expected to understand both Japan and the U.S., to be a bridge between the two countries, and to promote mutual understanding. In the Tule Lake Segregation Center, "they were searching for a way to become themselves in a culture that was neither Japan nor America. The only culture that was available for them was a culture of the camp, born out of boredom … that was, in fact, full of apathy, nothingness, and useless feelings; and they still felt the need for something worth living for" (Takita, 2007, p. 334).

In the past, members of the JACL had asserted that they were "genuine Americans" who had sworn an oath of loyalty to America, to the vast English-language world of America outside the camps, using the loyalty registration as a testiment of their principles. People driven into a corner by the loyalty registration began petitioning for re-segregation in the small Japanese-language community inside the camps, claiming that they were genuine Japanese inside and outside the camps. That was the ultimate expression of resistance to the U.S. government and nothing less than another kind of "loyalty registration." Just as the JACL had accepted only an unconditional "yes, yes" answer as indicating "loyalty to the United States," so the leaders of the re-segregation campaign would accept nothing other than agreement with re-segregation inside Tule Lake or segregation to another camp, eventually resulting in immediate repatriation, as proof of "loyalty to Japan." There was no room for those who had mixed feelings.

A re-segregation pamphlet asked people to sign for the following reasons:

> We cannot be loyal to two countries. As long as we are living here, why not make up our minds whether to be real Japanese or not? … Those who refuse to sign this will have people asking them, "Are you loyal to Japan or not? If you are not loyal to Japan, why don't you go out?" If they don't sign this, they will be known to be not loyal to Japan and will be so told in public. (Thomas & Nishimoto, 1946, p. 316)

Such threats, pressure, and violence prevailed at the center. People were at a loss. All they wanted was a secure, safe life until the war ended, but signing the petition might result in arrest and confinement by U.S. authorities. Failure to sign might mean that one would not be allowed to repatriate or expatriate. But many did not feel like returning to Japan immediately, either. Besides, re-segregation in the camp, which would require another move inside Tule Lake, was the last thing they wanted, yet there was no way of knowing what kind of harassment they might experience if they did not comply (Thomas & Nishimoto, 1946, p. 232). However, on the other hand, the parading and flag waving of the re-segregationists looked like cheap exhibitionism to them and a disgrace to the Japanese. They thought that they could "work things out in a gentlemanly fashion 'as proud people of a first-class nation'" (*Impounded People*, 1946, p. 186).

However, to those who promoted the cause of repatriation to the extent that they would "sincerely sacrifice themselves for a state under the reign of the Emperor, as its citizens," the "fence-sitters," who were unwilling to commit themselves wholly to being either American or Japanese, must have seemed like loathsome creatures.

"I don't know whether my father participated in coercing people to sign. He was already fifty years old then, so he might have been in the position of advisor or something like that," guessed Motomu Akashi.

Those who had unexpectedly been labeled "disloyal" in the past loyalty registration by their fellow Japanese and by the U.S. government were beginning to defend themselves by saying, "I guess I need to be a Jap if they treat me like a Jap." If someone takes on the label assigned to them by others or in fact acts as expected by those who assign the label, then they make a transformation from self-identification to self-fulfillment. The demand for repatriation must have been the ultimate form of such self-identification and simultaneously a process for self-protection and self-fulfillment.

Outsiders based their view of the "disloyals" on a fixed perception related to the war. Disloyalty to America could only mean that these "disloyals" were *evil*, that they were challenging the good nation of America, and that they were taking on the role of bitter enemies, on the side of fascist Japan. Needless to say, the authorities regarded the petition for re-segregation as nothing more than an underground activity on the part of those considered the most dangerous anti-American group. And this group was haplessly bound tighter and tighter together by the "disloyal" label, falling completely into the trap that was set for them.

Renunciation: A Trap?

On July 1, 1944, the Nationality Act of 1940 was revised and became the Denaturalization Act, which permitted *nisei* to renounce their citizenship during wartime. Some of the underpinnings of this change can be found in Bill Hosokawa's book, *JACL in Quest of Justice* (1982):

> Some of the [JACL] delegates charged that many of the renunciants were troublemakers who had disrupted the camps, condemned JACL stalwarts as WRA stooges, ridiculed volunteers for military service as "suckers" and opted to go to Tule Lake because they either hated America or wished to escape military service. These individuals, one delegate asserted, would be a constant reminder that there were Nisei who wavered in their loyalty to the United States and they would always be a disruptive element in Japanese American communities. JACL was urged to go on record as demanding the immediate deportation of those who failed to express loyalty.... Others expressed anger that if no distinction was made between those who stood on principle and those who wavered, the disloyal Tuleans would reap the benefits won through Nisei military sacrifice. (qtd. in Masaoka, 1987, p. 188)

The JACL's original suspicion of the *kibei* was based on their general acknowledgement that "among the more vocal and militant are Kibei who left Japan to avoid military service" and that the living expenses of *kibei* in Japan were supported by family remittances from the U.S. ("Factors Behind Citizenship Renunciation," Joe Masaoka, Colorado JACL, March 28, 1945).

Some see this revision of the Nationality Act as a kind of trap set by the U.S. government, who listened to the opinions of the JACL and then made decisions. This "trap" was designed to allow the government to expel subversive elements who might, in the future, put a blot on the Japanese American community. The renunciation program relied on the manipulation and intimidation of Japanese Americans by various U.S. government

agents (Takei, 2005, p. 95; Takita, 2007, p. 265). It was the expected consequence of the government's quest to identify "disloyals" and the many
different ways various government agencies had defined them:

> In truth, neither the WRA nor the PMGO [Provost Marshal
> General's Office] nor the WDC [Western Defense Command]
> ever managed to settle on a coherent definition of loyalty *even
> for itself.* Japanese American disloyalty became a chimera for
> each of these agencies, a wall on which each organization pro-
> jected a constantly shifting show of its own motivations, needs
> and experiences. (Muller, 2007, p. 3)

The renunciation program became good cover for all of these "embarrassing interagency conflicts."[27]

The application procedure for citizenship renunciation started on
October 6, 1944. The authorities were ready to "provide legal means to
denationalize between '300 to 1,000' persons…who had expressed a desire
to renounce their United States citizenship and have asked for expa-
triation" (Thomas & Nishimoto, 1946, p. 310), but the actual number of
applications the Department of Justice received was smaller — only one
hundred seventy valid applications during the whole of November — and
"by the middle of December, it was estimated that the total number of
applications received approximated 600" (p. 324).

---

27. Drinnon (1987) explains, "Charges that this was discriminatory class legislation
designed to secure renunciations of citizenship by native-born Americans of Japanese
ancestry, especially the Kibei, were corroborated by Tule officials. In his interviews
with men in the stockade, Besig discovered that Best and his staff 'had pressed such
renunciations upon them while they were imprisoned in the Stockade. Indeed, in
my conversations with … WRA officials, each of them stated quite frankly that they
had gotten rid of some alien Japanese by sending them to the Santa Fe, New Mexico,
internment camp, and that they expected to solve their Stockade problem by getting
the imprisoned men to renounce their citizenship and then send them on to Santa
Fe for internment' (Affidavit). In the overheard interviews Besig was thus warning
prisoners not to fall into the administration's trap by voluntarily becoming 'native-
American aliens,' a status that would subject them to the same arbitrary procedures
established by Edward J. Ennis's deal with the WRA for getting rid of troublesome
Issei" (p. 130).

However, on December 19, 1944, the government order to remove Japanese Americans from the West Coast was lifted. The news that most Japanese Americans would be released from the incarceration camps after January 20, 1945, whether they were "disloyals" held at Tule Lake or not, and that all camps would be closed as of January 2, 1946, threw people into a panic. They learned that the new policy was as follows: "Effective January 2, 1945, individual disloyalty, instead of race, would be used as the test for exclusion from the Pacific States" (Takei, 2005, p. 86). Paradoxically, the lack of evidence of disloyalty, such as neither having given negative answers to the loyalty question nor having requested repatriation, was also cause for detention.[28]

As such, people were again forced to face an uncertain future. They thought, "The war between Japan and the United States is not over yet. The mood outside the camps must be very hostile. We might be drafted. Is there any way we could stay inside? Will the camps really be closed? Isn't this a trick to kick us out? After all, nobody would believe in our loyalty to the U.S., so the best thing for us is to think about our future and family. Let our children and husbands renounce citizenship so we can keep the family together and protect our children and husbands from being drafted. By virtue of renouncing, we will be deemed hard-core disloyals, which should help us avoid release and relocation. Either way, we have nothing to lose, and it will be more advantageous to renounce now."

Renunciation of citizenship thus became a tool that a family could shrewdly employ in order to stay together and survive. Ironically, many *nisei* chose to renounce their citizenship on the basis of their "trust in the United States," bolstered by their faith in the absolute and unequivocal

---

28. According to Barbara Takei (2006), "By summer 1944 the Western Defense Command [had] a secret list of 3000 'disloyals' and 'troublemakers' at Tule Lake they wanted to keep in detention. Their worry was that if everyone was released, they would have trouble keeping track of the 'disloyal' because they 'all look alike.' ... They realized that if the 3000 on their secret list renounced their US citizenship, they would become 'alien enemies' not protected by the Constitution. The government could then detain these 'alien enemies' and not be concerned with their civil rights. ... [So] the Army put their denationalization plan in motion. Army personnel began interviewing male citizens, asking 'whether they wished to leave camp and resettle — or did they want to renounce their citizenship?'"

U.S. Constitution. Weglyn (1996) notes that "many Nisei naively acted on the assumption that renunciation was not a final act, that it could later be canceled" (p. 241). In fact, one of the re-segregationist leaders went so far as to say, "the Denationalization Bill is a wartime law, and I think it's unconstitutional.... After the war the entire picture will be changed. The United States will not deport those who renounced their citizenship" (Thomas & Nishimoto, 1946, p. 326).

As soon as people heard the news of the camps closing, renunciation applications suddenly increased. On December 26, the first day after the Christmas weekend, the Department of Justice in Washington D.C. handled a thousand requests for renunciation forms, and within a week received almost three thousand applications (WRA memorandum for the Attorney General, April 30, 1945).

Only those over seventeen years of age could renounce. According to Barbara Takei and Judy Tachibana (2001), "Military-age internees were incorrectly told by *Hokoku-Hoshi Dan* advisors that if they filled out the repatriation form they would not be drafted and could stay at Tule Lake until the war ended" (p. 18).

In the final accounting, about seventy percent of the U.S. citizens at Tule Lake were denationalized, with the greatest number among those twenty-five to twenty-nine years old, nearly fifty-six hundred citizens (Murakawa & Kumei, 1992, p. 30). Seventy-seven percent of all males renounced, compared to fifty-nine percent of all females. Over eighty percent of the *kibei*, thirty-seven hundred, renounced, compared with sixty percent, 1,870, of the *jun nisei* (Thomas & Nishimoto, 1946, pp. 357, 359, 360). There were some 4,390 families with at least one citizen member old enough to apply for renunciation. In seventy-three percent of these families, at least one member renounced (Thomas & Nishimoto, p. 358). It was reported that families having even one renunciant in the family became more solidly unified.

The Department of Justice was upset at the numbers, which greatly exceeded their original expectations. The DOJ believed that all renunciants would be expatriated to Japan, by force if necessary (Collins, 1985, p. 94). The DOJ had been against the incarceration from the beginning because of the possibility of its being declared unconstitutional, and they felt that they had to avoid the injustice of compelling people who were not really "militaristic disloyals," but had happened to be caught in the snare, to renounce their citizenship. They were aware that this would have seemed hypocritical for a nation that professed itself to be democratic and humanitarian.

Despite their earlier stance, they would accept only a strictly legal definition of coercion, i.e., a renunciation "would be coerced and hence void (only) if it were done under imminent or immediate threat of physical injury to one's self or to a member of one's family" (Collins, 1985, p. 95), and they disregarded the enormous social pressures that were gripping the camp. They needed a scapegoat that could cover up for the government's errors and the trap it had set in Tule Lake, where "confusions ... between cultural and political affiliation, between government and racism outside, between unity which spelled progress and unity which spelled defiance, were not clear" (*Impounded People*, 1946, pp. 216-217).

The *Hokoku Seinen-dan*

In August 1944, a month after it became possible to renounce citizenship, the *Sokoku Kenkyu Seinen-kai* [Youth Groups for Research on the Homeland], open to young *nisei* men between the ages of sixteen and thirty, was organized. The objective of the group was to study Japanese language, history, and culture in preparation for life back in Japan, to raise the members' ethnic consciousness as Japanese, to encourage a moral life and cultivate character, and to train the men physically to be able to serve their country immediately. In November 1944, when applications for renunciation were already being filed, the *Sokuji Kikoku Hoshi-dan* [Volunteers for the Immediate Return to the Homeland to Serve] was organized with the clear objective of a re-segregation campaign for repatriation. The *Sokoku Kenkyu Seinen-kai* changed its name to *Hokoku Seinen-dan* [Patriotic Young Men's Group to Serve the Homeland] "in order to reinforce their intentions in view of the situation and the establishment of a firmer foundation for the group over time, since the name initially chosen was relatively passive" (*Hokoku* [newsletter], December 6, 1944). About twelve hundred people attended the *Hokoku* inauguration ceremony, which was by invitation only: 650 members, 100 special guests, and 450 parents and guests (Akashi, 2005, p. 117).

In Motomu Akashi's chapter about his experience at Tule Lake (2005), there is a photograph of *Hoshi-dan* headquarters (p. 119). On the wall of the barrack, alongside a Japanese flag, a blueprint, and a slogan reading "Silence and Hats Off!," hangs a poster that reads: "Young people are the resources of a country, the source of its activities. They are creators of history and have an important mission. Therefore, each man should stay at his own post and break through this difficult time. A bright future will be born there."

In such statements were born a kind of cultural revivalism, a "retreat from defeat and frustration into the romantic world of the Issei … launched under the banner of unity, faced away from American soil for resettlement, and provided the solace of fighting against repression with the only weapons available, namely the world of custom" (*Impounded People*, 1946, pp. 209-210). The U.S. officials thought of it as something like a repeat of the Ghost Dance cult of cultural revivalism in the early stages of reservation life among Native Americans, an act "of defiance to 'white officialdom'" (*Impounded People*, 1946, pp. 212, 215).

On January 8, 1945, the *Hokoku Joshi Seinen-dan* [Patriotic Young Women's Group to Serve the Homeland] was organized. The *Hokoku Seinen-dan* boys were called the "Tule Lake GIs" and the young women in pigtails and middies the "Tule Lake WACS" ("A Lexicon of Center Terms," June 25, 1945, p. 7).

In those days, more than thirty percent of the inmates aged seventeen and a half or older were listed as members of the combined re-segregationist organizations (Thomas & Nishimoto, 1946, p. 328). At its height, the membership of *Hokoku Seinen-dan* reached fifteen hundred. All in all, ninety-one percent of the members of *Hokoku Seinen-dan* and *Joshi Seinen-dan* renounced their citizenship, compared with fifty-nine percent of non-members (p.360).

There are three major reasons that the *Sokuji Kikoku Hoshi-dan* and *Hokoku Seinen-dan* groups have been reviled in the Japanese American community (and to some degree still are even today). The first is, of course, the fact that they were vehemently "pro-Japan," and while their members may have disagreed about the use of violence, at least some of them did engage in it. But another reason, which I will discuss later, has to do with Japanese values, especially *bushido*, which the segregationists emphasized so much to prove that they were "real Japanese." And a third important reason is based on the American view of individualism.

From this standpoint, the way that the *Sokuji* and *Hokoku* groups pressured their fellow Japanese with the threat of physical violence to force them to renounce their citizenship was like bringing about the mass death of a group of American citizens. The use of violence by these groups to force individuals to follow a kind of group mentality magnified the fascist image of America's enemy, and the groups' members were viewed by the U.S. government and those who cooperated with it as "advance guards of the Emperor," in a word, evil.

Motomu Akashi remembered, "[I] frequently saw Kibei leaders intimidate young Nisei into joining and forcing them into renouncing their citizenships. Many young members, as well as elder adults, secretly complained about the Kibei leaders. Many, who I knew, became dissatisfied and disillusioned with the change and left the organization" (Akashi, 2005, p. 119).

However, Motomu stayed, as he didn't want to embarrass his father, since Sanae himself was distraught over the situation. According to Motomu, "Most people, including the administration, could not differentiate between the conservative members of the *Hoshi Dan* and the aggressive youths of the *Hokoku Dan*. They associated all militant activities with the hyphenated *Hokoku-Hoshi Dan*" (Akashi, 2005, p. 119). The *Hokoku Hoshi-dan* even complained to Director Best about "lawlessness in the Center, with attacks and violence by 'gangsters' carrying weapons. The letter requested that Internal Security investigate the illegal activities, and requested that the manufacture and sale of liquor be prohibited and that gambling and profiteering be prohibited. However, the WDC [Western Defense Command] chose to ignore the complaint, viewing it as a smokescreen by the devious Hoshi-dan seeking to blame others" (Takei, 2005, p. 81).

But even inside these "pro-Japan" groups, the members were split into two factions. One was composed of those who were "ardent supporters of the re-segregation movement, but vehemently opposed to the renunciation of US citizenship. This group felt that they were dissenters — anti-administration and pro-Japan and would work for betterment of the community — but they were not ready to give up their citizenship." The other "was strongly in favor of renunciation and pressured members toward that end" (Akashi, 2004, p. 174).

The "pro-Japan" groups asked the administration whether they could make group applications, which would help many *kibei* who could not read or write English, as well as family-unit applications that would keep families together:

> 4. Can we send in these applications as a group? If not, why is it not advisable to act as a group? There are many Kibei here who can't read or write English. We want to help them, and we want to act as a group to save money and to avoid red tape. We would like to send all of the applications in one envelope.
>
> 5. Is it all right to apply as a family group? May the father sign applications for his children? Should a child of 16 sign his own request or should his parent sign it? (Report of a call to the Project Attorney's office made by members of the *Sokoku Kenkyu Seinen-dan*, Barrack 5408-D, Newell, California.)

Regardless of the many times they asked the questions, they were never permitted to renounce as a group.

As time passed, various rumors began to circulate. Some leaders tried to force young people to enroll in the *Hokoku Seinen-dan* on the grounds that only members of this group could renounce citizenship. It was also rumored that children could repatriate with their parents only after renunciation. People spoke of the possibility of being drafted as well as the threat of being reported to the Japanese government, which could result in the Imperial government taking reprisal against sisters, brothers, and other close relatives in Japan (Weglyn, 1996, p. 236). The atmosphere was so stressful in the residential blocks that some of the inmates had to say they had renounced citizenship even though they hadn't or else they had to pretend that they had applied for renunciation and keep their heads shaved like *Hokoku Seinen-dan* group members. There were others within the camp "who kept curious watch to see who did or who did not receive letters from the Justice Department" (Thomas & Nishimoto, 1946, p. 355). Parents who felt pressured by the rumors had their children become members of the youth groups and made them renounce their citizenship.

At the same time, many people thought that they had to convince U.S. officials of their "loyalty to the Emperor." When answering the questions, they were asked to confirm their renunciations so that their applications would be acknowledged. The re-segregationist organizations opened what "Assistant Project Director Black referred to as a 'College of Renunciation Knowledge' and carefully coached those called for hearings on the questions that were to be asked and the answers that were to be given" (Collins, 1985, p. 101). The coaches taught prospective renunciants how to act when their turns came, and thus the answers became stereotyped. For example, "if a prospective renunciant was asked his opinion of the Japanese Emperor, he would almost always leap to his feet, stand at rigid attention, and assert that he regarded the Emperor as a Living God. Similarly, substantially every prospective renunciant who was asked if he believed Japan would win the war answered affirmatively and said that he hoped for that result" (p. 101). The young men gave exactly the same answers repeatedly, revealing the strong pressure exerted by parents, the group, and careful training.

Jun nisei are often seen as victims because they joined *Hokoku Seinen-dan* under pressure from parents and *Hokoku*, in line with their parents' wishes to return to Japan. They were forced to renounce their citizenship against their own will, without the right to really decide for themselves. But *kibei nisei* renunciants were often regarded with prejudice because it was thought that they were acting out of adherence to the militarism instilled in them during their education in Japan. They were thought to have renounced out of their own free will (Yamashiro, 1995, p. 47), not able to hide their inner preference for Japan.

Indeed, since most *kibei nisei* were older than *jun nisei*, there is no denying the fact that most chose renunciation of their own free will. However, the decision-making process of *kibei nisei* was actually fraught with complicated feelings of being torn between Japan and America. What should be remembered is that theirs was not a simple case of strict political loyalty to another country, as it has repeatedly been described in history textbooks to date. To get closer to the truth, the perspective of the *kibei* as ordinary citizens must also be considered.

Susumu Kako joined the *Hokoku Seinen-dan* with his younger brother and renounced his citizenship. He told me:

> My father answered "no, no" at Poston camp in Arizona because he wanted to go back to Japan. He had diabetes and was sixty-eight years old. I am the eldest son, so I thought by all means I had to take him back. My brother said he would go back, too, if I went back. Father joined *Sokuji Kikoku Hoshi-dan*, although he was not an active member. Under the umbrella of *Sokuji Kikoku Hoshi-dan* was the youth group *Hokoku Seinen-dan*, which we joined later. In the beginning, we didn't participate. My wife was also a member of *Seinen-dan*, but in name only. Once, when I went to the toilet, the *Hokoku Seinen-dan* members asked me, "Have you become a member?" "No," I answered. "Are you a Japanese? Really Japanese?" they said. They were trying to start a quarrel with me. "I am a Japanese but will not join *Hokoku Seinen-dan*," I replied. In the end, they threw the first punch at me. It was so irritating, so I joined.... I felt I had no alternative. And then I got dragged off to Bismarck.

The *Hokoku Seinen-dan* was organized into a central committee and three subcommittees: *shuyo* (Japanese cultural studies), *shako* (social relations), and *taiiku* (physical training). The group had seven ward branches (later eight), which were also organized into sub-branches (Kumei, 1996, p. 77).

Yoshio Nishikawa, who lived in the same residential area (Block 74) as Sanae Akashi, served as *shuyo* director. He told me:

> I did not have any intention of joining the group [*Hokoku Seinen-dan*] voluntarily. Working in the mess hall as a cook, I

heard a lot of talk. In particular, one of the top leaders of the group, Mr. Akashi, lived on my block and also worked in the mess hall. He was a fine man, vigorous and strongly built. He nagged us.... "Something must be wrong with us if we, who came from Japan, did not join *Hokoku-dan*," he said. My best friend Nakamura in the next room, who came from Hiroshima and was also working in the mess hall, said we should join the group; otherwise, Mr. Akashi would nag us even more. So, that's how we joined. In those days, I thought they might beat me up if I did not join. I had heard that a man living in one of the corners of the second barrack from mine did not join. He went to the laundry room in the middle of the night to do dishes after having a snack. It was said that someone in the group took a two by four and hit him in the back of the head and he died. That kind of thing happened all too often, and it seemed that whenever Mr. Akashi visited a barrack, the young men there all joined *Hokoku-dan*. We were at that rough young age in which we wanted to challenge everyone and everything. We had nothing else to do in the internment camp, and not everyone played baseball. Not having a lot of choice, the most we could do was work in the kitchen. If someone our age organized a group, we felt like joining. We didn't really think in terms of having any impact upon America. The group's name, *Hokoku Seinen-dan*, surely implies making an oath to Japan, but we never thought about it that seriously.

The *Hokoku Seinen-dan* was well known for its morning exercises. The members did their exercises, keeping forefront in their minds such ideals as, "Proper channels are no longer sufficient to achieve our objective of repatriation" (Murakawa & Kumei, 1992, p. 175); "We cannot be satisfied with merely expressing our feelings in words"; and "It is our explicit desire to make the authorities understand these facts through our conduct" (a letter to the WRA, October 23, 1945). But the authorities regarded these exercises as a demonstration of loyalty to Japan and as a form of dangerous "military training" on the part of the enemy, Japan.

Young men were awakened at five or six by the call of the bugle. In grey sweatshirts with the letters *Hokoku* ("serve our country") on them, wearing Rising-Sun headbands around their shaved heads, they bowed toward the Imperial Palace and did calisthenics. Tokio Yamane, one of the leaders, explained that the purpose of the shaved head was to "show others we were truly united in spirit," and added, "It was a self-imposed symbol of 'pro-Japan/disloyal' resegregation" (Takita-Ishii, 2005, p. 171). After exercising, they ran in columns of four to the sound of bugles, repeating the familiar Japanese "*wasshoi wasshoi*" running cadence. They even ran on icy roads during winter.

On the 8th of every month (Japan time, since December 7 in the U.S. is December 8 in Japan), they commemorated the Pearl Harbor attack and held a ceremony praying for the victory of Japan. It was said that to purify the mind and body before attending the ceremony, the leaders and block representatives took cold showers at 5:00 a.m. (Thomas & Nishimoto, 1946, p. 320). As the membership grew larger, the bugle unit grew from only a few to well over fifty members (Kumei, 1996, p. 78). Buglers were expected to "handle bugles carefully, thinking of the bugles as their souls, and to train themselves based on the Emperor's principles, keeping self-sacrifice in mind" (*Hokoku* [newsletter], December 6, 1944).

As director of the Japanese cultural studies subcommittee, Nishikawa also ran every morning. "People in my block ran in a group. Following the leader, who was the director of physical fitness, we ran all around the camp. My group had about thirty people. We ran even in the snow … for about an hour. And then we gathered at the starting place and did push-ups. After running, we went for breakfast."

For the record, it should be stated that members of *Hokoku Seinen-dan* were those who had a clear loyalty to Japan, agreed with re-segregation, possessed patience and strong minds, and were capable of bearing punishment with stoic indifference while meeting strict physical criteria. Most of the members were *kibei nisei*, but some were *jun nisei*. Motomu Akashi was a *jun nisei*, and he became a bugler at the age of fifteen, but he doesn't think that he was ever actually enrolled in *Hokoku Seinen-dan*:

My father might have submitted an application for me. I didn't think I was a member, though. But I did get up early; I did exercises, ran to the rallying call of *wasshoi wasshoi*, and bugled. We all marched to the Japanese military march or "*papparapa*" sound of the bugle. I just participated because my father said, "Hey, you should go out and get some exercise." It was cold in the morning, but I didn't feel it much, as I was young. I had no relationship with the *kibei*. I neither liked nor disliked them.

Japanese martial arts phrases that drifted back from the fragments of memory in Akashi's mind conveyed the abnormal atmosphere of the segregation camp:

> *Migini* [turn right], *hocho tore* [parade march], *kiotsuke* [attention], *mae muke mae* [face forward] … I had no idea who was saying what but just silently did whatever I was told to do. It was like being a Boy Scout.… I had fun. Within the group as a whole, there might have been some who were pro-Japan, but young participants probably just wanted to do something that was fun. We did not have any political motivation. "*Banzai* to Emperor"? Most of the *nisei* didn't even know what it meant. You know, "What on earth does that mean?" we wondered. We were just killing time. The *wasshoi wasshoi* run was really good exercise. I didn't know the meaning of what we were doing nor the meaning of *Hokoku*. I don't really even know it now, either.

Despite what he said to me, in his book Motomu Akashi expressed the joy of belonging:

> For the first time, I felt good about being Japanese, not in a political or loyalty sense but being part of the Japanese race. I was not taunted, harassed or treated as a second-class citizen. I could hold my head up high and be treated as an equal. I did not feel that I had to subordinate myself, feel inferior or show defer-ence to the whites as I often and subconsciously did when I was in Mt. Eden. I felt proud to be Japanese. (2004, p. 199)

Motomu could even remember observing camp administrators during the exercises, recalling "officials in their cars watching and doing nothing to stop us. In fact, they seemed to enjoy it. Our show of nationalism appeared to have their approval" (2005, p. 118).

One *jun nisei* said that he joined *Seinen-dan* to get away from his parents' control; another confessed in tears that he joined thinking it was a gymnastics club and that he accidentally hit an *inu*. Some parents were very pleased that their children had finally "become Japanese" by joining the group.

Tadahiko Okamoto, a *kibei nisei*, said laughingly that he joined the group upon invitation by his gang of friends and did some quite bad things. "I didn't hit anybody, but I threatened people that I would not collect their garbage unless they gave me something good, as I was in charge of garbage collection. We did some things that we cannot talk about with pride."

But Nishikawa did not concur with the violent image of the group. "Not all members of *Seinen-dan* did bad things; there were many good men. But with around twenty thousand people in the camp, there were bound to be interpersonal problems. Only a few people were not good."

In fact, as we learn from Barbara Takei (2005), several leaders of *Hokoku Seinen-dan* were actually against forced membership; they even closed off membership because some "individuals were insincere about their devotion to Japan" (p. 91).

Arrest as Equal to Re-Segregation

On December 27, 1944, just before a sudden increase in citizenship renunciation, the officials began to crack down on "right-wing radicals", with arrests, detainments, and transfers. Fearing for his safety, Tadahiko Okamoto left the *Hokoku Seinen-dan*, along with fifteen others, in January 1945, after only six months.

At 3:30 a.m. on December 27, in the pre-dawn darkness, seventy leaders of *Sokuji Kikoku Hoshi-dan*, including Sanae Akashi, were suddenly arrested by soldiers and taken to the Santa Fe Internment Camp for Enemy Aliens in New Mexico, which was under the control of the Justice Department.

On January 25, 1945, the activity of the *Hoshi-dan* was deemed illegal; on the next day, 171 more *Hoshi-dan* members, including Tsutomu Higashi, were transferred to Santa Fe. At this point, among the inmates "arrest" came to be regarded as a synonym for "re-segregation" and "the first step toward becoming a pure Japanese" (*Hoshi-dan Hokoku* [newsletter], No. 2, December 30, 1944), so it became a kind of honor or decoration for a Japanese American renunciant. "It also meant no relocation and no draft" (*Impounded People*, 1946, p. 214). As a result, in order to get themselves arrested, many young men behaved more extremely during the morning demonstrations. And in addition to those bearing the Japanese characters "*Hokoku*," T-shirts with the slogans "*mugen jikkou*" [silent action], "*sokoku nihon o shinnrai-seyo*" [believe in your country, Japan], and "*amerika o kui-tsubuse*" [eat up America] began to appear (Otani, 1983, p. 302). The newsletter also appealed to the members with "go for broke," the same spirit demonstrated in the brilliant military records of the Japanese American 100th Infantry Battalion, 442nd Regiment Combat Team (*Hoshi-dan Hokoku* [newsletter], No. 2, December 30, 1944).

However, the *Hoshi-dan*, expecting government action and afraid of losing influence and power in the center by having its leaders taken away, "had packed the records with wrong names" (Nakagawa, 2005b, p. 152).

On February 11, 650 prisoners, including Kako and Nishikawa, were sent to Bismarck, North Dakota, and on the night of the 12th, the authorities closed the *Sokuji Kikoku Hoshi-dan* and *Hokoku Seinen-dan* headquarters located in Barrack 8A of Block 54 in the 6th Ward. On February 15, a warning was released: "It is illegal to be a member of such groups" (*Tule Lake News*, February 15, 1945), and 125 more people were sent to Santa Fe on March 4. Citizenship renunciation kept increasing until mid-March, when all the major *Hoshi-dan* members were transferred to the internment camps under the control of the Justice Department. On March 16, bugles and Rising Sun flags were prohibited, but some of the young people continued bugling and were sent to the stockade.

However, the situation gradually changed. On April 7, representatives of *Hoshi-dan*, *Seinen-dan*, and *Joshi Seinen-dan* held a meeting with the authorities and demanded that all the remaining male members over eighteen years of age be sent to the Justice Department internment camps in exchange for an immediate discontinuation of their activities. The campaign for repatriation had been imperceptibly replaced by the wish to keep families together. Thus, while the four transfers carried out up until then were under the control of the Justice Department, on June 24 and July 3, an additional 424 young men were moved from Tule Lake to other DOJ internment camps by the War Relocation Authority. Legally, they were entitled to protection under the Geneva Convention as enemy aliens.

The mood had indeed changed from one of defiance to one of concern for the welfare of families. According to "The 5th and 6th Transfers of Tuleans to Justice Department Centers," a confidential report of the Department of the Interior dated June 30, 1945 (WRA Tule Lake Segregation Center, Community Analysis Section):

> The last two trips, by contrast, have had no relation to the renunciation program. There have been few rumors of draft, of forced relocation, or of forced labor for those who do not go to internment. There is no *taiso* out in front and no bugling. No sign-ups to replete the ranks.... "our trips" have been characterized by a final dwindling of Hoshidan ranks in which even a formal send-off ceremony has been dropped in favor of tearful farewells. Our trips, unlike those of the Department of Justice, bring the end of the Hoshidan in sight. They are characterized all around the circle by "reluctance to go."

These new prisoners at Santa Fe got up as early as six o'clock to exercise and took the initiative to carry out some of the more troublesome work at the barracks, so some of the internees started looking forward to the arrival of more members (Tana, 1989, p. 21). By contrast, there were others in the camp who felt antipathy towards those sent from Tule Lake because they were seen as arrogant, inflexible, and uncooperative. "An anonymous group called the 'Suicide Squad' threatened the camp censors with death," and those who could not stand such rioters "sent anonymous letters to the administration, naming the troublemakers and pointing out situations that needed attention" (Culley, 1991, p. 64).

The Department of Justice probably thought that Sanae Akashi was dangerous and "incorrigible" (Akashi, 2004, p. 159), as he was determined and manly, hating to leave things unfinished, and followed through with whatever he decided to do. Akashi was sent with fifty-seven other Japanese from Santa Fe to Fort Stanton Internment Camp, New Mexico. This camp, located about two hundred miles south of Santa Fe and controlled by the Bureau of Immigration, was known as "Camp Ichiban" and was Penitentiary Segregation Camp #1 for Japanese. At Fort Stanton, Akashi was detained in "Victory Hut," a square building with almost no windows (p. 159). Then, six months later, in September, he was transferred to an internment camp in southern California and finally sent to Portland, Oregon, at the end of the year.

It was on board the *USS General Gordon*, the second transport ship to Japan, leaving Portland with forty-five hundred repatriates, that Motomu Akashi and his family met up with their father:

> Father was finally released on the ship. We had been on board looking for him. We did not know if he would come or not. What was in our minds was going to Japan. Then we saw him coming along the pier. He was so thin that we could not recognize him at first. I looked at each man carefully hoping that one of them might be my father. The third man in line looked up. It was my father. He looked thin and old and carried a cloth bag in each hand, which held his sole possessions. He was not the arrogant man he was a year ago. He had lost his swagger and looked subdued. It was heartbreaking to see him so humiliated but I was relieved to see him again. (Akashi, 2004, p. 3)

This meeting occurred on December 29, 1945, a year after Sanae Akashi was arrested in the barrack.

Families Hesitate to Repatriate

"I could not be one hundred percent loyal to the United States ... my conscience did not allow me to ... so I answered 'no, no.' Besides, I was a member of *Seinen-dan*, so I thought I *had* to renounce my citizenship."

At this point in his life, Yoshio Nishikawa became stateless, for he had renounced his Japanese nationality before the war.

> If they had found out that I still had citizenship, my life would be in danger. I think most of the *Seinen-dan* members had renounced it, and even among non-members, many had renounced citizenship. Quite a few people were unable to make a decision. Rather than sticking to their own beliefs, they often hesitated when others said they should do such and such.... After all, all the conversations in the kitchen revolved around the same issue, something like, "You guys studied in Japan, so why are you holding on to your U.S. citizenship?" All the leaders of *Hoshi-dan* were *issei*. They didn't care about citizenship. They could come down hard on that issue because they were *real* Japanese.
>
> They might have felt that renunciation of citizenship was the final form of resistance they could take against the government ..., but in my opinion, not all of the people shared that feeling. I don't think people really thought seriously about the future before they renounced. They just instantaneously made up their minds ... like, "I have to do it," ... particularly the *kibei*. Those who did were probably resigned to repatriation, with a feeling of *shikataganai* [it can't be helped] rather than that they were all for it. I myself was resigned to it.

But Nishikawa, who had been educated in a U.S. high school before the war, never faltered in his faith in the United States as one of its citizens: "In my mind, I always thought America would not force me to go back to Japan even if I answered 'no, no,' because I was born here."

In Bismarck, Nishikawa decided not to return to Japan. After all, he had gotten married just before the war broke out, hoping to avoid the draft. So he had a family in the United States.

Some of the younger, unmarried *Seinen-dan* members often criticized the married members as being half-hearted because many of the married people "dropped out, one by one," and changed their minds, deciding not to repatriate for the sake of their wives and children (Kumei, 1996, p. 90).

As stated earlier, there was a second important reason that fellow speakers of Japanese detested the *Sokuji Kikoku Hoshi-dan* and *Hokoku-dan* — their hypocritical attitude, speaking with a "double-tongue," begged the question of whether the group members who claimed to be "genuine Japanese" really had "faith" that *bushido* would be rewarded in death (Nitobe, 1995, p. 65).

In deciding whether they should return to Japan after renouncing U.S. citizenship, the renunciants had to consider their parents' feelings and their own life plans. In particular, their planning for the future would be indescribably difficult if Japan were defeated, as each family's situation was different. They knew what life was like in Japan, so they wondered whether they should choose Japan for themselves and their families' future — or not. Could they get by if they remained in America? Could they support their families in a defeated country? The young men hesitated. The more aged *issei* had already passed on the decision-making authority in their families to their eldest sons. Consumed with almost animal-like instincts urging them to survive by any means, the *kibei nisei*, burdened with the responsibility of taking care of their families, had to decide on a place for themselves and their families, choosing between a defeated Japan and an abundant America. In most cases, political loyalty did not outweigh the economic incentives. Unlike the *jun nisei*, to whom filial piety meant obedience to their parents, to *kibei nisei* filial piety meant caring for their aging parents and carving out a new life for themselves and their families, comparing the advantages of living in Japan to those in the United States.

One such *kibei*, Jiro T., who renounced his citizenship even though he was not a member of *Seinen-dan*, had faith in America, like Nishikawa. Jiro T. who started high school in the Topaz camp, graduated from high school with top honors at Tule Lake and was very successful as an academic after the war. He recounted:

> In high school, I had a wonderful teacher named Ms. Gunderson. She taught us about American democracy and said that America is continuously in process, incomplete. She

said that we can't rest and feel reassured just because we have a Constitution; every citizen of each generation is responsible for making an effort to attain our ideals so that our country will not go in the wrong direction. "Don't abandon the Constitution, even if you are sent to camp. It is your responsibility to see that such things never happen again," she said.[29]

I had confidence in the democracy our teacher taught us about. I thought that it was not only for the United States, but a common value to be shared by all mankind. But then, just as he had when we were faced with loyalty registration, my brother said to me, "You are *kibei*, aren't you?" and my Japanese education resurfaced. I felt the pressure exerted by my brother more than from other family members. That's why I renounced.

Nevertheless, just before they were to leave for Japan, Jiro's brother, Ichiro T., told Jiro, "This time, do whatever you want to do." Jiro decided to stay in the United States and later was called up and went into military service.

Tadahiko Okamoto says he never initiated the procedure for renunciation. "Since there is a government record that I was a member of *Seinen-dan*, I was summoned. The officer in charge said rather contemptuously, 'You are a member of *Seinen-dan*. Why don't you shave your head?' Since I was upset, I said to him, 'If you want me to renounce citizenship, I will do so. Just give me the form.' I signed it and that's all." The date was February 5, 1945.

However, Okamoto, who was unmarried, changed his mind when he heard the news that Japan had been defeated.

Japan had accepted unconditional surrender. The Emperor had lost his value. The sight of the Emperor shaking hands with MacArthur meant Japan had already been destroyed. At that

---

29. Margaret Gunderson taught English and American history classes. Gunderson and her husband Martin, the principal of Tri-State High School, gave up their teaching positions outside of camp "to protest the decision to relocate and intern" Japanese Americans. In doing so, they were ostracized by other Caucasians (*Nichibei Times*, March 26, 1998).

moment, I thought it would be better to be an American and to live in America. The Japanese were defeated. I was a Japanese but I was not the citizen of a defeated country. I had never before felt so miserably ashamed. If I had been in Japan, I might already have been dead by now.

Okamoto demanded cancellation of his renunciation on September 15, 1945.

The *Nisei* Who Went Back to a Defeated Japan

Not all *kibei nisei* felt as Okamoto did. Some chose life in Japan.

The first of those who returned to Japan, 426 single men over eighteen years of age, left Tule Lake in trucks at 7:00 a.m. on November 23, 1945, "turning their thoughts toward Mt. Fuji, with expectations of a new Japan emerging from the feudal system" (*Tule Lake News*, November 23, 1945). The following day, the first transport ship, the *USS General Randall*, left Seattle carrying seventeen hundred Japanese returnees, arriving in Uraga, Japan, at 11:00 a.m. on December 6.

Masashi Nagai was one of the renunciants who chose life in Japan, which is where I interviewed him. He had not been a *Hokoku* member but was one of the *kibei nisei* renunciants returning on the *Randall*, and he said he had gone back with the goal of contributing to the reconstruction of his country.

I renounced my citizenship for personal reasons. I didn't do it because somebody told me to do it. I heard that I could return on the first ship if I renounced. Only foolishly honest people like me actually came back to reconstruct Japan.

I remember the night I told Mom I had made the decision. She said I didn't have to explain it because she had never said no to me. She had just one condition: that I take my youngest brother with me and leave my sister in America. I knew from the beginning that I would leave my sister, even though she had renounced her citizenship.

However, my youngest brother said he would go to Chicago with his *jun nisei* group. The second oldest brother in our family, who had studied *judo* and *kendo*, said he would go back to Japan, by all means, and that I should do whatever I wanted to do. My sister, who was an assistant nurse, said that if I went back to Japan, she would come with me to take care of the large number of disabled soldiers.

Mom said she could not come with us at the outset. She said I should let her know after I got settled in Japan and then she would make her decision. Even if Mom had said she would come, I would not have taken her with me. I knew from the beginning that life was not easy there because of the food shortages. As it happened, only the three men among us returned. Looking back on my life, I think I have contributed to the reconstruction of my country in my own way.

Nagai, who was seventy-eight years of age when I interviewed him in 1998, showed pride and self-confidence in choosing the words as he told me his story.

Masao Kawate, who was also on board the *USS General Randall*, shared similar feelings. He had applied for repatriation to Japan on July 1, 1943, at Leupp, Arizona. In January 1944, he wrote to the Spanish Embassy to ask for their help in getting him back to Japan as soon as possible. Excited about going back to Japan, he wrote in his diary:

> As it became clearer and clearer that the war was ending, I began to realize more and more that my task and duty were lying before me.... For the reconstruction of a better Japan, I knew I would be called upon to contribute something. As the war came to an end, my conviction was greatly strengthened. It came to my mind that it is for the good of Japan for us to stay where we were. It is clear that Japan has no economic resources to support her present population. I advised many people about this, but I knew also that I would be able to contribute more to Japan by going to Japan. Whether this was a mistake or not, only

time would judge. At any rate I am very anxious to help Japan
to rise again.

Bringing the American ideals of freedom and democracy to a new Japan
became a good cause for Kawate, who had initially hesitated to return to
defeated Japan but eventually pushed himself to keep what he had gained
from the U.S. and to think of his aged mother in Japan. Renouncing his
U.S. citizenship was Kawate's way of ensuring his return to Japan. Later, he
worked for an American oil enterprise, but he never set foot on U.S. soil
again, despite having later restored his U.S. citizenship in Japan (*Nichibei
Times*, November 20-26, 2008).

Ichiro T., who was known as the "General of the No, No Group" at
Topaz camp, also returned on the same ship, the *Randall*. He landed in
Japan alone, unaccompanied by any other members of his family.

My father asked me if he and my mother could come to
Japan along with me. Deep down in their hearts, my parents
wanted to return. But I said, "Wait a minute, Dad." I knew that
our ancestral home was in a mountainous region and that the
entire T. family could not make a living there. I thought I could
handle whatever situation arose, as I was educated in Japan, and
I returned by myself. I was very realistic. I never asked my other
brothers how they felt about going back to Japan. But I respected
the wishes of my parents and asked them to hold off on deciding
until after I had gone back first. I knew we could not make a living in Japan and that my family should stay in California rather
than return to Japan.

On witnessing so much misery after landing in Japan, Ichiro T. wrote
to his family in Tule Lake: "Please don't come."

Susumu Kako returned to Japan on the *USS General Gordon*, the third
repatriation ship, from Portland, Oregon.

They said that I could not repatriate unless I renounced my
citizenship. My wife renounced hers, too. Not many internees

at Bismarck returned to Japan. There was a hearing about repatriation, and the government asked me why I wanted to return. I asked my parents and wife what they wanted to do, and they said that they would return, too. Father was ill, so I thought that I could not let him go by himself. If Father went, I could not stay, so I said to my wife, "If you stay in America, then I will stay as well." Then she said, "Papa is ill, so let all of us go back together." My wife's parents said we should leave at least one child in America, if possible, but we could not. I had been separated from my parents when I was a child, so I did not want my children to have the same experience. I said I would raise my children. I was aware of the food shortages, but I thought, that's okay, and went back with my three children.

In the middle of our interview, the tone of Kako's voice suddenly changed. He began to mutter, as if trying to shake something off. The true feelings that he could not conceal finally gushed out: "We would have stayed in America if my father had not become ill." He continued:

> Father died on April 8, 1946, in his hometown in Wakayama Prefecture. He was able to reunite with his mother, after having been separated from her at the age of sixteen, but we had a hard time without sufficient food. Father was hospitalized once, but there was neither medicine nor equipment. We took him back home a couple of days before he died. He died on *tatami* [Japanese straw flooring]. That was good. It was really good to take Father back home.

He spoke as if trying to convince and console himself with the sense of relief he had salvaged from having carried out his responsibility as a son.

Motomu Akashi, a *jun nisei* who returned to Japan with his family, said frankly, "I didn't want to go to Japan at all, but I couldn't help it because my family said they would." He continued:

> Mother, a *jun nisei*, renounced her citizenship because she

wanted to go with my father. I didn't because I was too young. What I remember was Mother calling all of her four sons together to talk to us, saying we had to make a decision. After that, our uncle came to see us from Granada camp, Colorado. Uncle tried to persuade Mother to cancel the repatriation, saying, "Let your husband go by himself. You do not have to go because you are an American citizen. All of you should come to Colorado." But Mother said, "No. I will go wherever my husband goes." I think Uncle gave Mother money to go to Colorado because, just before we left, Mother bought all the children new clothes, which we had to sell immediately after we arrived in Japan.

The *kibei* also asked themselves about their ability to make a living on their own in the United States. Masashi Nagai, age twenty-three when Japan was defeated, said honestly that he was not confident that he could compete with *jun nisei* — native speakers of English — in the United States. Ichiro T. was of the same mind:

> In America, I could only become a gardener, which I really hated. My dream was to become an engineer. I did not talk about it to my parents, or to anyone else. That was because I thought that I had been educated in Japan to become a Japanese adult. I received a Japanese education to live in Japanese society. So I thought I would fare better in the future if I started a life where I could make the most of my Japan experience, and it would be even better if I could use English. I had been educated to survive back in Japan. My Japanese was at the level where I could make a living there. Another reason was that I thought I might be able to play some role, using my bilingual language skills, in rebuilding a defeated Japan that would have no other choice but to rise from the ashes.

After doing all he could as the eldest son, Ichiro T. returned to Japan by himself. To some, it looked as if he was abandoning his family, but his brothers all praised him.

"He is great because he really did return after repeatedly saying he would go back," said one brother. "There were many people who didn't return after all, in spite of urging others to return. Compared to them, my brother is great because he acted according to his own principles."

Although the United States government considered membership in *Sokuji Kikoku Hoshi-dan* and *Hokoku Seinen-dan* to be illegal, they did not try to charge the many group members who failed to repatriate to Japan after the war because the very fact that people had remained in America despite falling into the trap and renouncing their citizenship was proof that America was a wonderful country. The U.S. government even tried to stop those members who decided to repatriate from doing so. Nishikawa recalls a meeting at Bismarck:

> They had some final words for us. They gathered all of us together, even those who were not going back to Japan, in a large hall. "It is not too late to change your mind," they said. "America is not forcing you to return. If you do not want to go, you can stay." The U.S. government did not want to put itself in the position of forcing us to leave. They were probably wondering if renunciation was constitutional.

Susumu Kako, who was sent from Bismarck to Portland, heard similar words from the government on the train.

> The officers said, "If you want to stay, you can stay." If I wanted to live in this country, I should do so. Our family had already made up their minds to return to Japan all together, so if I changed my mind, my family would be at a loss as to what to do ..., so I said we would go.

Even on the ship, just before reaching Japan, some *kibei* were offered the option of returning to the U.S. as ships' crew members because of the shortage of hands (Murakawa & Kumei, 1992, p. 42).

With the long war finally over, the U.S. government, confident in its position as victor and world conqueror, resumed a paternalistic attitude, showing mercy toward the miserable underdogs who had made "loyalty" oaths to the defeated former enemy. Or was the U.S. government actually trying to "silence the returning Japanese who could complain over incarceration as if respecting their decision as individuals because their complaints could be threatening to MacArthur's occupation?" (Tana, 1989, p. 643). The U.S. government had categorized the "disloyals" who had expressed their desire to repatriate or to expatriate to Japan into two groups: one was made up of radicals who showed "complete hate and distrust of the US government by drastic actions," and the other was made up of those who wanted to be able to "say when they do go to Japan that they left friends in the United States.... They do not turn away from this nation in hate and passion" (*Impounded People*, 1946, pp. 183-185).

Members of the *Sokuji Kikoku Hoshi-dan* and *Hokoku Seinen-dan* who did not return to Japan were looked down upon by their fellow Japanese as "having no guts and only doing things halfway" because they accepted the "mercy" of the U.S. government, which was such that they were "required to express gratitude even for having been fleeced" (Tana, 1989, p. 644).

Tsutomu Umezu was disgusted and said, "Look what they [members of *Sokuji Kikoku Hoshi-dan* and *Hokoku Seinen-dan*] did after agitating so much for us to return to Japan. They went back for a while themselves, saying they would contribute to Japan, but then they turned around and returned to America in no time. Contemptible people."

The *kibei nisei* who had decided to stay in America from the beginning were firmly against renunciation of citizenship. Umezu was in this group; he had objected to the loyalty registration at Tule Lake in February 1943 and was sent to Leupp prison camp in Arizona.

> Our group was very angry and opposed to renunciation of citizenship, even to the point of getting into fights over it. We sympathized with Japan, but that was a separate issue. As a *kibei*, I had more attachment to Japan than the others. But it was not so simple a matter as being in favor of Japan because my parents were there. People knew that I had not registered, so they said that I was in support of Japan, but I had never said this. People

misunderstood at times, but I stood squarely against the *wasshoi wasshoi* demonstrations. After all, the right that remained with us to the very end was U.S. citizenship. We had citizenship rights, so we were U.S. citizens. If we renounced our citizenship of our own volition, to return to Japan stateless, without Japanese citizenship, leaving behind this rich America for a Japan where people scarcely had enough to eat, well then, how could we complain if someone "punched us out" because we weren't Japanese citizens? The group leaders were responsible for driving us into such a dangerous position without anyone to turn to.

They said, "Come with me. Come with me, and I will see to it that you can make a living after the war. We can all enjoy a life of prosperity with huge war payments from the Japanese government. You can buy as much land as you want. We will be given all the islands in the Pacific, and there we shall want for nothing. You will have more than enough money to educate your children and be able to send them anywhere you want. I have contacts. Just follow me." They made impressive speeches of this kind in front of people. That's why I can't forgive them. People did not have the knowledge or capacity to make good judgments, and, being in a vulnerable position, they simply believed and followed the group leaders. That's tragic. On arriving in Japan, they found that the leaders had simply disappeared.

Once the war was over, being "loyal" or "disloyal" did not matter. Regardless of status, everyone was just released from the camps. They talked big. They had renounced their citizenship, so I thought they would return to Japan, but they went back to the West Coast as soon as the exclusion order was rescinded.

Even those who went back to Japan as proud as peacocks, saying that Japan had won, returned to America immediately because America is better after all. The group leaders did not have any real convictions. Those people are not Japanese. A Japanese would think it was human to have convictions and act on them even though they turned out to be wrong.

On this point, when I interviewed him in 1998, Motomu Akashi agreed with special emphasis:

> That's why I feel proud of my father. I don't think my father thought Japan had won. But he did not change his mind about going back to Japan. And I am very proud of him. He had his convictions and acted on them. He said he was a Japanese, would be treated as a Japanese, and would continue to be a Japanese. Many people said they would go to Japan but changed their minds as soon as the war was over. They made excuses for themselves, such as that they had been forced to renounce their citizenship.

In his 2005 book, he emphasized the same point again:

> I was proud of my father. He stuck it out to the very end, holding on to his principles and not wavering. He showed he was a "true Japanese" even in defeat. He was not like many of the *Hokoku-Hoshi Dan* members who literally denied their involvement in the pro-Japan organization and claimed they were coerced, intimidated or tricked into joining. They blamed others for their actions; they sought reprieves and wanted to remain in America. I felt the strength of my father's presence and knew that everything would be all right. (Akashi, p. 129)

Restoration of Citizenship to *Nisei* Who Remained in America

About one thousand renunciants who decided to stay in America submitted revocation of renunciation requests on November 13, 1945. The "final phrasing of the theme — 'We are Japanese together' — died out, as fear of deportation and continued confinement became the final fears of Tule Lake" (*Impounded People*, 1946, p. 216). However, the attitude of ingratiating themselves with the U.S. government and the JACL, regarding the *dan* groups as the enemy, and shifting all the blame to the *dan* so as to sweep their past under the rug has remained deeply engrained in Japanese American communities up until the present. Unless they defined *Hoshi-dan* and *Seinen-dan* as radical pressure groups of disloyals and the renunciants as victims, they would not be able to placate anti-"disloyal" public opinion, restore their citizenship after the war, and "Americans in general would not have allowed those 'disloyals' to stay in or return to America as citizens" (Kumei, 1996, p. 82).

"The Department of Justice began reviewing requests to restore citizenship, expediting applications of those who claimed the pro-Japan people forced them to renounce. People were astute in realizing there was a 'right' answer, the 'loyal' answer, that would speed up restoration of their citizenship. The 'right' answer scapegoated the pro-Japan groups, thus absolving the U.S. government of blame in the matter" (Takei, 2006).

> The Department of Justice persisted in laying blame for the renunciation on the pro-Japan group, and in 1956 they announced that citizenship would be restored to those who were willing to blame their renunciation on the coercive influence of fellow Japanese Americans at the Tule Lake segregation center. For example, a wife blamed her husband for coercion, and a son blamed his father and his friends for coercion. On May 20, 1959, the Department of Justice held ceremonies to end a governmental program for the restoration of citizenship. By that time, 4,987 out of 5,409 who applied for citizenship restoration had been successful in nullifying their acts of renunciation. Only about 50 renunciants did not apply for restoration at all. (Takita, 2007, p. 267)

One thing is perfectly clear: continued manipulation and pressure from both the U.S. government and the Japanese American community have probably done more to hinder than encourage a real understanding of the suffering of people caught between Japan and the United States, including those who changed their minds about repatriating to Japan.

One renunciant spoke of what a hard decision it was to change his mind about repatriation after traveling all the way from Tule Lake to Santa

Fe with a shaved head. He fully anticipated a cold reception as a "turncoat" (Tana, 1989, p. 656). Some thought that they could contribute to Japan by remaining in America and supporting Japanese development overseas once the war was over (p. 468). On the other hand, there were also some who bet their future on Japan, encouraged by news accounts of Japan's victory on the shortwave Radio Tokyo news that aired every afternoon. Some returned to Japan with a firm determination that they would never change, even if the Stars and Stripes fluttered over Boso Peninsula near Tokyo, because they had family in Japan (p. 442), and others stubbornly stuck to the idea of "Japan's victory," as if accepting the actuality of defeat as an opportunity to change their minds would reflect badly on their manhood (Murakawa & Kumei, 1992, p. 147).

There were just a few "pure-minded people who thought about the meaning of their life, dedicated themselves to justice, and chose a disadvantageous, steep path" (Murakawa & Kumei, 1992, p. 159). A good example is *kibei nisei* Kinzo Wakayama (1895-1999), who is unfortunately remembered in history mainly as a "pro-Japan radical."[30] Wakayama was known to have quoted a Japanese proverb, probably "*Taigi shin o messu*" [To further the great cause of our country, we will not hesitate to sacrifice the lives of parents and brothers]. A group of social scientists interpreted the proverb differently: "To help the great cause, we have to *kill those who stand in its way*" (Thomas & Nishimoto, 1946, pp. 319-320; italics mine).

The problem lies in the ambiguity of the proverb. By the "great cause," Wakayama probably meant the ideal of U.S. democracy, but authorities most likely thought that he meant the "great cause" was the Emperor of Japan. And because he incited others to violence, the word "sacrifice" was interpreted as "kill," so many people must have assumed that Wakayama was justifying "killing" those who stood in the way of his "great cause,"

---

30. Born in Hawaii and a veteran of World War I, Wakayama was secretary-treasurer of the Western Fishermen Union in Terminal Island, California, and, with his wife June, the first to file a writ of *habeas corpus* at Santa Anita Assembly Center, challenging the unconstitutionality of confinement of citizens without due process of law for duration of the war. "Short and stout: effeminate appearance; small features; beard; soft spoken and courteous to Caucasians; boastful and egotistical with fellow evacuees. Good command of both English and Japanese" (Thomas & Nishimoto, 1946, pp. 375-376).

which they assumed was the Japanese Emperor. But he was actually choosing a more difficult path, suggesting that one should give up his own parents and brothers for "the great cause." The more we understand the contradictory views recorded in the history of a people divided by language, the less we can blame a person for the choices he or she makes in order to survive.

As I dug even more deeply into the Bancroft Library archives, I found a poem entitled "Kibei Blues," written in a kind of pidgin English, the words of a conflicted soul:

I'M A SHORT HAIRED LITTLE KIBEI
AND I'M LONGING FOR JAPAN
MAYBE THIS WILL BE MY D-DAY
PRAYERS SENT TO BUDDHA SAN
ALL MY BROTHERS, UNCLES, COUSINS
HAVE DEPARTED — ALL BUT ME
THEY LEAVE TULE BY THE DOZENS
BOUND FOR SUNNY SANTA FE
I DO GOOSE STEP; I SHOUT BANZAI
I BLOW BUGLE VERY WELL
EVERYBODY GO AND LEAVE ME
HERE I STAYING — WHAT THE HELL?
MR. BEST, HE BLANKY-BLANKY
MR. BURLING, BLANKY TOO
NO LIKE TULE; LIKE GO NIPPON
ALL BY LONESOME — WHAT TO DO?
ALL ALONE I BLOW THE BUGLE
TOOT LIKE HELL, BUT NO ONE COME
BY MYSELF THE ONE-MAN GOOSE STEP
NO ONE HERE TO HELP ME SOME
NOW I'M ADMIRAL, GENERAL, PRIVATE,
BOTTLE-WASHER — EVERYTHING
ONE SMALL KIBEI, WEARY, DREARY
ALL IS GLOOM — I NO CAN SING

Who could ridicule the sorrow of these *kibei* whose nerves were frayed by the tension between their expectations for and resistance to America and who, at the end, were driven to renounce their citizenship? Ultimately, if they had remained in the United States, they would have had to live with the stigma of having been identified as "disloyals" (Kumei, 1996, p. 96).

As a matter of fact, even after returning to Japan, renunciants came under scrutiny. U.S. General Headquarters (GHQ) issued a directive to dismiss, repatriate, and expatriate *nisei* who were working as interpreters and translators there (*Pacific Citizen*, July 26, 1947). Was it true that the JACL and the *nisei* veterans "wrote a letter to the Secretary of War and asked that the 'Disloyal and Citizenless Nisei' be fired from their employment with the US government" when they heard the news of employment of *kibei* and *nisei* in Japan and that "on September 30, 1947, all Nisei and Kibei were fired from their employment"? (Kojima, 1996).

Mitsuo and Masatoshi Aoyama, both *jun nisei*, returned to Japan on the *USS General Gordon*, following their mother, who wished to be united with her eldest son in Japan. In order to support their family in Nagoya, the brothers went to Tokyo and did odd jobs. Mitsuo, who had renounced citizenship, lost his jobs at Atsugi Airport and the Daiichi Hotel in Shinbashi, the entertainment facility for GHQ, due to another *nisei* reporting on him, using words to the effect of "He's a renunciant," or "We are superior to them." In fact, Masatoshi was not even old enough to be a renunciant at Tule Lake.

Kawate was also discharged from his job as a translator/interpreter to the occupation forces at Kure, Hiroshima, in the summer of 1946. He was the only one who was discharged even though there were many others who were of the same status as he was, according to his letter to Wayne Collins, dated December 2, 1958.[31]

Life was not easy for the Akashi family either; they returned to Japan on the same ship as the Aoyama brothers. Motomu Akashi recalled:

---

31. On the other hand, Tokio Yamane had a completely different story. He was offered a job by a high-ranking American officer, but Yamane declined the offer, replying, "I understand what you wish, but we renounced our American citizenships and came back to Japan as Japanese. It is impossible for us to work for the United States" (Takita-Ishii, 2005, p. 173).

We had a house and land in our hometown that we inherited from Grandfather, but as Father's brother was still alive, we
went into the mountains and my father cleared new land. Our
relatives were not kind. They did not want to share food with
us. Meanwhile, Father was offered a job at the prefectural office
because he spoke English. The office was controlled by the GHQ.
Father said he would not work for the damned foreigners and did
not attempt to flatter them. At the end, he badly hated America.

Sanae Akashi taught English at junior high and high schools in his
hometown from 1947 to 1979, when he died. Somehow, despite his feelings about America, he had the habit of saying that Japanese children
should study English.

On February 6, 1948, the *Chicago Shimpo* reported that the number of
nisei who could not return to the U.S. when the war broke out was about
fifteen thousand. Of those, about seven thousand lost or were about to
lose their U.S. citizenship. Out of them, about seventeen hundred lost citizenship because they were drafted in the Japanese military (most of them
unwillingly conscripted), about fifteen hundred renounced to work for the
Japanese government because they had to make a living, and about seven
hundred lost their citizenship because they voted in the first Japanese Diet
election, believing that the election was conducted according to American
democratic principles. "Since January 1946, the citizenship of about thirty-five hundred *nisei* in Japan has been restored. About fifteen hundred
nisei returned to the U.S., and two thousand *nisei* are working for the US
Occupation Forces."

A few years after President Ronald Reagan signed the Redress Bill of
1988, the *nisei* in Japan who had renounced their U.S. citizenship received
an apology from President George H.W. Bush and twenty thousand dollars in compensation for their incarceration. Some of the recipients are
reported to have cried to interviewing researchers, "Only America could
have done it!" (Murakawa & Kumei, 1992, p. 161).

As an *issei*, despite having been educated in the U.S. and having
dreamed of living a successful life in America, Sanae Akashi could never
become an American citizen. Although he proclaimed that he detested

America close to the end of his life, the fact that he felt such a great need to teach English in Japan resonates across the decades and across the Pacific.

"Only America could have done it."

CHAPTER SIX

BETWEEN BILINGUAL AND BICULTURAL: CHILDREN IN THE CAMPS

I outlived my son
who wrote a letter in broken Japanese
to a mother who does not understand English

—Yaso Ueno

Children, the Primary Victims of the Internment Camps

In February 1943, a thirty-two-year-old *jun nisei* mother who rejected the loyalty registration was asked by the authorities to state her reasons. She answered, "I have American citizenship. It's no good, so what's the use?" And when further pushed about whether she wanted her children raised in Japan, she replied, "It's too late for me, but at least I can bring up my children [in Japan] so that they won't have to face the same kind of trouble I've experienced [here]" (Thomas & Nishimoto, 1946, pp. 95-96).

In December 1945, leaving Tule Lake Segregation Center to return to Japan in a repatriation ship after the war, a small girl said to her parents, "So, we are going back to America" (Kumei & Murakawa, 1988, p. 68). For those children who had grown up in the desolate incarceration camps without any chance of seeing other Americans, Tule Lake had become a veritable Japan. Anything outside the camps *must* be America. Other children thought that Japan itself must be a frightening place. On board the *USS General Gordon*, a fourteen-year-old girl expressed her fear about going to Japan: "I thought Japan was going to be like those Samurai movies where they came out of the dark and killed people" (Nakagawa, 2005, p. 155).

In the Tule Lake camp stockade, when asked whether he ever wanted to return to the U.S., one youth answered, "No, I don't think I ever want to come back." But neither was he interested in living in Japan: "I don't want to stay in Japan. None of us do." When asked where he wanted to go, he replied, "Maybe Australia. We'll want to go where there are new frontiers." But at that point, Australia admitted no Asians (Otani, 1983, p. 284; *Life Magazine,* March 20, 1944, p. 32).

Masashi Nagai, a *kibei nisei* and one of the teachers at *Dai Toa Juku* (the Greater East Asia School at Tule Lake Segregation Center), summed up the effect of internment on children in the following words: "I think the first victims of the camps were children and young people. Children became victims of their parents, which was common in those days."

Were they really victims? And if so, were they victims of their parents?

Religion and Language — Yardsticks of Assimilation

Early in April 1942, when the forced removals started, JACL leader Mike Masaoka asserted that the incarceration camps should not become "Japantowns." Masaoka recommended to the U.S. government that the camps should not have Japanese language schools since they had to serve as facilities to prepare Japanese Americans to become one hundred percent American after the war, prior to their release and transfer (Lim Report, 1990, pp. 58-59). To Masaoka, the Japanese language itself was not only an obstacle to Japanese Americans' assimilation into English-speaking white American society; it was also a blot upon the future of the Japanese American community.

To underscore this point, General John L. DeWitt, head of the Western Defense Command, who enforced the removal of Japanese Americans in March 1942, concluded in his final report that the Japanese language schools were "one extremely important obstacle in the path to Americanization of the second generation Japanese." The report also claimed that the Japanese Society for Education of the Second Generation in America, which supported these schools, was contrary to American interests because it was "founded to Japanize the second and third generations in this country, for the accomplishment of establishing a greater Asia in the future" (TenBroek et al., 1958, p. 269).

Since language and religion are so closely tied to identity, they are regarded as major elements in determining the difficulty of assimilation into mainstream society. During the loyalty registration of February 1943, inmates were asked questions about religion and Japanese language skills as part of the examination to determine who could and could not be released from the incarceration camps. One's answers to these questions were regarded as a measure of one's intentions, as well as that person's prospects for assimilation into Anglo-American society. Applications for release from those who said they believed in Shinto, the native Japanese religion, were rejected; Buddhism and other Oriental religions were considered a minus and Christianity was a plus (Takezawa, 1994, p. 110). Inmates were even asked whether they would "avoid the use of the Japanese language except when necessary" (Weglyn, 1996, p. 179).

What lay at the bottom of the deep-rooted suspicion about the relationship between Japanese religion and language was probably the English-speaking Christian community's prejudice about issues such as language and religion. Whether or not they admit it, most Americans feel that religion plays an important role in providing cohesion to an ethnic group (Nakamaki, 1989, p. 234). For that reason, especially in wartime, they regarded Buddhism and Shinto as ethnic religions that run counter to Christianity and as vehicles for propaganda fanning "the Japanese spirit." Shinto, in particular, was regarded as dangerous in its status as the Japanese state religion (Kumei, 1992, p. 179), and it was so detested that there was a movement to consider it grounds for depriving Japanese Americans of U.S. citizenship and expatriating them (TenBroek et al., 1958, p. 312). In the incarceration camps, even Seicho-No-Iye, an amalgam of Christianity, Buddhism, and Shinto, was reported to the U.S. government to be a type of fanatic cult allied with Shintoism, not a religion in its own right (Government document in the private collection of Harry Ueno).

In the Japanese American community, however, gathering places such as Buddhist temples were not sites intended to foster solidarity based on religious beliefs, as Christian churches often are. They functioned rather as community centers where people tried to find some inner peace of mind by confirming their own origins and sharing with others (Inoue, 1986, p. 111) and came to be the central meeting places of Japanese American communities. Because of their higher learning, the priests of these temples were highly respected. "When most Japanese immigrants had not completed their high school education, almost all the priests had a university degree, ... they were ... the recognized leaders in community affairs when there was a need for community spokesmen. Their duties thus transcended their religious obligations" (Kashima, 1977, p. 69). Religious communities provided a small and different world where Japanese — the minority language in the larger community — became the primary language.

These Japanese-speaking places, floating like islands in the ocean of the English-speaking community, were subject to a great deal of prejudice and misunderstanding. As we shall see, it was the difference in the role and function of language in these two cultural spheres that caused this level of mistrust.

In most American communities, where people espouse individualism and assume that they may not share a common culture and values with others, language is merely a tool for communication — a means of expressing ideas and getting across a point of view. In an ethnically homogeneous society like Japan, where the state is equated with race, and people are obsessed with the idea that they should share a common culture and values, language has a tendency to become ideological. Japanese, as the language of Japan, thus became a symbol of the national spirit, the foundation of *yamato damashii*, the brave and stalwart national character of the Japanese (Yamashita, 1996, p. 78) and synonymous with Japan itself.

In any case, the suspicions of the United States toward the Japanese language moved toward outright paranoia. In this hostile climate, Japanese language education for *nisei* could not evade serious scrutiny. Since it was at the Buddhist temples that many of the Japanese language schools had started, and since Buddhism was "continually misunderstood or deliberately mistaken for or lumped together with the state Shinto religion" (Kashima, 1977, pp. 31-32), Americans got the impression that Japanese language education was somehow related to emperor worship.

The war magnified the differences between the roles and functions performed by the English and Japanese languages, to the extent that family ties and the futures of persons of Japanese ancestry were severely tested by the resulting prejudices. This was the real tragedy of the Japanese language during the war.

Japanese Language Education
for Japanese Americans

Japanese language education for Japanese American *nisei* began just after Japanese emigration to California increased in the second half of the nineteenth century. By 1903, Japanese language schools had already opened in San Francisco and Sacramento. In 1910, there were more than thirty schools in California that provided Japanese language education to thirty-five hundred Japanese children born in the United States (Suzuki, 1930, pp. 8-9).

When the U.S. government passed a law prohibiting Japanese immigration in 1924, *issei* sought a more permanent residence status. By the 1930s, the Japanese American population totaled about one hundred thousand. Less than half of the population had been born in Japan, and with those born in the United States making up the majority, education for *nisei* inevitably became a big concern in the Japanese American community. There were as many as 130 Japanese schools in northern California alone, with 246 teachers teaching 9,862 students (*Nichibei*, June 14, 1936).

Before the war, Japanese language education focused on educating the *nisei* culturally as Japanese. *Issei* parents and teachers tried very hard to pass on the essence of the Japanese language as a form of culture to their children because of their own bitter confrontations with racial discrimination. *Issei* educators hoped that *nisei* would overcome this discrimination by taking pride in being Japanese, and this pride was considered an inherent attribute of the language. More specifically, educators thought that if *nisei* could learn the characteristics of an Oriental culture prominent in world history, as well as celebrate and exercise Japanese traits of "loyalty, righteous indignation, patience, sacrifice, grace, and refinement" (Terakawa, 1930, pp. 345-346), they would make good American citizens and be accepted in the United States. To *issei*, this was how the *yamato* [Japanese] spirit could complement the spirit of the American Founding

Fathers, and it was also seen as a way of fulfilling the duties of an American citizen (Kumei, 1995, p. 220).

What kept this ethnic pride from becoming exclusionary or from displaying a distorted sense of superiority? It was the fact that the immigrants and their children had infinite faith in the concept of democracy embraced by America, as well as in America's commitment to upholding that democracy. Even though the *issei* had suffered from discrimination, many of them could not believe that true Americans would discriminate; they believed that only a small group of rather coarse people harbored this sort of "Japanophobia." Such was the high respect the Japanese had for Anglo-Saxon people, and such was their trust in America (Kumei, 1995, p. 187). However, the U.S. Army propagated strong racial suspicions about these people and went so far as to suggest that Japanese Americans had an "inverted inferiority complex" in that "many have been taught to look down upon white people and have learned that anything not Japanese is to be despised" (Muller, 2007, p. 43).

Japanese language education in the U.S. was meant to help Japanese Americans overcome the pain of racial discrimination that had deeply scarred them and to allow them to attain the strength "to become foremost in *representing non-white races* for justice, humanity, freedom and equality" in the United States (Kumei, 1995, p. 187; emphasis added). However, in this definition of Japanese language education, we detect some of the hierarchy implicit in *hakko-ichiu* (a slogan used in militarist Japan that justified Japan's advancement overseas based on the claim of bringing "the whole world under one roof") and *dai toa kyoueiken*, the Great East Asia Co-Prosperity Sphere. The more the Japanese suffered from discrimination from the white community, the more attractive *hakko-ichiu*, the idea of a Pan-Asian world, became and the greater validity there seemed to be to a Great East Asia Co-Prosperity Sphere, which had the goal of liberating Asia from the oppressive control of imperialist Western powers so that Asia could pursue co-existence and co-prosperity. As a consequence of discrimination, Japanese immigrants were receptive to these ideas as an antidote to the pain imposed on them. Who could blame these *issei*, especially when they could not become citizens, no matter how much they contributed to the country?

The *issei* believed in teaching the goodness of America to help their children survive, and no matter how often they heard nationalistic Japanese slogans, they never thought of encouraging Japanese empire building. These slogans were intended only to give their children self-confidence. Their pride in their Japanese-ness and their cultural morale was based on the fact that they had Japanese blood, but this pride was very different from the nationalism felt by Japanese who lived in Japan (Matsumoto, 2007, p. 253).

It is inconceivable to me that *issei* parents would educate their own children, who were American citizens, in the Japanese language with the political objective of having them pledge allegiance to Japan and sacrifice their own lives for the Emperor in order to establish the Great East Asia Co-Prosperity Sphere. In the case of *issei* parents and teachers, the ideal of *hakko-ichiu* and *dai toa kyoueiken*, i.e., "to make Asian countries respect Imperial Japan as their parent state based on the ethical values of loyalty, filial piety and compulsory subordination" (Eizawa, 1995, p. 116), was distilled into an essence and sublimated as pride in their ethnic group, particularly when they physically moved out of militarist Japan, with its vertical hierarchical principles of order, into democratic America, a society founded on nonhierarchical horizontal principles.

The Japanese teachers thought that an American citizen "nourished with Japanese characteristics," and thus having a Japanese mind, would be able to add "color to the civilization of the United States" and "promote harmony of the Eastern and Western civilizations" (Minutes of Gakuen Kyokai, qtd. in Kawamura, 1930, pp. 27-28). They did not connect either *yamato damashii* or *hakko-ichiu* with emperor worship or militarism but instead regarded them as ideas that would contribute to America (Kumei, 1995, p. 221). In sum, Japanese language education for *nisei* was expected to form the foundation of a comprehensive approach, teaching that "Japanese pride" would allow the *nisei* to contribute to the United States, maintaining a relative balance of power between their Japanese ancestry and mainstream U.S. society. The *issei* of those days anticipated what became the current American spirit of multiculturalism.

With their Japanese spirit, *nisei* were expected to become "bridges" in the community by using their English ability to teach Japanese culture and values to mainstream America. In fact, it was considered the *nisei*'s responsibility to bridge two countries for mutual understanding and prosperity (Mizuno, 2005, p. 221). But the more the *issei* emphasized the importance of *yamato damashii* in the assimilation of *nisei* into American culture, the more the Americans became suspicious of the Japanese Americans.

Parents Spoke Japanese; Children Spoke English

As much as their parents and teachers would have liked them to study Japanese willingly, in reality the *nisei* children were forced to learn Japanese and did so grudgingly. As a consequence, "their Japanese was very poor," and "their sense of the Japanese language was quite weak" (Abiko, 1930, p. 310).

When children attended American schools, their English vocabulary increased dramatically, and their interest in the world expanded, but their Japanese vocabulary did not. As a result, aside from daily conversations at home, deep communication with their parents became difficult. It is true that traditional Japanese fathers usually did not converse very much with their wives and children at home, but communication between children and mothers, particularly between mothers and sons, also began to fail. It was no wonder that children who could argue well in English in the American community gradually began to feel disdain toward their parents, who were oppressed and considered to be at the lowest level of society due to their inability to communicate in standard English.

Japanese language schools were responsible for bridging the gap between culturally distant parents and children through *nisei* education. The underlying principle of these schools was supposed to allow "parents and children who were different from each other in all aspects [to] proceed in the same direction without disappointing each other, thereby promoting their mutual interests and welfare" (*Nichibei*, January 1, 1927). Furthermore, the Japanese language schools were supported by the Confucian tradition brought by the *issei* to the United States, entailing strict filial relationships and honoring education. Even though parent-child communication was difficult, hierarchical discipline between parent and child or older and younger brothers and sisters was accepted as part of life, along with loyalty and filial piety, which built firm family bonds. While *nisei* might have been irritated at their parents' instructions, they rarely opposed them. Children still had a sense of "Japanese-ness"— reluctantly attending Japanese language school without talking back if their parents told them to do so.

Kenji Takeuchi clearly remembers the frustration he experienced while teaching at a Japanese language school before the war. Children came to his school directly after American public school closed, at around two thirty. From Monday to Friday, about twenty-five children from grades one to six studied mainly Japanese for about an hour and a half every day.

> They briefly studied *shushin* [discipline], which included *joshiki* [common sense], proper behavior, mental discipline, and how they should behave as Japanese. The students, however, only spoke English and we teachers, only Japanese. We could hardly communicate with each other, and I got tired of teaching in a week or so. I spoke in Japanese, and they understood to some extent, but they did not respond in Japanese, only in English. I, on the contrary, did not understand English. "Don't you understand what I am saying?" I shouted, which did not work. They didn't seem to get it because their minds worked differently.

At the time, Takeuchi was only twenty years old.

In March 1942, Tetsuo Asano and his family moved from California to his friend's farm in Colorado in a "voluntary evacuation," so the Asano family did not undergo a life of incarceration. Tetsuo, born in 1928, was thirteen when the war between Japan and the U.S. broke out. Beginning in his elementary school days, his parents sent him to a Japanese language school at a Buddhist temple.

> We had a [text]book and I remember that I brought my writing [homework] to school, copying "*Saita saita sakura ga saita*" [Blooming, blooming, cherry blossoms are blooming] in my notebook. Class was only on Saturdays from nine in the morning to four in the afternoon. We were children, so there really

wasn't much else to do but study Japanese. School was not so
enjoyable. It was a lot of work to write *kanji* [Chinese characters
used in written Japanese]. Parents sent children to school to
study, fearing that they would become unable to communicate
with their children. That was a time when people thought every
Japanese child should attend Japanese language school. It was
not in preparation for their parents to return to Japan. I attended
for five or six years. It's not really that I liked studying. Probably
I wanted to go and play with my friends. Though we learned
hiragana [phonetic Japanese characters] and *katakana* [phonetic
Japanese characters used in writing foreign words], I did not
wish to go to Japan in the slightest. I talked with my parents in
Japanese, with my brothers in English.

For about an hour every weekday, Motomu Akashi also reluctantly
attended the Japanese language school where his father was teaching.

I think there were forty to fifty students. We attended from
elementary school to high school. We studied *hiragana* and
katakana with flash cards... it was difficult. It was something
like helping my father, that I had to do [it] by all means.
Enjoyable memories were a samurai movie that Father showed
with a projector he brought from somewhere, a performance
of "Peach Boy," the Boys' Festival in May, *Bon* Festival dancing,
and New Year's Day celebrations in the community. The movie
Chushingura — Father explained the story at the beginning,
but I could not understand much of it. Japan was somewhere
overseas ... that was the feeling I had about Japan. If I had really
known anything about Japan, I would not have gone there after
the war.

Mitsuo Aoyama, who grew up in Seattle, also learned composition and
dictation at a Japanese language school every day after regular school.

I heard the words *yamato damashii* [Japanese spirit] and *oya kôkô* [filial piety] very often. We did *kendo* [bamboo sword martial art] on New Year's Day and listened to a talk on how we had to respect the Emperor and the Imperial Rescript on Education. But I just thought of [the Emperor] as someone in a foreign country.

In Japan, *kendo* was "explicitly linked to Japanese military training and worship of the emperor. In the United States, however, ... [the *kendo* clubs] toned down or even eliminated the attention to the emperor and focused instead on physical, moral and spiritual development" (Muller, 2007, p. 12).[32]

Mike Masaoka and General DeWitt vilified Japanese language schools, but their error was in failing to notice that the primary language of Japanese American *nisei* was English and that the approach of these *nisei* to language and culture was virtually the same as it was for other English speakers in mainstream American society. For *nisei*, Japan and its emperor were just abstractions, something existing only in their imagination, like fairy-tale lands and heroes.

---

32. Kiyota clearly remembered how the *kendo* lessons he had taken in his San Francisco days had raised FBI suspicions at the Topaz camp, to such an extent that his request for leave was denied.

> When they questioned me, I repeated that I did not belong to any organizations. The FBI agent said, "Liar! You were a member of the *Butoku-kai* [Martial Arts Association], were you not?" I said, "I just took some *kendo* lessons. I guess the San Francisco *Kendo* Club was affiliated with the *Butoku-kai*, but I never knowingly became a member of that." He then asked, "I am not asking you what you knowingly did. I am telling you that the *Butoku-kai* is a reactionary organization. What kind of training did they give you? What sort of orders did you have when you came into this camp?" I retorted, "I took *kendo* lessons as a sport!" He then shouted, "Why do you lie? The head of the *Butoku-kai* is General Araki Sadao. What orders did Araki give you? Orders to commit sabotage, right? You speak Japanese—you're a perfect candidate for sabotage. You're a *kibei*, and a member of the *Butoku-kai*. You are a dangerous individual! And you are not getting out of this camp!"... If I had possessed a knife at that moment, I have no doubt that I would have plunged it into the FBI man's heart. From my *kendo* training, I knew how to kill another and to kill myself in the tradition of the ancient *samurai*. And *kendo* had trained in me the determination to accomplish what I willed. (Kiyota, 1997, p. 82)

To these *nisei* children, Japanese was merely a tool for communication with their parents, a language they only understood from the perspective of English speakers, as something foreign. As a result, for them, Japanese was never linked with Japanese nationalistic views or Japanese pride. Japanese American *nisei* born and raised in the United States were already assimilated into the United States in terms of their capacity for language and their sense of values; Japanese language capabilities, whether they had them or not, never governed their thoughts. Most of them would agree that "Japanese" was really only a synonym for the Confucian value of "filial piety."

To *issei* parents, Japanese language education was actually a manifestation of their parental love for their children, a way of seeking a comfortable mode of communication with them rather than an attempt to impart ethical discipline in the face of the reality that their children were less and less able to speak Japanese. The children's sense of language had been transformed from the Japanese emphasis on pride in the language itself to the English emphasis on results, on measurable learning, springing from its practical nature. Japanese language education, which started from early childhood, had another, more practical aspect: it offered potential economic opportunities working with other Japanese in the Japanese American community, in light of the reality that even the *nisei* might not find any other work because of racial discrimination, no matter what level of education they eventually achieved.

Nonetheless, the U.S. government was preoccupied with the *issei*'s Japanese beliefs, viewing the Japanese from an ethnic ideological perspective. After Pearl Harbor, Japan was regarded as "outrageous and unpardonable" for challenging the United States and an "evil power" to be hated. Use of the Japanese language in the United States was regarded as a kind of Japanese invasion challenging American democracy.

During an interrogation at the Justice Department internment camp in Missoula, Montana, an *issei* teacher who had taught at a Japanese language school in Seattle and been sent to the camp just after the war broke out was asked about the textbook used at his former school. He was asked whether he had "used a Japanese language textbook designated for use by the Japanese government" (Itoh, 1982, p. 96), suggesting the sense of fear felt by the American side of indoctrination through language.

If we look at the Pacific War as a war of ideas between the Western worldview, with its horizontal principles of liberty and equality, and the Japanese worldview, with its vertical principles of master/subject, filial piety, veneration, and service (Eizawa, 1995, p. 207), one might say that speakers of the Japanese language in the United States were fighting a similar war of ideas in their enemy's land. "Parental love for their children" was thought to be a propaganda tool of Japanese nationalism, and understanding or speaking Japanese meant that the person was contaminated by the emperor system or Japan's militarism. Thus, U.S. authorities regarded Japanese language education for Japanese American *nisei* as a process of creating "contaminated persons," in their minds similar to the policy of assimilating and/or naturalizing people in the Japanese colonies of Korea and Taiwan into the Japanese Empire. They viewed the Japanese language education movement as an act of "inculcating the Japanese spirit, making local citizens understand the spirit of the Emperor's state in order to cultivate the foundation of the Great East Asia Co-Prosperity Sphere" (*Monthly Nihongo*, August 1993, p. 7).

Children Wavering Between Two Languages

This "war of ideas" started with the family.

In his report, Western Defense District Commander DeWitt insisted that *kibei nisei* had originally been sent to Japan for nationalistic "indoctrination" and that they frequently returned to the United States more fanatically Japanese in their disposition than their own parents (TenBroek et al., 1958, pp. 279-280). In reality, however, the primary reason for sending these children to Japan was economic necessity because of the illness or death of parents or grandparents. Parents, relieved of the necessity of caring for their children, could continue working in the United States, sending money to Japan. Only families of some means could afford to send their children to Japan for educational purposes alone.

When children raised by their grandparents in Japan returned to the United States after several years, what awaited them was not only a sense of distance from and cultural conflict with their parents and Americanized brothers and sisters but also the formidable walls of the language barrier, culture shock, and the stormy period of adolescence as they sought their own true identity — i.e., a place where they actually *belonged*.

At the age of eighteen, Kenji Takeuchi was forced to attend an American secondary school. Culture shock magnified his conflicted feelings and sense of shame. He commented, "Oh! Everything I saw or heard irritated me. No one [in the street] walked straight and tall. People walked arm in arm, chewing gum ... which irritated me."

Studies of bilingual young people have found that those who have lived overseas between the ages of six and twelve experience problems of adjustment both upon their arrival overseas and after their return to the homeland. For these young people, the language used in the elementary school overseas is likely to have a crucial bearing on their subsequent educational career and life. On the other hand, young people who live overseas between the ages of thirteen and eighteen may acquire a firm grasp of a new language, but they are also likely to show emotional instability, overwhelmed by the dual stress of adolescence and the clash with a foreign culture (Nakatsu, 1989, p. 58).

In the case of *kibei nisei*, individuals who were only a year apart in age at the time of their return to the United States, depending upon the age at which they went to Japan, the length of time they spent there, and the age at which they came back to the United States, had very different life development experiences.

Jiro T., who went to Japan with his brother Ichiro at the age of eight after finishing third grade in the United States, found himself exhausted by the psychological conflict he experienced. Once, after the war, he asked his mother why she had sent him to Japan.

> I thought I would not have suffered so much if I had not been to Japan. Then Mother said that she had thought I should get a job in Japan because I would not be able to find one in the United States, even if I graduated from college. In order for me to get a job in Japan, she thought she should send me to Japan at an early age to receive an education identical to that of other Japanese. It was not that she thought the Japanese educational

system was better; she acted purely out of economic concern, considering our future.

After spending six years in Japan, Jiro T. returned to the United States with his brother at the age of fourteen, only to experience difficulty in adjusting. "As I had not used English at all for six years, I forgot it completely, and because of that I hated life here. Mother told me later that she had been planning to send me back to Japan and would have done so had it not been for Pearl Harbor."

Jiro started his American education all over again, beginning with the first grade of elementary school.

> I did not feel any gap with my parents but was disappointed that *nisei* were so Americanized. Japan was at war with China then, you know. I had no concept of citizenship then, so I couldn't understand the way these fellow Japanese (*nisei*) thought at all. Things were very austere in Japan, but these brothers and sisters of mine seemed awfully soft. I was really nonplussed, but the feeling didn't last long.
>
> For example, we had a show-and-tell once at the Japanese language school. We were to read what we wrote or talk about whatever we wanted to. I feel a little embarrassed to admit this now, but at the time I could not stand girls who had permanent waves in their hair. That sort of hairstyle was not allowed in Japan then. It was the militarist period. They called these permed heads "sparrows' nests." So I used the show-and-tell to make fun of these hairstyles. It was a little after I came back to the States. I gradually became Americanized, though superficially so.

Saburo T., eight years younger, related his complicated feelings toward his *kibei* brothers:

> We had grown up in the United States, so, for example, we talked back a lot. I was scolded all the time. I had a bad habit of saying a lot of offensive things. They frequently would say,

"Don't talk back," or "How dare you speak to your parents like that?" My father was a quiet person, so probably he left it to my brother Ichiro. I was more scared of my brother Ichiro than of my father. He [Ichiro] had just come back from Japan and had the most authority in my family. While my brothers were in Japan, Mother sent a package there once a month, food and stuff. I envied that; they were lucky. I was a child, you know, so packages reminded me of Christmas. Kids like packages. I was envious. My brothers were, on the contrary, envious of us because we were with Mother.

The vertical hierarchy of the Japanese family structure dictated that parents send to Japan the sons who could support the family in the future, so that they might be educated; these sons, raised in Japan, in turn absorbed and brought back the very same vertical hierarchy to the United States. But inevitably, the Confucian superior/subordinate relationships (parents/children, older/younger brothers, and husband/wife) under which family members stayed in fixed positions and fulfilled the duties that came with those roles (Eizawa, 1995, p. 111) clashed with the American liberalism and individualism that had already encroached upon Japanese American families, sometimes dividing them. Jiro's second youngest sister went back to Japan with her mother and two other brothers, but she could not get used to life in Japan at all, so she returned to the States with her mother after only six months.

Sister was so tall that she was bullied. She was clumsy and her Japanese was not good. Mother worried about her and decided to leave only the boys in Japan. I heard that when the teacher of her class asked her if she would come back to Japan, my sister answered, "I will never come back."

Jiro laughed gleefully as he recounted this story. Usually the daughters of the family preferred the American sense of values, and "most frequently, they kept their feet planted in America, the sons in Japan" (Thomas & Nishimoto, 1946, p. 359). This was no accident since even in the mid-twentieth century American women had far more freedom than Japanese women.

When families faced complicated situations that could split them apart, like the loyalty oath questionnaire of February 1943 or the citizenship renunciation movement extending from 1944 through the spring of 1945, it often came down to a rivalry between Japanese and American values within the family. Male or female, family members were forced to choose and adopt a set of values that would afford them the best conditions in the future.

Controlled Usage of Japanese

While the use of Japanese was strictly prohibited at first in most, if not all, of the camps until about the middle of the war years, after the loyalty oath and segregation the policy changed, but only for some whom the U.S. government wanted to control.

When I interviewed Saburo T., a *jun nisei*, he immediately introduced himself in fluent Japanese. "*Boku no nihongo wa meido in USA desu*" [My Japanese is made in the USA], he said, and then proceeded to recite the opening of the Imperial Rescript on Education in rapid-fire Japanese:

> *Chin omouni waga koso kosokuni o hajimuru koto koenni toku o tatsurukoto shinko nari wa ga shinmin yoku chu ni yoku ko ni okucho kokoro o itsu ni shite yoyo so no bi o naseru wa kore....*
> [I (Emperor Meiji) conceive that it was in the remote past that *amaterasu oominokami,* our imperial ancestor/founder, and successive Emperors created the country, and the virtue of the Emperors, generation after generation, is deep and vigorous. Our Japanese people have made a concerted effort to honor the virtues of loyalty and filial piety....]

When asked about the meaning of the words he had recited, he answered with a laugh that he didn't know.

In 1943, Saburo T. was in the fifth grade of *Dai Toa Juku* (Greater East Asia Japanese Language School) at Tule Lake Segregation Center.

The Imperial Rescript on Education, which he memorized while sitting up very straight, cross-legged on the floor, during the one-hour *shushin* [discipline] class held twice a week, still remained in his brain like a code after more than half a century. He also recited the names of the successive emperors with amazing speed. He had at one time been able to remember all the names of the hundred emperors up to Showa, but now he could only recall up through the sixteenth. "Why up until the sixteenth?" he asked, sadly. "Because I repeated them from the beginning whenever I forgot," he laughed.

Almost all the history books say that the Japanese language schools in Tule Lake Segregation Center were "set up as means of indoctrinating their *nisei* students with pro-Japanese sentiments in an effort to transform them from Americans into Japanese" (Collins, 1985, p. 77). These books claim that Japanese language schools were turned into propaganda outlets where pro-Nippon proselytizers exalted the doctrine of Japan's national destiny ("to free the Orient of the domination of Western nations") and where youths were daily exhorted to return to the moral and spiritual values of their Oriental heritage — i.e., "to the spirit of self-denial and sacrifice" (Weglyn, 1996, pp. 233-234). In fact, the day at schools like *Dai Toa Juku*, the most prominent school in Tule Lake (Collins, p. 77), *did* begin with a ceremonial bow to the East (Weglyn, pp. 233-234).

But from another point of view, these schools were a kind of trap set up by the U.S. government, a trap that involved the "Japanization" of the Tule Lake Segregation Center to force people to make difficult choices. Through the schools, the WRA enacted its policy to foster activities aimed at encouraging repatriation (Takei, 2005, p. 85); this policy was cleverly set up to dovetail with the Department of Justice policy of sending all Japanese and Japanese Americans in Tule Lake back to Japan. *Issei* parents were thus trapped by having to choose an American or Japanese path to ensure their children's future. While "Japan" lay at the core of the parents' existence, the center of life for the children was simply their "parents." The ones who suffered the most, being caught in the trap, were the children, who could not help being involved with Japan because of a fate that they did not choose.

People in power often regard a language they do not understand with suspicion and treat it as if it were an evil conspiracy. In the camp, this meant that even basic signs such as "Men," "Women," and "Do Not Waste Water" had to be translated into English (Mizuno, 2003, p. 852). No exceptions. Those in power also tend to ignore the simple fact that for most people the mother tongue is the only means by which real feelings and consciousness can be conveyed. Because they cannot understand other languages, those in power force others to use only *their* language. Many Americans, including not only white people but also Japanese American *nisei* born and raised in the United States, could not understand the ease and comfort that human beings can find *only* in their mother tongue.

The use of Japanese for both reading and writing had been prohibited at temporary detention centers prior to the incarceration camps. Fearing that the unfamiliar "enemy language might be misused for propaganda, agitation, or conspiracy, or simply disliking its foreignness, camp authorities prohibited Japanese American evacuees from reading, writing, publishing, discussing, worshipping, and even singing or playing in their ancestral language" (Mizuno, 2003, p. 860). Use of Japanese at meetings and in newspapers was not allowed. Informal grade-school classes were immediately organized so that youngsters would not be entirely deprived of an education, but classes could not be conducted in Japanese unless taught by a Caucasian, and "all books written in Japanese, even nonpolitical light ones, except religious ones, were confiscated" (Weglyn, 1996, p. 83).

Takeya Mizuno (2003) recounts the frustrations of one inmate when his classic Japanese novel was confiscated. "If the 'Tales of Genji' written in the tenth century AD is to be considered subversive in twentieth century America I'm afraid that all literature pertaining to any phase of Japanese culture — whether written in English or in Japanese — must be condemned" (p. 856). The seemingly arbitrary confiscation of the very few, precious books that inmates had been able to bring with them was a "terrible blow on the morale of the Japanese-reading residents" and was likened to fascism (p. 857).

Furthermore, services held during Buddhist meetings, and recreation such as plays and talent shows at temporary detention centers had to be conducted in English (Kashima, 1977, p. 53; Mizuno, 2003, p. 860). And for a while at some camps, administrators even censored private letters written in Japanese (Mizuno, 2005, p. 264). Even the English newspapers issued in the temporary detention centers were censored, prohibited from publishing news associated with Japan or with anything remotely Japanese. "Discussion of the international situation, war news, national news, even hometown news and politics was taboo" (Mizuno, 2003, p. 99). In this way, newspapers merely functioned as "the camp administration's mouthpiece" (p. 102). This situation even further frustrated the inmates, who had been forcibly evicted from familiar places only to be confined in makeshift barracks converted from stables. It was even worse for those who spoke only Japanese; they were denied the opportunity to gather together and share information in their common language through Japanese books, newspapers, or entertainment.

In July 1942, more than ten Japanese and Japanese Americans, including Kinzo Wakayama, at Santa Anita temporary detention center in southern California were arrested and accused of conducting a meeting in Japanese in violation of center regulations and of conspiring to circulate a petition demanding publication of a Japanese-language newspaper (*Pacific Citizen*, July 2, 1942). Because most *issei* and *kibei* were not very good at English, the alienation and cooped-up feeling of being forced to use English must have been stifling. What could they do to retain their identities? They felt as if they were dragging around empty bodies, forced to be deaf, blind, and mute. They felt like dolls (Mizuno, 2005, p. 263).

The situation was similar in the incarceration camps; any use of Japanese, even for entertainment, had to be approved.[33] At the Manzanar camp, a meeting of *kibei* held in Japanese allowed inmates to voice "sen-

---

33. "...when an entertainment group put on a variety show in the mess hall, the emcee spoke only in English. The Issei did not like this. When the shows were in Japanese, the programs first had to be translated into English for approval. If they weren't approved, they couldn't be staged. It was humiliating enough that their native language had to yield to English, but because many Issei were weak in English, their humiliation was doubled.... One evening when the Issei knew that the Caucasian in charge of entertainment was away on business, the Issei seized their chance-in-a lifetime opportunity to stage an extremely pro-Japanese show called 'Call to Duty.' This was a cathartic victory for the Issei, who relished every minute of it, but the next day word got back to the administration. Needless to say, the Issei entertainers were reprimanded. Who would have informed the authorities? It must have been a Nisei *inu*"(Shirai, 2001, pp. 76-77).

timents that had been steadily crystallizing ever since evacuation" and aroused a great deal of emotion. In reaction, "the project director pronounced the meeting 'disgraceful' and thereafter the use of the Japanese language in public gatherings was prohibited" (*Impounded People*, 1946, p. 75).

Being forced to use a foreign language, English, was a rather severe form of punishment for non-native speakers. In April 1943, at Moab prison camp in Utah, a rule was established under which prisoners had to get the director's permission to visit other buildings and once permission was granted could do so only accompanied by a guard. Only the use of English was permitted during visits (Harry Ueno's private autobiography). Harry Ueno, a *kibei* who protested against prohibition of the Japanese language at Manzanar (*Hokubei Mainichi*, December 13, 1995), recalled a security officer whom internees called "Seamy" because he often said, "If there is anything you want, see me. See me." "See me" set up the rules, saying, "You can't talk in Japanese; you've got to speak in English" (Embrey et al., 1986, p. 73). This created such outrage that one-third of the prisoners demonstrated against the new rule.

In human beings, the mother tongue is so strongly connected with the speaker's identity that it shapes his or her personality. The mother tongue is involuntary and very much a matter of fate, not choice, similar to not being able to choose one's own parents; in this sense, it is "one of the most irrational things we encounter in our life" (Tanaka, 1975, p. 54). Therefore, adding insult to the injury of forced removal and incarceration, the government's suppression and prohibition of Japanese and Japanese Americans' self-expression in their mother tongue became an added human rights violation. And, as Takeya Mizuno has argued, this suppression was a violation of the inmates' First Amendment freedoms of speech and expression (Mizuno, 2003, p. 860).

The Japanese Language at Tule Lake

In contrast to the temporary detention centers and most other camps, the Tule Lake Segregation Center was an environment in which Japanese could be used quite naturally without restraint. Authorities allowed the use of Japanese at Tule Lake as if acknowledging the mistakes made at other detention centers and camps. The Tule Lake camp was a lively Japanese-speaking world where a variety of dialects could be heard in every direction. For instance, a *kibei nisei* might be heard making a speech in a Hawaiian dialect of Japanese incomprehensible to the crowd (Weglyn, 1996, p. 133). At times, children could not communicate with each other because of the mutually incomprehensible dialects they spoke, a result of the different dialects that their Japanese immigrant parents brought with them to the U.S. With *issei* parents mostly engaged in agriculture, as family units spread over the vast land area of America, naturally the language *nisei* children picked up was the dialect of their parents. Government observers noted that "the gradual disuse of English by the Issei in camp makes for a greater development of Japanized English" and that "a knowledge of both Japanese and English is necessary to completely appreciate the richness and the succinctness" of *issei* and *nisei* language at the camp. They spoke "neither good English nor good Japanese" ("A Lexicon of Center Terms," June 25, 1945).

Kinzo Wakayama, who saw the Stars and Stripes fluttering on the flag pole at the center of the Tule Lake central plaza from the train carrying him there, protested, "Pull down the flag. Otherwise, I will never get off the train. Why do we have to worship the Stars and Stripes morning and night at a place interning Japanese who did not take a loyalty oath to America? I came here with the intention of being a total Japanese in mind and body. Why do you harass us?" (Murakawa & Kumei, 1992, pp. 128-129). Soon thereafter, the Stars and Stripes disappeared.[34]

---

34. Tokio Yamane from Jerome, Arkansas, also told the exact same story to an interviewer: "When we arrived in Tule Lake from Jerome, even before getting off the train, we saw an American flag fluttering in the sky. We were greatly disturbed by that sight. We had traveled all the way from Jerome to Tule Lake believing this was the segregation center to house those who were loyal to Japan. My immediate reaction to the situation: 'We don't need the American flag, a symbol of loyalty to America.' I negotiated with the camp administration, threatening them that we would not get off the train if the American flag remained flying. After about half an hour they agreed to pull the flag down so that we would all leave the train. Later I heard that we were the only group that was successful in pulling the flag down, even though similar attempts were made before us" (Takita-Ishii, 2005, p. 166).

In the meantime, doorplates bearing titles such as *"Hawaii kibei honbu"* [Hawaii Kibei Head Office] and *"dainippon shinmin _____"* [_____ of the Citizens of Great Japan] were posted enthusiastically on the doors of the barracks. One huge billboard read, *"gakujuku"* [private school]. Graffiti such as *"dai nippon teikoku banzai"* [*banzai* for Great Imperial Japan] and *"ichioku isshin"* [literally, "one hundred million, one heart"] could be found on the black walls of the barracks. At one point, inmates stormed the administration office demanding that the administrators speak Japanese because the protestors did not understand English very well.[35] Swept up in the Japanization process, the name of the camp's central market was even changed to *toa ichiba* [East Asian market]. Then, at the high school, the *kibei nisei* broke up a dance held by the *nisei* because they thought it irreverent during wartime, and after that incident, no public dances were held.[36] Finally, in yet another instance of pro-Japanese behavior, a man in charge of the public address system at a basketball game was forced to stop playing American jazz and instructed to play the Japanese national anthem (Thomas & Nishimoto, 1946, p. 111).

In accordance with their petition for re-segregation, some Japanese speakers radically elevated their belief in the power of the Japanese language, becoming more militant about speaking Japanese and making their dependence on the Japanese language a form of self-defense. For example, on the wall of *Sokoku Kenkyu Seinen-kai* (Youth Group for Research on the Homeland) office, one could see Japanese flags and a sign to the effect that any person speaking English in the office would be fined at the rate of one cent per word (Thomas & Nishimoto, 1946, p. 320).

In a more extreme example, Yoshio Nishikawa, the *shuyo* [discipline] director of *Hokoku Seinen-dan*, was directed by leaders of *Sokuji Kikoku*

---

35. There were also quite a few bilingual people among the inmates, which worried the administrators. Bilinguals had power because they could operate in both English and Japanese worlds.

36. Tokio Yamane remembers, "One night I and other youth from the Kai group made a raid on a dance party held at the camp mess hall. We screamed at those who enjoyed dancing, 'Hey, we are at war now! Those soldiers were fighting in the front line. Stop partying and do other more constructive activities.' We called the party off" (Takita-Ishii, 2005, p. 166).

Hoshi-dan to ask for an interpreter at an inquiry carried out by authorities, telling them that he could not speak English, although in fact he was bilingual. "When I look back now, it really sounds stupid because at the interview they had all my records. They knew I had graduated from high school in the United States. Notwithstanding, I asked for an interpreter on the grounds that I could not speak English. And then they whipped out the document and called me on it."

This emphasis on Japanese language and culture continued at frequent meetings of *Sokoku Kenkyu Seinen-kai*, where Buddhist priests presented lectures with titles such as "War and National Philosophy" and "On Japanese Culture" (Kumei, 1996, p. 78) based on information gleaned from Radio Tokyo emphasizing the significance of emperor worship and the Greater East Asia Co-Prosperity Sphere. Susumo Kako, a *kibei*, admitted that he had once sneaked out of a lecture and was discovered and beaten for having left. He commented:

> The lecturers were highly educated, often graduates of what was called "high school" under the old system. Those Buddhist priests were eager. They taught us *yamato damashii* [Japanese spirit], urging us to become Japanese through and through. You know, people can become awfully overbearing when they combine religion and politics.

A speech contest held at a high school auditorium featured such themes as "the young men who have constructed the great empire are fighting a sacred war," and many of the speakers lectured passionately on subjects of their own choosing, such as "live loving your country," "let us go and take up our great duty," "shatter our three-year silence," and "you wake up when you hear the national anthem and feel that you are a Japanese," all speaking with the single-minded sense of justice characteristic of youth (*Hokoku* [newsletter, English translation], December 6, 1944).

Passion for the promise of the young was a central theme of the slogans that proclaimed the hopes for the "pro-Japan" group. Ichiro T., who had met several young members of *Hokoku Seinen-dan* for the first time in the hospital, said of them, "They were all serious. In a group, they might have said that they would go back to Japan to fight for the Emperor, but individually, they were nice people. They were just full of self-righteousness and innocence."

"Japanese Tolerance": A Clever Trap

The camp administrators' ploy of ignoring or even approving of the "Japanization" of the center was so clever in its ability to fan the anger and righteousness of youth that even a Japanese correspondent commented ironically, "America may well boast of its world-famous reputation as a country of democracy and freedom; its generosity is beyond our expectation" (Kumei, 1996, p. 76). Even a "pro-Japan" hard-liner was fooled into writing the following in a statement for *Sokoku Kenkyu Seinendan*: "Fortunately, the government, whose national policies are based on democracy, humanity and liberty, has now proclaimed by legislation that it officially approves our indignation. We are, indeed, delighted with this recognition" (Thomas & Nishimoto, 1946, p. 312).

As part and parcel of this generosity, the segregation center was officially permitted to establish schools in which classes were taught in Japanese in December 1943. As a result, Japanese schools were set up in each ward, from one through eight, making use of mess halls, recreation halls, and even washrooms for facilities, and children were required to attend daily. As part of this trap of Japanization, children could study in Japanese, but, "according to the FBI, after segregation took place during the summer of 1943, no public schools operated at Tule Lake" and "it wasn't until martial law was lifted in February 1944 that public schools were finally opened" (Takei, 2005, p. 85). So, for more than six months, these American children were denied the opportunity of American public schooling in which they could speak English; instead, they were encouraged to become more Japanese.

As of July 1944, there were almost forty-seven hundred school-age children and students from five to nineteen years of age at Tule Lake, a quarter of the total population of 18,600. By the fall of 1944, approximately forty-three hundred students were enrolled in Japanese language schools (James, 1987, p. 148).

One reason that the Japanese schools in Tule Lake were reviled by many as places for Japanese militaristic propaganda may be that there were two kinds of schools, clearly distinguishable from each other by their different emphases: one kind of school taught Japanese as a tool of communication and the other focused on arousing Japanese pride, reflecting the increasingly pro-Japanese sentiment within the center. But since not everyone in the center agreed with them, the schools emphasizing Japanese pride led to infighting and posed a challenge to parent-child relationships, which grew weaker and weaker during incarceration.

Other aspects of camp life also contributed to the weakening of family ties. Meals were announced by the sound of a bell and eaten in the mess hall by all residents of a block, denying families the chance to bond over dinner at home. The inevitable cultural and emotional distance between parents and their adolescent children was compounded by the fact that parents could not really be the main providers for their children during their stay at the incarceration camp. Thus, parents inevitably lost control of their children, and the children lost the sense of respect that they would ordinarily have for their parents. Mothers lamented, "We bear the children, but we do not give birth to their minds" (Saki, 1999).

Motomu Akashi, who was a student of Tri-State High School at the center, had a busy daily after-school schedule:

> I never got bored at all. I played football and had a lot of things to do. I played, ate at the mess hall, came back to the barrack and slept, went to Japanese language school…. My parents didn't tell me to do this or that. Nobody was at home, so I was always out with my friends. I was not a gang member, though, but a teenager, you know. Some were in gangs. I was more interested in sports. Even when I went to eat at other mess halls far away, I had friends there. We had a good time.

In this camp atmosphere, children became self-indulgent, living a life beyond their parents' reach. Likewise, many adults who had been working nonstop since they had come to the United States also had an easy life, just killing time the whole day. Although they felt that they were wasting time, relieved even of the need to cook or do dishes, nobody complained about their lives of leisure or being able to do whatever they wanted (Saki, 1999).

With time hanging heavily on their hands in the stifling surroundings of the camp, some parents might have had hopes that the Japanese language school would bolster the weakening bonds between parents and children to help them unify as families again. For such parents, the ideal of "Japan" in the segregation center became a cultural "Promised Land" in which they thought they might be able to rebuild communication with their children and regain the unity their families had lost.

U.S. and Japan — Two Conflicting Worlds

The incarceration experience also exacerbated another conflict: many parents found themselves emotionally torn between the traditional Japanese maxims, "Children should obey their parents" and "When old, obey your children." They found themselves comparing the two worlds, thinking, "The war will be over sooner or later, and then we can choose either Japan or America. It will not be too late." Striving to avoid being affected by the winds of fate and opinion, and hoping that their children would have as many options as possible in the future, parents daily sent their children off into two conflicting worlds: "America," taught at American public schools in the morning, and "Japan," taught at Japanese schools in the afternoon. As of fall 1944, about twenty-three hundred children attended both American public schools and Japanese schools (James, 1987, p. 148) and suffered from the complications, frustrations, and contradictions of living in constant tension between two cultures.

What annoyed the children most was that they were supposed to learn American ideals, values, and laws at the American school with inadequate books and teaching materials, in classes that were only a half day, and that they were not required to attend. The government deemed this sufficient, though, as it met the minimum standards set by state education departments. But no matter how much the ideals of "freedom, equality, and justice" were praised in these morning classes, the reality was that these students found themselves being held in incarceration camps. Under such circumstances, how would American education be of use to them?

Distrustful of American hypocrisy, the children would have been more likely to take note of how to survive in authoritarian Japanese society in the afternoon. In addition to the Japanese language, boys were trained in discipline, and girls learned Japanese customs such as *seiza* (sitting on the floor in proper Japanese style), manners, and sewing. As children in Japanese schools would, they practiced gymnastics to recorded Japanese music and worshipped the Imperial Palace every day. They also read aloud the Imperial Rescript on Education on every possible occasion. Even so, these schools did not particularly emphasize the "Japanese spirit" or teach the Japanese language to the point where students showed dramatic improvement.

According to Harry Ueno, at the Tule Lake Fourth [Ward] National School, *shushin* [morals], reading, writing, comprehension, dictation, penmanship, stroke order in Japanese calligraphy, speech, mathematics, geography, Japanese history, and gymnastics made up the curriculum. One woman I met at the Tule Lake pilgrimage, who also attended the Fourth National School, can still smoothly pronounce the words "*amaterasu-oominokami*" [the Sun Goddess], perhaps the most important Shinto deity in Japanese mythology and also considered to be directly linked in lineage to the Imperial Household of Japan and the Emperor. "I haven't uttered such words in decades," she said in English, smiling sweetly.

However, children were suffering from the obligation of changing their personalities like chameleons, becoming different people in the afternoon from the ones they were in the morning. Some children were scolded by the American teacher for drawing an airplane with the Rising Sun flag or the Statue of Liberty waving the Rising Sun in her hand. One *nisei* girl shocked her Japanese teacher when she reacted to the stress by refusing to sing the Japanese national anthem at Japanese school and instead loudly sang, in English, "Pistol Packing Mama," a popular song at that time (James, 1987, pp. 100, 152). The bilingual and bicultural world the children lived in was nothing but a source of confusion — a place where they could not tell right from wrong — and it became a heavy burden on them.

Most of the National Schools were run by the moderates, inmates who had lived in the Tule Lake camp before it became a segregation camp and who looked for compromise with the authorities. These moderates recommended that parents send their children to American schools. But some other teachers urged parents not to send their children to the American schools.

The Japanese schools located in wards where leaders of *Sokuji Kikoku Hoshi-dan* and *Hokoku Seinen-dan* were dominant were known as bastions of resistance to WRA policy at Tule Lake, such as Ward 7, where Sanae Akashi (who petitioned for re-segregation) lived, and Ward 8, across camp from Akashi's place, where Kinzo Wakayama lived (James, 1987, p. 151). Children there were prohibited from attending American public schools and were taught discipline, obedience, and respect for elders at the Japanese schools. Students had to bow to teachers when approaching them, which, from the standpoint of Americans, smacked of nationalistic indoctrination, fostering loyalty to Japan.

Motomu Akashi recalled attending the Seventh [Ward] National School half a day every day for a short period of time, noting that students had their heads shaved and were prohibited from speaking English:

> There were about twenty-five students. The teachers were strict but I did not want to study, and actually, I did not study so much. I do not think the other students studied either. I went to school every day, as my parents told me to, but I did not learn anything there, [which was evident by the fact that] I could not speak Japanese when we went back to Japan. I only understood very basic Japanese, which was good enough for me to work as an interpreter for the U.S. Occupation. I was called a "third-rate national," though.

Motomu clearly remembered a *kibei nisei* teacher saying, "Let's study Japanese popular songs!"

> The songs had names like "*Nanatsubotan*" [Seven Buttons], "Song of the *Kamikaze*," "*Harunokaze*" [Spring Breeze].... We practiced singing them, probably as a part of our cultural studies. They told us to memorize *oyakoko* [filial piety] or *waga koso* [our imperial ancestors], and the teacher explained what they

meant, but I could not understand the poor English of the *kibei*.
And bowing ... we always had to bow. "*Kiotsuke, keirei*" [Stand
at attention and salute!], we were told.

Motomu Akashi's crisp and clear Japanese words, interspersed with
conversational English, sound dated, and talking with him felt like traveling back in time to those days. Motomu himself, however, had no strong
feelings either positive or negative towards militarist Japan.

Dai Toa Juku – The Greater East Asia School

Dai Toa Juku was started at Tule Lake in October 1943 as a Japanese
language school by Kenji Takeuchi, who shared a room with Ichiro T. At
the time, Ichiro was twenty-one and Takeuchi was twenty-three years old.
Monthly tuition was twenty-five cents per child. In the beginning, it was
just a small group of students, and classes were held in a room in the barracks, but the number of students suddenly increased over a short period
of time. Later the school expanded to include junior high grades and
night classes, making use of other spaces. There were about twenty-five to
thirty students in a class, one class for each grade level, but students' ages
and levels of Japanese language ability varied. Sometimes teenagers were
placed among first graders.

From the very beginning, Tule Lake inmates had a guarded attitude
toward *Dai Toa Juku,* which was located in Block 30 of Ward 2 (Barrack
3003-D). A few months after the school opened, in early December 1943,
the inmates requested that it be closed on the grounds that it was extrem-
ist, that it would obviously worsen relations between the inmates and the
authorities, and that it was insulting to the principals of the other Japanese
schools (WRA Internal Security Follow-up Case Report, September 28,
1944). Following the protest, the *juku* was quiet for a while, but it soon
resumed operation.

Dai Toa Juku has been described in various ways in history books. Some
books state that *Hokoku Seinen-dan* members were forced to attend the
juku (Shirai, 1981, p. 193),[37] whereas others say that all of the *juku* teachers

---

37. The leaders of the re-segregation and repatriation groups thought that in order

were arrested and sent to Santa Fe along with the *Sokuji Kikoku Hoshi-dan*
and *Hokoku Seinen-dan* members (Memorandum by W. Collins, 1954).[38]
In response to these accounts, Ichiro T. and Kenji Takeuchi said that the
reports of arrests and being "sent to Santa Fe" were serious misrepresen-
tations of the situation, though they admit that both of them had been
called in for questioning by the authorities.[39]

According to Ichiro T.:

> I was brought in and they said they would blindfold me. They
> threatened me, saying that I would be executed … taken out and
> shot! I said, "Okay, I don't care, go ahead, do whatever you want
> to do." Then one of the parents, who was *nisei* and could speak
> Japanese fluently and also president of the PTA of the *juku*,
> negotiated with the authorities, explaining in detail that the *juku*
> was just a place to prepare for the return to Japan, unrelated to
> politics. We were released within three hours and came home.

After that incident, the name of the *juku* was changed to Tule Lake
Gakuen [Academy], but its educational principles never changed. The *juku*
continued in operation until its closure in mid-August 1945, when the war
ended. In the last commemorative photo taken in front of the barracks,
there are nearly 130 students and seven teachers.

Why were the inmates so cautious about the *juku*? It was probably because this supplementary school practiced strict military training
together with corporal punishment. As Takeuchi retells it, "Sometimes we
hit the students with our fists. That seemed incredibly severe and violent

---

to become "true Japanese," young people must not only reject their U.S. citizenship
but also refuse an American education. These leaders asked students to quit the
public schools and enroll in either the Peoples' School (Kokumin Gakko) or the
Greater East Asia *juku* (*Dai Toa Juku*). These were the only schools approved by the
movement's leaders (Shirai, 1981, p. 149).

38. Motumu Akashi attended *Dai Toa Juku*, and what he learned at the school
is described in his book *Betrayed Trust* (2004, pp. 209-216). He also claims that
Takeuchi was arrested and sent to Santa Fe (p. 216).

39. In my interview with Takeuchi in September 2013, he admitted that he was in the
stockade for a few hours.

to students who had grown up in America." Ichiro T. said that he intentionally made conditions severe for the sake of students, in consideration of the fact that they would have to go to Japan, where life was harsh and probably had become even more difficult, compared to the way it had been in the years he himself was there. But ultimately, he believed that the harsh *juku* training was the only way for students to learn Japanese.

On September 28, 1944, a few days before the *juku's* first anniversary on October 1, a camp inmate made the following report to the authorities:

> For the past several weeks the attention of the internal security officers on patrol in the colony have been attracted to an intensive drill being carried on by children of all ages, from six to about sixteen, which had the appearance of a semi-military drill. This culminated in a large outdoor demonstration that took place September 27 and lasted nearly all day.... Questioning the spectators, the investigating officers were told that the entire procedure was for the purpose of building up the physical health and muscular activity of the children engaged in the ceremonies, and had no reference to anything military. Our informant [opined that] this drill is of decidedly military character, and because of the strenuousness, is to build up a Spartan spirit among prospective residents of Japan. The process of training at the school consists of long hours and very severe discipline, to the extent that the children are slapped, struck with sticks, and otherwise severely chastised for the smallest infraction of discipline or mistake in a drill or ritual. The informant states that the parents of most of these children are of rather low mentality, and therefore consider this method of teaching as being the true Japanese method. For this reason, they give the schoolteacher free rein and one hundred percent support in anything he does in a disciplinary way. (WRA Internal Security Follow-up Case Report, September 28, 1944)

Kenji Takeuchi was known for leading the drills at the segregation center, according to the report. "*Dai Toa Juku* was the first school to do the morning radio gymnastics and to have the students run while shouting, 'Wasshoi wasshoi,' in cadence. The *Hokoku Seinen-dan* started doing the same thing, and I didn't want to be associated with them, so I stopped," said Takeuchi.

According to Ichiro T.:

> At the athletic meetings, we did gymnastics. All of the male students had their heads shaved and wore headbands with the Rising Sun symbol and the characters for *Dai Toa Juku*. They marched in to the *aikoku koshinkyoku* (a patriotic song) that about two hundred students, including males with close-cropped hair and females in braids, would sing in unison with their heads turned to the right. They performed the pyramid, bridge, and other exercises that I learned in junior high school. I was directing from the stage, giving the command, "Turn your heads to the right!" Then the MPs came by in a Jeep. They asked who the leader was, and then they took me away with them.

The WRA's report on *Dai Toa Juku* continued: "… the anniversary of the incident of November 3rd is tentatively set as the zero hour for the kick-off of a demonstration toward which this school and various other organizations seem to focus. [The informant] emphatically warned the investigating officers to be especially watchful about November first, second, third and fourth." The report concluded, "The informant definitely indicated his conviction that unless the school and the drilling were stopped or controlled they would shortly build up in volume to sufficient proportion to be a decided menace to the peace and tranquility of the colony, if not to the WRA itself" (Internal Security Follow-up Case Report, September 28, 1944).

Perhaps the main reason that the *juku* was misunderstood, even reviled, could be related to Takeuchi's educational philosophy. He was a graduate of *Kokushikan* Middle School, which demanded absolute obedience in an outright militarist manner. So, to those not accustomed to this approach, it was not so much that the curriculum seemed militaristic as that it was simply too incompatible with the spirit of the American education system, which emphasized individuality and more gentle discipline.

However, in the eyes of Takeuchi and Ichiro T., who had experienced Japanese education in the 1930s, their system represented Japan as they had experienced it. This "Japan" was neither good nor bad, but deep in the roots of and forming the core of their beings. All the elements they recalled from their Japanese education were there — from the name of the school, invoking "Greater East Asia," to the patriotic song sung at the athletic event commemorating the first anniversary of the school's founding (*Tule Lake Shimpo*, October 5, 1944), to the headbands bearing images of the Rising Sun and the Japanese characters for *Dai Toa Juku* and even the daily morning radio gymnastics. To the American authorities, however, these signs of Japan all smacked of Japanese militaristic propaganda and thus were regarded as dangerous and evil.

But let us entertain a different scenario: What if the Japanese educational spirit that Takeuchi and others had absorbed during their most impressionable years actually represented, for them, a level of human dignity, taken wholesale from its original Japanese setting and interwoven with the American principles of democracy and equality in the complicated context of the internment camp? To put it another way, could customs formerly bound to the Japanese soil have been transformed into a kind of free-standing "Japanese pride" supporting a collective vision and identity much more important than loyalty to a country or an emperor?

Here is Takeuchi's account of what they attempted to accomplish:

> We talked about *yamato damashii* at the *juku* but never told the students to go against the country they were born in. We never told them to fight. What we taught at the *juku* was that they should live an honest life, headed in the right direction, and believing in themselves as Japanese because they had the same blood flowing in their veins as ours. We wanted them to be Americans who were also equipped with "genuinely Japanese" minds. The matter of loyalty or disloyalty to the state had nothing to do with this. Through Japanese language, I taught them about the human heart, what to do as a human being, what is right and what is wrong, namely, to go straight for what they

believe in, never to tell a lie, to venerate their parents and get along with their brothers and sisters, and how to contribute to the world. To present a balanced picture, we gave examples from both Japan and America. I talked about the heroism of Washington and Lincoln as well as the vengeance of the Ako warriors ..., how righteous vengeance was one of the sentiments characteristic of the ancient Japanese. We also taught them that once they start something, they should persist in finishing it. If they gave up in the middle, they would be losers.

This is a very Japanese way of thinking, isn't it? The Japanese spirit is inherent in its language ... in words such as *shojiki* [honesty], *kinben* [diligence], *omoiyari* [sympathy for others], *kenkyo* [humility], *tsuyosa* [strength], *isagiyosa* [good grace], *kihaku* [spiritedness], *seijitsu* [sincerity], *shinnen* [firm convictions]. And I think that Americans can understand these Japanese ways of thinking pretty well.

With great conviction, Takeuchi made the point that the universal values of the Imperial Rescript on Education, if detached from association with the Japanese Emperor, could be the salvation of modern-day America in a way that transcends specific time periods or racial and ethnic groups:

The Imperial Rescript on Education is at the core of the Japanese heart. If the United States provided a moderate education that combined the Christian teachings of love for one's fellow man with the Japanese spirit as embodied in the precepts of the Imperial Rescript on Education — all nicely integrated from the pre-school level or elementary school onward — the United States would undergo a great change in the space of ten years. It would be a wonderful country.

Classes at *Dai Toa Juku* were conducted with a strong awareness that many, if not all, Tule Lake inmates would be forced to repatriate to Japan. With no real political motivation or regard for the outcome of the war, parents who saw some hope for a better life in Japan wanted their families to repatriate and thus sent their children to a *juku* in preparation. They strictly adhered to the principle of educating their children in classes that allowed only the Japanese language, from 8:00 a.m. to well into the evening, so that these children might be able to master Japanese. The students were not allowed to attend American public school and were prohibited from using English both in the *juku* and at home.

Ichiro T.'s brother Saburo explained that he was frequently hit by his teacher at school, to set an example to other pupils. "A friend of mine who could not speak Japanese visited me, so I could not help speaking in English. Someone heard me, and the next day the teacher hit my shaved head. I was hit frequently," he admitted with an embarrassed smile.

The strict Japanese education presented at the *juku* reflected the strongly critical mindset shared by Ichiro T. and Takeuchi, who had both had bitter experiences in Japan, where they had been discriminated against as Americans due to their inadequate language skills.

> We didn't tell our students, "Don't study English." Instead, we said that if they wanted to study English, they should do it on their own time. Since we thought that these children would go back to Japan, take the entrance exam for college, get jobs, and build their future, we felt that the Japanese language would be the most important subject for them. If they were handicapped by deficient language skills, they would not be able to find jobs that paid decently and would have to settle for doing manual labor, which would be no different from their life in America, don't you see?

Ichiro T. spoke in a spirited voice. He was only being realistic in saying that he thought primarily of the survival and practical needs of families who would be settling in Japan. In his opinion:

> The Japanese reading they taught in National Schools was not at a high enough level to allow them to make a living in Japan. And the Japanese study they did in their spare time was also insufficient. We thought that they should study math, geography, and science in Japanese as well.

At the *juku*, students were taught subjects such as Japanese, math, history, geography, science, calligraphy, and *shushin* [discipline], along with children's and military songs, gymnastic exercises, and (for girls) sewing and etiquette. There were a lot of highly proficient teachers for those subjects in the camp, and they were studying too. Among other courses, Ichiro T. himself studied English during the day while teaching Japanese at night.

> Japanese Americans who had graduated from the University of California were giving lectures at the college level, so I took courses in math, physics, and chemistry. But why did I study English, although I had decided to go back to Japan? I thought that if Japan were defeated, it would be occupied, so to survive we would have to know English. Besides, Japanese people would naturally assume that I spoke English, as I had come from America.

After Japan's defeat in the war, Ichiro T. and Masashi Nagai were the only *juku* personnel who returned to Japan. In post-war Japan, Ichiro T. played an active role as an executive at an international company, making good use of his proficiency in English. Masashi Nagai became a contract interpreter for Yamaguchi and Aichi Prefectures and later was involved in an international trading company.

Takeuchi got married while still in the camp and decided to stay in the United States. Most of the *juku* schoolchildren remained in the United States as well. One former student said, "I fell behind everyone else in English because I attended *juku*, but I think that it was a good idea to have studied Japanese after all."

The Importance of Bilingualism

Long before the December 7, 1941, attack on Pearl Harbor, in the 1920s, having discovered that Japanese language schools were actually run not for the sake of the *nisei* but for the *issei*, Yusen Kawamura wrote an article titled, "The Future of the Japanese Language School." He began thus: "The Japanese language school is destined to meet its end soon. Its future consists only in waiting for its self-destruction, like a flickering candle light" (*Nichibei*, January 1, 1927).

Because of a 1924 law prohibiting new Japanese immigration, the population of *issei* would dwindle and the needs of English-dependent *nisei* would take over. Nearly twenty years later, when World War II ended with the defeat of Japan, Mike Masaoka declared, "We will abolish Japanese language schools. We will reject the values of the *issei*" (Yamashiro, 1995, p. 109). In this way, the *jun nisei*, who were English speakers, became the key players in the Japanese American community, and the roles of Japanese-speaking *issei* and *kibei nisei* were downplayed and even disparaged. In such a climate, the words "Tule Lake" became taboo; people who had resided there were pigeonholed as "disloyal" and hidden from sight after the war. It was an era in which "even most of the *kibei nisei* who had been the biggest troublemakers at Tule Lake came to a kind of settlement with their past and did not send their own children to Japanese language schools" (p. 109). Bilingualism, and with it the Japanese language, had become a badge of shame.

Fifty years after the war, Japan has grown into a leading economic power, and at the time of this writing, in the 1990s, there are about fifty thousand people learning the Japanese language in the U.S. At Golden Gate Institute, which opened in 1911 in San Francisco, about one hundred students, ranging from pre-school to high-school age, study Japanese language and culture for three hours every Saturday morning. They are the children of the *shin issei* who have come to the United States after the war, including many mixed-race children who reflect the majority of Japanese Americans who marry outside their race (Kitano, 1993, pp. 126-127).

Viewed from the perspective of its function to foster communication, bilingualism undoubtedly has its economic advantages. But this logic only works for those in the mainstream, those in power, i.e., in the U.S., American speakers of English. If the speaker belongs to a minority group, his or her mother tongue is relegated to the status of an "ethnic language," despite the deep power of bilingualism in human affairs beyond the realm of economics.

Masao Yamashiro, a *kibei nisei* columnist who calls himself a "poorly made Japanese," writes, "It is possible to teach Japanese Americans born and raised in the United States about their parents' roots and culture, but it is impossible to give them any sense of a homeland they have no memory of" (1995, p. 140). Perhaps this sense of a "homeland" can only be experienced through the images of childhood, remembered in and formed by one's mother tongue.

Of his life in America, Yamashiro says that he "viewed the mountains with Japanese spirit and the seas with Japanese feeling, learned about rural and urban life with a Japanese mind, and shared friendship with a Japanese heart" (1995, pp. 77-78). America thus became his own version of Japan, created by what he calls his "pure subjectivity as a Japanese."

American society encourages individuals to maintain connections to their ethnic cultures, but white, English-language culture still prevails. Children who are in the minority by virtue of their language (having a different mother tongue) and ethnic/racial background (having a different physical appearance) grow up with discrimination and must navigate a multicultural and multilinguistic environment from the time of their birth. Growing up under these circumstances puts them at risk for a kind of bicultural ambivalence that can lead to loss of identity. In other words, if they are unable to feel an unshakable pride in their own ethnic cultures, they will experience conflicting emotions of love and hate toward both ethnic and mainstream cultures and ultimately will be unable to feel that they belong to either. Thus, they lose the sense of having their own place in the world — the complicated notion of "homeland."

As these young people assimilated into English-speaking mainstream culture, some fell victim to a darker side of American society rarely observed in previous generations of Japanese Americans. According to Michi Weglyn (1996), "Drug abuse and delinquency are among the problems perceptibly on the rise, notably among youth whose Nisei parents have little or no sense of ethnic or racial pride" (p. 278). More than anything else, what children need is a sense of pride in themselves, the pride to accept exactly who they are. But foreign-born parents can only convey their own pride to their children in their native language, which is part of their core identity and enables them to express themselves. Sadly, they cannot express this same pride — not an exclusive, racial pride, but simply a pride in their own identity — in English, which is a foreign language to them.

Saburo T., one of relatively few Japanese Americans to hold an important office in the California state government, told me that he uses Japanese quite often in his work and deeply values the education he received at Tule Lake:

> I feel thankful about having attended *Dai Toa Juku*. I heard that the *shushin* [discipline] curriculum was discontinued in Japan after the war, probably because of the controversial issue of emperor worship. Even so, I think we still need to study basic human relationships, and because it focuses on such principles as respect for parents or helping each other, I think that a curriculum based on *shushin* is still appropriate for Japan. Frequently, when I'm around other Americans, I become aware of my Japanese-ness. I am proud of it ..., I am different. I know that I have a different background, a different way of thinking.
>
> In daily life, most issues and decisions are neither black nor white. There are a lot of grey areas, but many Americans seem to make decisions in terms of black and white. They think, "If my opinion is stronger, then my opponent must be wrong." In Japanese culture, people listen and let others say everything they have on their minds, and the listener will step back rather than collide with the speaker. This principle has been very useful in my managerial work.

Jiro T. raised his daughter with the discipline to study more seriously than other children; consequently, she applied herself to studying the Japanese language in college. He said that she has pride in being a Japanese American. In a similar vein, Ichiro T. had his son practice *kendo*. "I did not deliberately stress that he should adopt the Japanese spirit, but he seems to have mastered patience, politeness, a will to overcome, and the confidence that he can succeed if he tries," he said, speaking as a proud father.

Kenji Takeuchi said that he cherishes family bonds more than anything else:

> I had a lonely childhood separated from my family, so I made it a rule to eat dinner with my family. I never allowed my sons

to eat at their friends' houses, however eagerly they were invited. Until they graduated from high school, we were always together, even while traveling. I did not let my children complain. My sons could not say "but!" or make excuses. On my part, I never interfered in their daily conduct. We parents become role models, showing the children how they ought to act. Children grow up imitating their parents. This idea does not seem to have currency in the American family, where the family itself is just a gathering of individuals and parents educate children to be independent.

Takeuchi suddenly raised his voice and uttered Meng-tzu's words, *"fugyo tenchi ni hajizu"* [nothing to be ashamed of in mind or conduct]. Fairness and courage — feeling no shame before anyone and harboring no grudges, no self-doubt — this spirit must have found something in common with the culture of extreme individualism of America, giving Takeuchi the strength and conviction to survive in this country.

It was Mike Masaoka who announced the name of Takeuchi's eldest son, Derrick, as the first JACL Thomas T. Hayashi Law Scholarship recipient in Philadelphia in 1976 (*Pacific Citizen*, October 8, 1976). Having learned that Derrick Takeuchi planned to make use of both English and Japanese in his future work on legal issues between Japan and the United States, Masaoka clearly stated to the Takeuchi family: "I regret that I did not study the Japanese language."

EPILOGUE

THE NO NO GIRL

Exactly ten years after my first pilgrimage, I found myself standing at Tule Lake Segregation Center again. On July 4, 2008, with fifty others in the early morning on Independence Day, I climbed Castle Rock for the first time. The craggy mountain that had overlooked row after row of black barracks at the camp towered into the sky before my eyes, unchanged since my first visit.

Huffing and puffing from want of regular exercise, I hiked the trail leading up the mountainside, weaving my way through sagebrush. Watching the dragonflies flit to and fro above the sagebrush, I would now and then take a deep breath of the bracing fragrance of the sage. I looked up to see a swallow dancing against the impossibly blue sky.

In front of me, two elderly men with walking sticks were hiking along slowly, talking all the while in hushed tones in heavily accented English. Their voices, now audible, now beyond the threshold of my hearing, were low, with an extremely subtle boldness and richness. Judging from the words that I was able to make out here and there, I gathered that they were talking about their families. In their voices, intentionally kept to a low murmur, I could sense some sort of private understanding between them. Something secret, with a soft, subtle quietude coming from their shared memory, something unique to those who had experienced life in the camps. The deeply voiced, faltering English exchanged between the two seemed out of place amid the arid terrain that surrounded us.

A Caucasian woman who had caught up with the two old men from behind began asking questions of one of them. Turning to answer her, the old man suddenly raised his voice an entire octave. He began to speak in a bright, cheerful tone, as if the incarceration camp experience was something that had happened to someone else. It was the voice one uses to address a guest, clearly audible and comprehensible even to me. Having lost his conversation partner, the other old man silently began to follow the trail on ahead. The muffled memories that had hung in the air between the two old men for a few moments, hanging from the threads of spoken language crisscrossing between them, vanished instantly into the surroundings, as if by magic. I hurried along in silence, but I was no longer able to catch up to the old man who had gone on ahead.

From the summit of Castle Rock, reached with much sweat and grim determination, I looked down upon the remains of the Segregation Center. Looking out in the direction marked by a large white cross at the peak, I could see the land at the foot of the mountain dotted with what looked like a large number of buildings. In this brownish expanse of land, offering little in the way of greenery, the buildings of the Newell Elementary School and its surrounding residences, the silos of a faded white storehouse, and the Segregation Center prison stood out in stark relief. In the intervening years, the number of buildings standing at the former site of the Segregation Center had undeniably increased.

But even more surprising was the dense, vivid green of the landscape around the camp ruins that I saw below. No doubt due to economic development in the area, the neighboring farmland had expanded far beyond its reach of ten years ago; what's more, it was a lush green so fresh and exuberant it almost hurt the eyes. Hadn't the Segregation Center been built on land as barren as a desert, where the harsh climate of the interior would never support agriculture? Yet now, the abundant greenery surrounding the remains of the camp on all four sides seemed to be encroaching upon the camp little by little. Would what was left of the camp someday be buried in this bounty of green? And what would be left of the dismal thoughts entertained by the many people who had spent time here — the kind of thoughts that seem to have no place and leave the holder uncomfortably burdened? Would they, too, come to be sealed within the confines of the sterile, inorganic name engraved upon a single metal plate marking the ruins a "Historical Landmark"?

After descending the mountain, I spoke to Kenji Takeuchi about my impressions of the view from the summit, with the lush greenery encroaching on the remains of the camp. Mr. Takeuchi was the founder of *Dai Toa Juku*, the school whose name went down in the history of Tule Lake as a breeding ground for "pro-Japan radicals." After listening to what I said, he replied, "That's just proof of the fact that the Japanese worked hard to turn this into good farmland."

As part of the pilgrimage, Mr. Takeuchi was visiting Tule Lake for the first time since being released from the camp. He was setting foot in the place for the first time in over sixty years.

"What is it like for you?" I asked.

He replied to my clichéd question in a tone laden with sentiment. "The first thing that came to me was the memory of so many people's faces." But he didn't go into much detail. "At that time, we were only thinking, 'What are we going to do from here on in?' That was really the only thought in our minds."

"You were young, weren't you?" I asked.

Mr. Takeuchi nodded silently. Then suddenly, on some impulse, he let slip a trace of deeper emotion: "Yes, but still...." His words broke off there, and he did not try to elaborate. The thought that could not be put into words was no doubt for him the unvarnished truth. How could I, an outsider, imagine the nature of those feelings he could not voice?

Unlike my first pilgrimage, the memorial service was held in the remains of the camp cemetery. Joining hands together in prayer in front of a model of the Tule Lake camp depicting eleven black barracks in the shadow of a miniature Castle Rock, the pilgrims each offered flowers to the spirits of the deceased. The eleven miniature barracks bore the names of ten incarceration camps and the words "Department of Justice."

From the mood and discussion on this pilgrimage I got the sense that finally, slowly but surely, the community was beginning to respect and attempt to understand the experiences of the "pro-Japan radical group" consisting of the *kibei* "No No Boys" who had been sent to Justice Department camps. This healing of past wounds had taken longer than the total sum of years I had been alive. I felt bad that there were so many from this group who had ended their lives still conflicted, still feeling estranged because of a decision they made long ago, under duress. Of the *kibei* "No No Boys" I had interviewed twelve or thirteen years ago, Mr. Takeuchi was the only one I had been able to contact again. While thinking it unlikely that I would ever meet with the others again, I recalled their faces and voices while I added my flowers to the offering and put my hands together in prayer: "Thank you. I'm glad to have met you. You gave me the courage to live in the United States. I'm truly grateful to you."

The last morning of the pilgrimage, one of the pilgrims who had been born and brought up in Hawaii spoke to me in the cafeteria. "Takako, I moved here to the mainland from Hawaii, but I've found that the Japanese Americans on the mainland are totally different from the Japanese in Hawaii. In Hawaii, we just say, 'We are Japanese.' We don't even bother saying 'Japanese American.' The other day, at a museum in Los Angeles, a Caucasian asked me, 'Are you from Japan?' That really bothered me! After all, we've been in this country for over one hundred years!" He spoke with a look of frustration at the difference between Hawaii, where Japanese Americans are in the majority and have some political power, and the mainland, where they have to live in an uneasy compromise with the mainstream Caucasian society, sometimes playing up to its paternalistic attitudes. Hearing him speak, I impulsively reached out and tapped him on the shoulder, saying, "The spirit of Harry Ueno and Joe Kurihara is alive in you," and laughed. He laughed it off too, nonchalantly. But without question their spirit does live on, as do the spirits of Kinzo Wakayama and all the other *kibei* "No No's" who had pride in the core of their identity.

The evening before in Klamath Falls, Oregon, we had watched a showing of *The Cats of Mirikitani*, a moving film about Tsutomu "Jimmy" Mirikitani, a *kibei* "No No Boy" who had given up his U.S. citizenship and been branded an enemy alien. When I first saw the film in Chicago and learned that Mr. Mirikitani had refused Social Security payments, saying he was not about to accept aid from a government that had taken everything he owned from him, I was impressed by the spine he showed in following through on his convictions. During the three days of the pilgrimage, Mr. Mirikitani kept largely to himself, silently working with a ballpoint pen and a pad of paper, conversing with no one. He was sketching the scenery of the Tule Lake camp, with Castle Rock in the background. As I watched, he tirelessly and precisely added shading to the barracks with his ballpoint pen. Amid the shrubbery in front of the barracks emerged one of the cats made famous by the film.

After the screening, Mr. Mirikitani took the stage. He immediately launched into a series of three old Japanese songs, including "Tokyo Ondo"[40] and "Battleship March," dancing and gesturing expressively. Mr. Takeuchi, who was sitting next to me, murmured, "These songs were popular around 1933 or '34 in Japan." Hearing such a spirited Japanese song sung for the first time in quite a while, I felt happy and found myself laughing. "Is that so?" I said. "I often used to hear these songs as I passed by *pachinko* parlors [game arcades] back in Japan."

When the songs were over, Mr. Mirikitani suddenly began to speak in clear, fluent Japanese. "This was a gathering place of eighteen thousand people who were certain Japan would win ... must surely prevail. I told them, 'Don't do anything foolish.'" From out of his eighty-eight-year-old body, the Japanese flowed without hesitation. I wondered when was the last time he had spoken so openly and grandly in Japanese. The mother tongue that had been drilled into his body from the earliest age, the songs remembered from youth — these were the things that stood as proof of his existence, the things he would carry with him throughout life, things of the sort that would never fade away.

Looking up at Mr. Mirikitani on the stage wearing a red beret just like the one he wore in the movie, Mr. Takeuchi spoke quietly, suddenly the picture of seriousness. "He, too, followed the path he believed in in life. I'm amazed at his lack of avarice. I respect those feelings that prompted him to stick close to his original dreams and intentions."

It was true that as an artist Mirikitani never lost sight of his original intentions. Even while homeless, he continued to sketch and sell pictures on the sidewalks of New York City, outside night and day in all seasons, despite the bitter cold winters.

The Japanese word that Mr. Takeuchi had used to describe Mirikitani's "original dreams and intentions" was *shoshin* — literally, "one's first heart." It had been a long time since I had heard that word spoken. "Remaining true to one's original intentions" — these were not the kinds of words I often heard from the lips of Americans.

---

40. *Ondo* is a kind of call and response, where a leader sings the first line and the group chimes in on the second.

Just before leaving the stage, Mr. Mirikitani called out clearly to the audience in a loud voice, this time with a slight trace of a regional accent (perhaps Hiroshima?) in his speech. "Everyone, I would truly like to thank you for coming here today. I offer you my deepest gratitude." At the sound of his robust voice, I felt my heart tremble. In his words I encountered something that had somehow gone missing from those of us who had been through the postwar Japanese education system, first influenced by the United States Education Missions to Japan right after the war, then later flattered by the "Japan as Number One" wave of economic prosperity. That missing something was the backbone of a person who had a vision and stuck with it to the end.

This steely spirit of the *kibei* always made me think of my own father. Having witnessed Japan's defeat in World War II at the impressionable age of 17, he was a man who lived through a time of confusion when Japan's defeat forced its people to undergo a 180° change in direction — a complete overhaul of their value system. Brandishing his authority as father, prepared to tell me that white was black and never permitting a word of protest, he unilaterally imposed obedience upon me, only to later thrust me away with the words, "You are free. Do as you like; your life is your responsibility." As a daughter, I felt as though I had fallen through the cracks, caught between the values of pre-war militaristic Japan and the postwar values that America imposed on defeated Japan. Feeling that my home was no place for me, I spent the days of my girlhood in confusion.

During one of the discussion sessions at the pilgrimage, the middle-aged *sansei* (third-generation Japanese Americans) lamented that their parents had never spoken to them of life in the camps, though they had wished they would. I thought of my own parents. I knew nothing of my parents' childhood or youth or even of their married life. Back then, parents didn't speak openly to their children about themselves, let alone their feelings. Was that just a part of Japanese culture? We have an old saying, "A child grows up looking at her parent's back." The parent teaches the child what is important in life through the sight of his or her own back. The parent's way of life is transmitted to the child not through words in face-to-face conversation but naturally, so that the child absorbs it from the parent's entire body. To put it another way, the parent must display his way of life to his children through his body. The parent is silent, and without speaking the relationship between parent and child is formed from the grit and generosity of the parent, which are never put into words. It was in such an atmosphere that I spent my youth.

Some of the *sansei* on the pilgrimage said that their parents had mentioned only the good aspects of camp life, and they wondered why. I can only imagine how great the shame must have been for inmates, after building a life through hard work, only to lose it all by forced removal and incarceration! It is only natural that those who experienced this loss felt as though the entirety of their own lives had been rendered null and void. And yet, the *issei* parents swallowed their own pride, saying, "*Shikata ga nai*" [It can't be helped] or "*Gaman dekiru*" [We've just got to bear it]. If we ask why, the answer seems obvious: Weren't they thinking about their children's future? What good would it do these children, who would live their lives in this country as Americans, if their parents complained about the United States? The children needed to take pride in their own country and in the fact that they were Americans. What good would it do to saddle the children with the burden of the parents' resentment toward the United States or their vexation, sorrow, and laments?

The truly painful things that cause the greatest suffering can never be expressed in words. The reason that so many of the *issei* and *nisei* left this world without ever complaining to their children about what happened to them was none other than the strength that moved them to try to protect their children, along with a fierce kind of love, intent on only one thing: to make their children's future a happy one. *Kodomo no tame ni* [for the sake of the children] has survived in the Japanese American community.

While on the Tule Lake pilgrimage, I noticed that although some *nisei* can understand and speak Japanese perfectly well, they often hide this fact from others. This reticence to admit speaking Japanese is most likely a result of the incarceration camp and postwar experience.

Nevertheless, during the trip, it was obvious to me that the participants on the pilgrimage were different from Caucasian Americans. Not just in their physical appearance — a fact of racial difference — but also in their behavior. Although many of them no longer understand much Japanese at all, having lost their superficial "Japaneseness" through years of assimilation, something remains inside them that is different. I think that Mr. Takeuchi must have felt the same way I did. Just once, as if the observation had sunk into his heart and left a visceral trace, he remarked, "These people are Japanese, aren't they? They are behaving like Japanese — they are living and breathing it." It is as if something of the earnestness of their parents, who had loved them deeply but who had been unable to present the "stuff of life" in words, had been passed down to them in an unbroken thread.

Since my last pilgrimage in 1998, I have changed as well. I no longer feel the sense of familiarity upon seeing Japanese American faces and hearing Japanese American voices that I felt then. Now I have just one question to ask of this self who is finally beginning to separate from "Japan" and the concept of self as a "person of Japan": as I move forward in life, what is left within me that I can truly take pride in, a simple pride in myself as a human being and as one who speaks Japanese, no matter how far I may be physically and mentally removed from Japan? If such a thing exists, what might it be? However I may be ridiculed for being unable to speak English clearly and eloquently or for having the face of a "person of Japan," however I may encounter prejudice and discrimination, I think it's best to become a "No No Girl" who lives life with dignity and without apology for what I am.

In 1996, when I was researching the relationship between pre-war South Dakota and Japan, I wrote:

> It was a prairie night of the kind that made me feel as though I was the only person in the world who was awake. I listened to the sound of the wind outside the window. While praying that the waves that separated me from Japan would never grow rough, I trained my ears upon the hum of the jet-black prairie night in which I could not see so much as one small light. I thought that there was nothing so sad yet sweet as the sound of waves heard in the place farthest removed from the ocean.

Today, my heart is no longer shaken by the sad but sweet music of the vast ocean that lies between Japan and the United States. Becoming a

"No No Girl" means taking the entire world into my heart, as one human being, aiming for empathy and solidarity with others.

I am a "No No Girl." And what ceaselessly encourages and cheers me on is the Japanese phrase I learned from a "No No Boy": *Fugyo tenchi ni hajizu*. I believe I have "done right in the sight of God and man."

BIBLIOGRAPHY

PRIMARY SOURCES

Community Government in War Relocation Centers. (1946).
Washington D.C.: United States Department of the Interior, War
Relocation Authority.

Impounded People: Japanese Americans in the Relocation Centers. (1946).
Washington, D.C.: United States Department of the Interior, War
Relocation Authority.

A great many documents, including official reports, memoranda, correspondence, unpublished autobiographies, and family histories are held in the private collections of individuals who were interned or their heirs. These materials are frequently photocopied and passed on. Such documents are cited in the text to the extent possible. I am indebted to Haruo Kawate for access to Masao Kawate's personal diary and correspondence, to Motomu Akashi for access to the papers of Sanae Akashi, and to Harry Ueno for access to his personal collection.

Some general archives of the primary materials are found in the Bancroft Library at the University of California–Berkeley and the National Archives and Records Administration, Washington, DC. The Harry Y. Ueno Papers are held in the Stanford University Library, Stanford, California.

NEWSPAPERS, MAGAZINES, AND NEWSLETTERS

The Bismarck Tribune

Chicago Daily Tribune

Chicago Shimpo

Hoshi-dan Hokoku [newsletter]

Hokoku [newsletter]

Hokubei Mainichi

Japanese American News [San Francisco]

Life Magzine

Monthly Nihongo

Nichibei [San Francisco]

Nichibei Jiji Shinbun

Nichibei Times

Nikkei West

Pacific Citizen

Rafu Shimpo [Los Angeles]

Topaz Times News Daily

Tule Lake News

Tule Lake Shimpo

Utah Nippo

The Zephyr

Secondary Sources

Abiko, K. (1930). Hogo gakuen ni taisuru ichi shiken. In Y. Kawamura (Ed.), *Beikoku kashu nihongo gakuen enkaku-shi* (pp. 309-312). San Francisco: Hokka Nihongo Gakuen Kyokai.

Akashi, M. (2004). *Betrayed Trust.* Bloomington, IN: Author House.

Akashi, M. (2005). Tule Lake Segregation Center: Resegregation and Pro-Japanese Movement. In *A Question of Loyalty: Internment at Tule Lake.* Klamath Falls, OR: Journal of the Shaw Historical Library.

Arrington, L.J. (1991). Utah's Ambiguous Reception: The Relocated Japanese Americans. In R. Daniels, S.C. Tayler, & H. Kitano (Eds.), *Japanese Americans: From Relocation to Redress* (rev. ed., pp. 92-97). Seattle: University of Washington Press.

Chin, F. (1991). Come All Ye Asian American Writers of the Real and the Fake. In J.P. Chan, F. Chin, L.F. Inada, & S. Wong (Eds.), *The Big Aiiieeeee! An Anthology of Chinese American and Japanese American Literature* (pp. 1-92). NY: Meridian.

Christgau, J. (1985). *Enemies: World War II Alien Internment.* Ames, IA: Iowa State University Press.

Collins, D. (1985). *Native American Aliens.* Westwood, CT: Greenwood Press.

Culley, J. (1991). The Santa Fe Internment Camp and the Justice Department Program for EnemyAliens. In R. Daniels, S.C. Taylor, & H. Kitano (Eds.), *Japanese Americans: From Relocation to Redress* (rev. ed., pp. 57-71). Seattle: University of Washington Press.

Drinnon, R. (1987). *Keeper of Concentration Camps: Dillon S. Myer and American Racism.* Berkeley: University of California Press.

Eizawa, K. (1995). *Dai-toa kyoei ken no shiso.* Tokyo: Kodansha.

Embrey, S.K., Hansen, A.A., & Mitson, B.K. (1986). *Manzanar Martyr: An Interview with Harry Y. Ueno.* Fullerton, CA: The Oral History Program, California State University.

Hattendorf, L. (Director). (2006). *The Cats of Mirikitani* [film]. USA: Lucid Dreaming.

Hosokawa, B. (1982). *JACL in Quest of Justice.* NY: Morrow.

Ina, S. (Producer & Director). (2005). *From a Silk Cocoon* [film]. USA: Hesono O Productions.

Inoue, J. (1986). *Umi o watatta nihon shukyo.* Tokyo: Kobundo.

Itoh, K. (1982). *Amerika shunju hachi-ju nen.* Tokyo: PMC Shuppan. [*Eighty Years in America.* Seattle, WA: The Seattle Japanese Community Service].

James, T. (1987). *Exile Within: The Schooling of Japanese Americans 1942-1945.* Cambridge, MA: Harvard University Press.

Kajita, M. (1997). *I bunka ni sodatsu nihon no kodomo: amerika no gakko bunka no naka de.* Tokyo: Chuo Koron-sha.

Kashima, T. (1977). *Buddhism in America: The Social Organization of an Ethnic Religious Institution.* Westport, CT: Greenwood Press.

Kawamura, Y. (1927, January 1). Nihongo gakko no shorai. *Nichibei.*

Kawamura, Y. (1930). Gakuen kyokai sokai kiroku. In Y. Kawamura (Ed.), *Beikoku kashu nihongo gakuen enkaku-shi* (pp. 24-38). San Francisco: Hokka Nihongo Gakuen Kyokai.

Kitano, H. (1993). *Generations and Identity: The Japanese American.* Needham Heights, MA: Ginn Press.

Kiyota, M. (1997). *Beyond Loyalty: The Story of a Kibei.* Honolulu: University of Hawaii Press.

Kojima, T. (1996, November). Enlightenment Between an Elder Ex-JACL Official and a Liberal Revisionist. *Nichibei Times.*

Kumei, T. (1992). Senji tenjusho karano "sai-teiju" — nikkei amerika-jin no chusei o meguru ichi oboegaki. *Nagano Tanki Daigaku Bulletin, 47,* 177-188.

Kumei, T. (1995). *Gaikoku-jin o meguru shakai shi.* Tokyo: Yusen Kaku.

Kumei, T. (1996). Skeleton in the Closet: The Japanese American *Hokoku Seinen-dan* and Their "Disloyal" Activities at the Tule Lake Segregation Center During World War II. *Japanese Journal of American Studies, 7,* 67-102.

Kumei, T., & Murakawa, Y. (1988). Fu-chusei kumi to yobareta sengo sokansen kikokusha ni kansuru ichi kosatu. *Rekishigaku Kenkyu, 581,* 62-72.

Kurashige, L. (2000). The Problem of Biculturalism: Japanese American Identity and Festival Before World War II. *Journal of American History, 84*(4), 1632-1664.

Kuwayama, N. (1996, April). Series tabunka no shoho sen #1. *Gekkan Nihongo.*

The Lim Report. (1990). Report Prepared for Presidential Select Committee on JACL Resolution #7. (D. Lim, author). 31st Biennial Convention of the JACL, June 17- 22, San Diego.

Lyon, C. (2012). *Prisons and Patriots: Japanese American Wartime Citizenship, Civil Disobedience, and Historical Memory.* Philadelphia: Temple University Press.

MacWilliams, C. (1944). What About Our Japanese Americans? [pamphlet]. NY: Public Affairs Committee.

Masaoka, M., with Hosokawa, B. (1987). *They Call Me Moses Masaoka: An American Saga.* New York, NY: William Morrow.

Masaoka, M., with Hosokawa, B. (1988). *Moses to Yobareta otoko Mike Masaoka.* Tokyo: TBS Britanica.

Matsumoto, Y. (2007). *Tsukurareru amerika kokumin to "tasha": amerika-ka jidai no citizenship.* Tokyo: Tokyo University Shuppan-kai.

Mizuno, M. (n.d.) *Nikkei amerika-jin no bungaku katudo no rekishiteki hensen: 1880 nendai kara 1980 nendai ni kakete* (Unpublished dissertation). Kyoto University

Mizuno, T. (2003). Government Suppression of the Japanese Language in World War II Assembly Camps. *Journalism and Mass Communication Quarterly, 80* (4), 849- 865.

Mizuno, T. (2005) *Nikkei amerika-jin kyosei shuyo to* journalism: *liberaru-ha zasshi to nihongo shinbun no dainiji sekai taisen.* Tokyo: Shunpusha.

Moen, F. (1946, February 23). Ft. Lincoln Internees Led Well-Fed, Regulated Existence. *Bismarck Tribune.*

Muller, E. (2007). *American Inquisition: The Hunt for Japanese American Disloyalty in World War II.* Chapel Hill: University of North Carolina Press.

Murakawa, Y., & Kumei, T. (1992). *Nichibei senji kokan sen, sengo sokan sen kikoku sha ni kansuru kiso teki kenkyu.* Tokyo: Toyota Foundation.

Nakagawa, M. (2004, January 1). Back to Bismarck: The Little-Known Story of the Ft. Lincoln Internees. *Hokubei Mainichi.*

Nakagawa, M. (2005a, February 16). Filmmaker Sheds Light on Why Parents Renounced Citizenship. *Hokubei Mainichi.*

Nakagawa, M. (2005b) Renunciants: Bill Nishimura and Tad Yamakido. In *A Question of Loyalty: Internment at Tule Lake.* Klamath Falls, OR: Journal of the Shaw Historical Library.

Nakamaki, H. (1989). *Nihon shukyo to nikkei shukyo no kenkyu, nihon, amerika, braziru.* Tokyo: Tosui Shobo.

Nakatsu, R. (1989). The Trials of Bilingual Children. *Japan Echo, 16* [special issue].

Power of Words Handbook: A Guide to Language about Japanese Americans in World War II – Understanding Euphemisms and Prefered Terminology. National JACL Power of Words II Committee, April 27, 2013. Retrieved from http://www.jacl.org/documents/Rev.%20 Term.%20Handbook.pdf.

Niiya, B. (Ed.). (2001). *Encyclopedia of Japanese American History: An A-Z Reference from 1868 to the Present.* NY: Facts on File.

Nitobe, I. (1995). *Bushi-do* (52nd ed.). Tokyo: Iwanami-shoten.

Nozaki, K. (2007). *Kyosei Shuyo to* Identity Shift. Kyoto: Sekai Shiso-sha.

An Oral and Documentary History of the Japanese American Internment in Ten Camps During World War II. (2000). Powell, WY: Heart Mountain, Wyoming, Foundation.

Otani, I. (1983). *Japan Boy: Nikkei Amerika-jin tachi no taiheiyo-senso.* Tokyo: Kadokawa-shoten.

Park, R. (1922). *The Immigrant Press and Its Control*. NY: Harper & Brothers.

A Question of Loyalty: Internment at Tule Lake. (2005). Klamath Falls, OR: Journal of the Shaw Historical Library.

Riggins, S. (Ed.). (1992). *Ethnic Minority Media: An International Prespective*. Newbury Park, CA: Columbia University Press.

Robinson, G. (2009). *A Tragedy of Democracy: Japanese Confinement in North America*. New York, NY: Sage.

Rogers, K. (2003, September 21). Remembering "Snow Country Prison." *Bismarck Tribune*.

Saeki, S. (2004). *Senjo no seishin-shi: bushido to iu gen-ei*. Tokyo: Nihon Hoso Shuppan kai.

Saki, H. (1999). Tule lake junrei: watashi no tsuioku no hibi. *Heisei, 34*.

Shirai, N. (1981). *California nikkei-jin kyosei shuyo sho*. Tokyo: Kawade Shobo Shinsha.

Shirai, N. (2001). *Tule Lake: An Issei Memoir*. Sacramento, CA: Muteki Press.

Shishido, K. (1998, September). Beinichi no hazama ni ikita nikkei 442 rentai. *Ronza*.

Snow Country Prison Exhibit Guide. (2003). Bismarck, ND: North Dakota Museum of Art.

Suzuki, T. (1930). Kashu ni okeru nihongo gakuen. In *Beikoku kashu nihongo gakuen enkaku-shi* (pp. 8-9). San Francisco: Hokka Nihongo Gakuen Kyokai.

Takei, B. (2005). Legalizing Detention: Segregated Japanese Americans and the Justice Department's Renunciation Program. In *A Question of Loyalty: Internment at Tule Lake* (pp. 75-105). Klamath Falls, OR: Journal of the Shaw Historical Library.

Takei, B. (2006, August 9). Dignity and Survival in a Divided Community. *Hokubei Mainichi*.

Takei, B., & Tachibana, J. (2001). *Tule Lake Revisited*. Sacramento: T & T Press.

Takeshita, T., & Saruya, K. (1983). *Yamato damashii to seijo-ki: nikkei amerika-jin no shimin-ken toso-shi*. Tokyo: Asahi shinbun-sha.

Takezawa, Y. (1994). *Nikkei amerika-jin no* ethnicity. Tokyo: Tokyo University Press.

Takita, S. (2007). *The Tule Lake Pilgrimage and Japanese American Internment: Collective Memory, Solidarity and Division in an Ethnic Community* (Unpublished dissertation). UCLA, Los Angeles.

Takita-Ishii, S. (2005). Tokio Yamane: A Renunciant's Story. In *A Question of Loyalty: Internment at Tule Lake* (pp. 161-185). Klamath Falls, OR: Journal of the Shaw Historical Library.

Tana, T. (1989). *Senji tekikoku-jin yokuryu-sho nikki (kan)*. Tokyo: Sanki-bo Bussho-rin.

Tanaka, K. (1975). *Gengo no shiso*. Tokyo: NHK.

TenBroek, F., Barnhart, E.N., & Matson, F. (1958). *Prejudice, War and the Constitution*. Berkeley: University of California Press.

Terakawa, T. (1930). Shushin ka no tokusetu ni tsuite. In Y. Kawamura (Ed.), *Beikoku kashu nihongo gakuen enkaku-shi* (pp. 343-353). San Francisco: Hokka Nihongo Gakuen Kyokai.

Thomas, D.S., & Nishimoto, R.S. (1946). *The Spoilage*. Berkeley: University of California Press.

Tomita, M. (1995). *Dear Miye: Letters Home from Japan, 1939-1946*. Stanford, CA: Stanford University Press.

Vyzralek, F. (2003). *The Alien Internment Camp at Fort Lincoln, North Dakota, During World War II: An Historical Sketch*. Bismarck: State Historical Society of North Dakota.

Weglyn, M.N. (1996). *Years of Infamy*. Seattle, WA: University of Washington Press.

Yamashiro, M. (1995). *Kibei nisei: kaitai shiteiku "nippon-jin."* Tokyo: Gogatsu Shobo.

Yamashita, A. (1996). Senji-ka ni okeru tekisei-go kyoiku. *Ningen Kagaku, 13*(2). Mito, Japan: Tokiwa College, Department of Human Science.

Yanagisawa, I. (2006). Fort Lincoln "tekisei gaikoku-jin" shuyosho ato. In *Hokubei no chiisana hakubutsukan* (pp.30-37). Tokyo: Sairyu-sha.

Yanagisawa, I. (2007). Fort Lincoln "tekisei gaikoku-jin" shuyosho to "yukiguni no keimusho" ten: Doitsu-jin to Nihon-jin to Senjumin tono jiku o koeta deai. In *Transnational Identity to tabunka kyosei* (pp.144-170). Tokyo: Akashi Shoten.

Yoneda, K. G. (1984). *Ganbatte: Sixty-Year Struggle of a Kibei Worker*. Los Angeles: Asian American Studies Center, UCLA.

TAKAKO DAY, originally from Kobe, Japan, is an award-winning freelance writer who has published six books and hundreds of articles in the Japanese language. In 1986 she moved to the San Francisco area where she worked for the New York *Yomiuri*, a subsidiary of Japan's largest newspaper company, the *Yomiuri Shimbun*, and the *Nichibei Times*. This work culminated in her 1992 book, *Challenge to America: Bicultural Women Bridging the Pacific* (Tokyo: Akashi Shoten, 1992).

In 1992 Day relocated to South Dakota, where she continued writing for the above newspapers and a number of other periodicals in Japan. She published *Bananas and Apples: A Japanese Person's Experiences in South Dakota* (Tokyo: Gogatsu Shobo, 1993) and began doing research on the historical relationship between South Dakota and Japan, which led to her 1997 article "Mizuho Takahashi: The Dream of a Japanese Woman in South Dakota," published in English.

Day then focused on Native American issues because of her interest in the nearby Pine Ridge Indian Reservation, then considered the poorest Indian reservation in the US. This research resulted in the publication of *American Indians Today: Contemporary Oglala Lakota People Through a Woman's Eyes* (Tokyo: Dai San Shokan, 1998).

A visit to Bismarck, North Dakota led her to research on the history of Japanese Americans in internment and prison camps during World War II. Day's experience in the Dakotas and her interviews with Japanese Americans who had been incarcerated at the Tule Lake Segregation Camp in California became a book titled *I Cannot Shoot A Japanese Soldier: The Hidden History of the Japanese American Incarceration Experience* (Tokyo: Fuyo Shobo Shuppan, 2000).

In 1999, Day and her family moved to Illinois. She published the book *Chicago and Illinois Off the Beaten Path* (Tokyo: Kobunken, 2008) and a half-autobiographical account, *Proof of Existence of a Tall Woman – If Cinderella Had Big Feet* (Tokyo: Sairyusha, 2005), in which she traced the psychological background of discrimination against tall women in Japan. Day started a support group for tall women in Japan in 2006. Through her writing she hopes to change Japanese society.

Day enjoys reading, swimming, *taiko* drumming, traveling, gardening, and hunting down pre-war Japanese antiques. She and her husband Michael live in the Chicago area. They have one daughter.